Modern Greek

by Eirini Argyrouli

A Wiley Brand

Modern Greek For Dummies®

Published by: **John Wiley & Sons, Inc.,** 111 River Street, Hoboken, NJ 07030-5774, www.wiley.com

For general information on our other products and services, please contact our Customer Care Department within the U.S. at 877-762-2974, outside the U.S. at 317-572-3993, or fax 317-572-4002. For technical support, please visit https://hub.wiley.com/community/support/dummies.

Wiley publishes in a variety of print and electronic formats and by print-on-demand. Some material included with standard print versions of this book may not be included in e-books or in print-on-demand. If this book refers to media that is not included in the version you purchased, you may download this material at http://booksupport.wiley.com. For more information about Wiley products, visit www.wiley.com.

Library of Congress Control Number is available from the publisher.

ISBN 978-1-394-34274-7 (pbk); ISBN 978-1-394-34276-1 (ebk); ISBN 978-1-394-34275-4 (ebk)

Printed and bound by CPI Group (UK) Ltd, Croydon, CR0 4YY

C9781394342747_191125

Table of Contents

Introduction

D ear reader, the book you hold in your hands isn't just a tool for learning a language. It's a small key that will help you unlock an entire world — the world of Greek. It's the beginning of a grand and enjoyable adventure, a game with sounds and letters, with words and tenses. And yes, that is exactly how I want you to approach learning the Greek language — with enthusiasm, with joy, with determination — to explore it, to understand its secrets, to listen to it, to sing it, to love it, to make it a part of your daily life, and ultimately, to master it.

As you turn the pages of this book, as you navigate the challenges of the Greek language, I want you to think of beautiful images of Greece: a sunrise over the Aegean Sea, a dive into the blue waters, a hike on Mount Olympus, or an afternoon coffee beneath the Acropolis. So, dear reader, it's time to begin your journey, and I hope you grow to love the Greek language and enjoy this book from beginning to end.

About This Book

Modern Greek For Dummies follows the teaching methodology developed at my online school, the Greek Learning Hub. This method aims to help you understand the Greek language in all its aspects: writing, reading, vocabulary, grammar, speaking, and listening skills. All these components of the language are developed simultaneously throughout this book.

Each chapter is independent, meaning you don't need to read the book (or even the individual chapters) from beginning to end. Instead, you can browse the table of contents or index, find the topic that interests you, and study it on its own. Cross-references guide you to other sections and chapters if you want to expand your knowledge or revisit something you may have forgotten.

It's important to note that this book serves as an introduction to the Greek language, providing basic grammar and vocabulary essential for your first visits to Greece. After you've completed this book, if you wish to reach higher levels of proficiency in Greek, you can take the online courses offered at the Greek Learning Hub (https://greeklearninghub.com/) or any other school of your preference.

Conventions Used in This book

Greek words appear in Greek letters and are highlighted in **bold** to make them easier to distinguish. You can see the Greek alphabet in Chapter 2.

Next to each word written in Greek characters, you'll find its phonetic transcription using Latin characters. Chapter 2 explains how each Greek letter corresponds to the Latin alphabet. Each syllable is separated by hyphens to help with pronunciation. Additionally, the syllable that should be stressed more is written in *italics*. For example: **καλημέρα** (ka-lee-*me*-ra).

After the Greek word and its transcription, you'll find its English meaning, which helps you understand and learn the word. For example: **καλημέρα** (ka-lee-*me*-ra) (*Good morning*).

Greek verbs have ten forms: I, you (singular), he, she, it, we, you (plural), they (masculine), they (feminine), they (neutral). The verb endings change depending on the form. Special attention is needed when learning verbs to ensure the correct endings are used. (Find out more about verbs in Chapter 4.)

Here are a few other features you find in this book:

>> **Talkin' the Talk:** These features contain everyday dialogues that will help you better understand what you learned in a given section of a chapter.

>> **Words to Know:** The key vocabulary included in a "Talkin' the Talk" dialogue is presented in a vocabulary list. By learning this vocabulary, along with the rest of the content in the chapter, you gradually build the essential foundations for speaking Greek.

>> **Fun & Games:** The end of each chapter offers a simple and enjoyable exercise to test how well you have absorbed the chapter's topics.

Foolish Assumptions

Before I started writing this book, I began thinking about who might be interested in reading it. So I started by making some assumptions about who you, dear reader, might be.

>> You've never had the opportunity to learn Greek in a structured way, but you feel that the time has come for any number of reasons: You have Greek

heritage, your partner is Greek, you live in Greece or you want to move there, you're a polyglot who loves learning languages, or something else.

>> You want to learn basic words and phrases that will help you communicate with Greeks when you visit the country as a tourist or on business.

>> You want to learn in an engaging, fun, and effective way, without having to memorize long vocabulary lists or endless grammar sections.

Icons Used in This Book

Like all *For Dummies* books, this book features icons to help you navigate the information. Here's what they mean.

REMEMBER

If you take away anything from this book, it should be the information marked with this icon.

TIP

This icon highlights especially helpful advice about the Greek language and culture.

WARNING

This icon points out situations and actions to avoid when you visit Greece or when you use the Greek language.

GRAMMATICALLY SPEAKING

Greek grammar has plenty of quirks, and this icon points them out.

CULTURAL WISDOM

Heading to Greece soon? Check out the information marked with this icon for details about Greek culture.

PLAY THIS

This icon accompanies "Talkin' the Talk" dialogues you can listen to online. They are a great way to hear Greek speakers in action.

Beyond the Book

This book is packed with valuable insights, but there's even more to explore online. For more tips and tricks for speaking the Greek language, including helpful questions and phrases to use in a variety of settings, check out the Cheat Sheet. Just go to www.dummies.com and search for "Modern Greek For Dummies Cheat Sheet."

Want to perfect your pronunciation? You can listen to Talkin' the Talk dialogues in this book to get a more natural feel for the sounds — something that's useful when learning Greek, with its distinct melodic intonation. You can find recording of the dialogues at www.dummies.com/go/moderngreekfd.

Where to Go from Here

Now that you have this book in your hands, you can explore Greek at your own pace. Whether you want to skim through or dive deep into each chapter, it's entirely up to you. Simply find the topic that interests you, check the index or table of contents, and discover the key phrases you need to speak Greek confidently.

If you're new to the language, I recommend starting with Chapters 2, 3, and 4 — they cover the essentials of Greek pronunciation, the Greek alphabet, and basic grammar. Learning the Greek alphabet — το ελληνικό αλφάβητο (to e-lee-nee-*ko* a-*lfa*-vee-to) — will help you read and write with ease. Come back to these chapters whenever you need a refresher on building Greek sentences or deciphering handwritten notes.

So, are you ready? Flip to the chapter that interests you or listen to the online audio tracks to get a feel for the language's rhythm. Take steady steps. Learning a language requires consistency, perseverance, and practice. Speak Greek at every opportunity, and incorporate the language into your daily life. It's easier than you think! Πάμε! (*pa*-me) (*Let's go!*)

1
Getting Started with Greek

Explore the Greek alphabet and discover Greek grammar basics, including nouns, verbs, and cases.

Understand basic Greek expressions.

Get a handle on numbers, times, and dates.

Speak about your everyday life in Greek.

Chapter **1**

Greek in a Nutshell

This chapter gives you a sample of some of the topics and vocabulary you'll encounter in the rest of the book. It's like dipping your finger into a jar of honey — and in this case, the honey is the Greek language itself.

Introducing the Basics

A few topics are essential as you begin learning Greek: the alphabet, grammar, useful expressions, and numbers, among others. The following sections give you the scoop on basic Greek.

The Greek alphabet

Check out this list: **A, B, E, I, K, M, N, O, T.**

Do you recognize these letters? They're some of the letters in the Greek alphabet. So, we're off to a good start! Are there more? Of course! The Greek alphabet has 24 letters waiting for you to discover them. And some of them might be completely unfamiliar to you: Take for example the letter **Ξ**, which sounds like "x," or the letter **Π**, which sounds like "p." Have you seen those before?

If you're eager to begin learning Greek, you don't have to wait long. Chapter 2 dives right into the Greek letters. After you complete that chapter, you'll be able to recognize any Greek text.

Basic and not-so-basic grammar

After introducing you to the Greek alphabet in Chapter 2, I guide you through simple grammar topics in Chapters 3 and 4. The reason grammar is important and is placed at the beginning of this book is because by understanding how basic grammar works, you'll be able to create correct sentences — so you can speak, express what you want to say, and be understood by your conversation partner.

It's different, for example, to say:

> **Εμείς πήγαμε στο μουσείο.** (e-*mees pee*-ga-me sto moo-*see*-o) (*We went to the museum.*)

> **Εγώ πηγαίνω στο μουσείο.** (e-*go* pee-*ye*-no sto moo-*see*-o) (*I'm going to the museum.*)

> **Εσύ δεν πήγες στο μουσείο.** (e-*see* den *pee*-yes sto moo-*see*-o) (*You didn't go to the museum.*)

TIP

Each of these sentences, even though they seem quite similar, gives different information about a visit to the museum. To adjust a sentence to say exactly what you want, you need to know at least basic grammar. If you don't know it already, I'd recommend studying Chapters 3 and 4 fairly early on.

Useful expressions

In Chapter 5, I provide you with the most essential expressions — those you can use during your first visit to Greece (and beyond!). These are, after all, the first phrases one learns when picking up any new language. For example:

» **καλημέρα** (ka-lee-*me*-ra) (*good morning*)

» **γεια** (ya) (*hi, hello*)

» **Τι κάνεις;** (tee *ka*-nees) (*How are you?*)

» **Πώς σε λένε;** (pos se *le*-ne) (*What's your name?*)

» **Από πού είσαι;** (a-*po* poo *ee*-se) (*Where are you from?*)

» **ναι** (ne) (*yes*)

>> όχι (o-hee) (*no*)

>> ευχαριστώ (ef-kha-ree-*sto*) (*thank you*)

In Chapter 5, I also give you words and phrases that help you talk more about yourself in Greek. That way, you learn vocabulary for εθνικότητες (e-thnee-*ko*-tee-tes) (*nationalities*), επαγγέλματα (e-pa-*ge*-lma-ta) (*professions*), and οικογένεια (ee-ko-*ye*-nee-a) (*family*).

REMEMBER

Building your vocabulary alongside grammar while learning a language is extremely important. Personally, I believe languages should be learned holistically, meaning that all aspects should develop together: grammar, vocabulary, writing, reading, speaking, and listening comprehension. This book has been designed to offer you just that.

Numbers, dates, and measurements

Want to count your money?

Say a date?

Weigh fruit at the greengrocer?

All of these tasks require knowing numbers. In Chapter 6, I teach you the numbers from 0 to 1,000 — the ones you need for everyday conversations. But since you might be eager, I go ahead and share the numbers from 1 to 10 here:

>> 1 — ένα (*e*-na)

>> 2 — δύο (*dee*-o)

>> 3 — τρία (*tree*-a)

>> 4 — τέσσερα (*te*-se-ra)

>> 5 — πέντε (*pe*-nde)

>> 6 — έξι (*e*-ksee)

>> 7 — επτά (e-*pta*)

>> 8 — οκτώ (o-*kto*)

>> 9 — εννιά (e-*nya*)

>> 10 — δέκα (*de*-ka)

CULTURAL WISDOM

The ancient Greeks were among the first civilizations to develop mathematical thinking, and some of the earliest mathematicians have gone down in history — you may have heard of Pythagoras or Archimedes.

Greek at home

Our home is the place where most of us spend the majority of our time. It's where we have our daily rituals and habits, where we relax, work, and create. So, expanding the vocabulary related to the world around us, Chapter 7 talks about our daily routine as well as the home and its furnishings.

Putting Greek into Action

In Part 2 of this book, you learn Greek that helps you in your everyday life in Greece — whether as a tourist or a more permanent resident. It covers a range of essential topics you need to speak in shops, on public transportation, at work, or even during a visit to the doctor.

Going places

When visiting a new city, you definitely need to get around. You might use the αυτοκίνητο (af-to-*kee*-nee-to) (*car*), λεωφορείο (le-o-fo-*ree*-o) (*bus*), τρένο (*tre*-no) (*train*), or another means of transportation. You may also need to ask someone for directions:

> Πού είναι η Ακρόπολη; (poo *ee*-ne ee a-*kro*-po-lee) (*Where is the Acropolis?*)
>
> Πού είναι το κέντρο; (poo *ee*-ne to *ke*-dro) (*Where is the center?*)

And you need to understand the directions they give you:

> Στρίψε δεξιά. (*stree*-pse de-ksee-*a*) (*Turn right.*)
>
> Στρίψε αριστερά. (*stree*-pse a-ree-ste-*ra*) (*Turn left.*)
>
> Προχώρα ευθεία. (pro-*kho*-ra ef-*thee*-a) (*Go straight.*)

Check out Chapter 8 for more information about getting around Greece.

Shopping

Chances are that during your trip to Greece, you won't skip visiting some local shops for clothing, souvenirs, or groceries. You may have questions:

>> How do you ask for the right clothing size?

>> How do you ask for a discount?

>> How do you find things and shop at the supermarket?

A quick look through Chapter 9 answers all your questions.

Dining and entertainment

Do you prefer a ταβέρνα (ta-*ve*-rna) (*tavern*) or an εστιατόριο (e-stee-a-*to*-ree-o) (*restaurant*)? And what are the differences between them? Would you like ζάχαρη (*za*-kha-ree) (*sugar*) and γάλα (*ga*-la) (*milk*) in your καφές (ka-*fes*) (*coffee*)? Do you want a χορτοφαγικό μενού (kho-rto-fa-gee-*ko* me-*noo*) (*vegetarian menu*)? What do you do on a night out at μπουζούκια (boo-*zoo*-kya) (*bouzoukia*) or during a traditional Greek πανηγύρι (pa-nee-*yee*-ree) (*festival*)?

All of this and much more is explored in Chapter 10, where you find words and phrases related to nightlife, food, drinks, and entertainment in Greece.

Health

Our health is very important, which is why we do everything we can to stay healthy. We go to the doctor, eat healthy foods, and exercise. If you'd like to learn vocabulary related to this topic, then Chapter 11 is for you. Here is some vocabulary to get you started:

>> ο γιατρός (o ya-*tros*) (*the doctor*)

>> το νοσοκομείο (to no-so-ko-*mee*-o) (*the hospital*)

>> Πονάω. (po-*na*-o) (*I'm in pain.*)

>> Είμαι άρρωστος. (*ee*-me *a*-ro-stos) (*I'm sick.*)

>> υγεία (ee ee-*yee*-a) (*health*)

Business

Do you want to move your business to Greece? Work at a Greek company? Do you have Greek colleagues and want to speak with them in Greek? Chapter 12 helps you with all of that. Let's look at some basic and very useful vocabulary:

>> Δουλεύω. (doo-*lev*-o) (*I work.*)

>> δουλειά (doo-*lya*) (*work, job*)

>> εταιρία (e-te-*ree*-a) (*company*)

>> υπάλληλος (ee-*pa*-lee-los) (*employee*)

>> συνάδελφος (see-*na*-de-lfos) (*colleague*)

>> συνέντευξη (see-*ne*-def-ksee) (*interview*)

>> συμβόλαιο (see-*mvo*-le-o) (*contract*)

Taking Greek on the Go

There's no better way to get to know Greece than by traveling it from corner to corner. Alongside everything else, don't forget to pack this book in your suitcase! It will help you immensely, as Part 3 provides all the vocabulary you need for preparing and enjoying your holidays in Greece.

Planning a trip

What do you need to travel?

>> διαβατήριο (dya-va-*tee*-ree-o) (*passport*)

>> εισιτήριο (ee-see-*tee*-ree-o) (*ticket*)

>> βαλίτσα (va-*lee*-tsa) (*suitcase*)

>> ξενοδοχείο (kse-no-do-*hee*-o) (*hotel*)

>> κράτηση (*kra*-tee-see) (*reservation*)

These and many other essentials are things you need to keep in mind when planning a trip to Greece. And all the relevant vocabulary can be found in Chapter 13.

Transportation

But how will you travel? And once you arrive in Greece, how will you get around? Will you go to the airport and take a plane? Or perhaps to the station to catch a train? How will you find a taxi, and from where will you catch the ferry to the islands? Where can you buy tickets, and where do you ask for information? And how will you do all of this in Greek? With the help of Chapter 14.

Sightseeing

Greece has so many things to see!

>> το μουσείο (to moo-*see*-o) (*the museum*)

>> ο αρχαιολογικός χώρος (o a-rhe-o-lo-gee-*kos kho*-ros) (*the archaeological site*)

>> το θέατρο (to *the*-a-tro) (*the theater*)

>> το οινοποιείο (to ee-no-pee-*ee*-o) (*the winery*)

>> τα αξιοθέατα (ta a-ksee-o-*the*-a-ta) (*the sights*)

If you'd like to practice your Greek, you could choose a tour led by a guide who speaks Greek. It's a fantastic opportunity! Find out more about sightseeing in Greece in Chapter 15.

Enjoying traditions

Chapter 16 includes what I consider the most interesting part — it features vocabulary related to the most important Greek traditions. And you'll certainly get to know Greece much better if you have the chance to experience some of these:

>> ο γάμος (o *ga*-mos) (*a wedding*)

>> η ονομαστική γιορτή (ee o-no-ma-stee-*kee* yo-*rtee*) (*a name day celebration*)

>> το ελληνικό Πάσχα (to e-lee-nee-*ko pa*-skha) (*Greek Easter*)

>> οι παραδοσιακοί χοροί (ee pa-ra-do-see-a-*kee* kho-*ree*) (*the traditional dances*)

Chapter **2**

Checking Out the Greek Alphabet

t's a beautiful spring morning. You're sitting at your desk, drinking your coffee while listening to Django Reinhardt. You're very happy because it's time to book your vacation in the Greek islands. You open a Greek website with information and see the following word: ΜΥΚΟΝΟΣ . . . Wow! You recognize almost all the letters and can read the word MYKONOS. You look at the next island: ΚΕΑ . . . you recognize this, too. You read more: ΣΙΚΙΝΟΣ, ΚΑΣΟΣ . . . Wow, is the Greek alphabet really this easy? And why do people say Greek is difficult? Then you think, "If the alphabet is this simple, why not start learning it, so I can read the signs when I'm in Greece?"

Very good idea! And now, I'm here to tell you, my friend, that the Greek alphabet has some letters that resemble the Latin alphabet but also quite a few different ones. Certainly, the alphabet is the first step to start learning Greek, and this chapter tells you what you need to know. Are you ready?

Meeting the Full Greek Alphabet (Some Letters Will Look Familiar!)

The alphabet of every language is the beginning of the challenge but also the start of an exciting journey of knowledge. Knowing the alphabet, you can then read and write words, thus learning vocabulary and starting to speak the language. Therefore, learning the alphabet is the most important first step.

CULTURAL WISDOM

I don't want to tire you with too much historical information, but I want to tell you this: The Greek alphabet began to take shape during the Iron Age, around the 9th to 8th century BC. This means that knowing Greek letters allows you to read an ancient Greek inscription you might see in a museum. The Greek letters carry an ancient history that continues to this day. And you, right now, can become part of this ancient tradition.

REMEMBER

Let me tell you some basic things about the Greek alphabet. It has 24 letters: 7 vowels and 17 consonants. Each letter has a capital and a lowercase form. Also, each letter has only one sound, and you read exactly what you see. That means there are no surprises in pronunciation.

PLAY THIS

I've created Table 2-1 for you with the alphabet. In the first column, you see the capital letter. In the second, the lowercase letter. In the third column you can see the name of the letter. (Yes! Greek letters have names.) In the fourth column, I've added a description of the sound the letter makes to help you pronounce it. In the fifth column, I tell you whether it's a vowel or a consonant. In the last column you see how this letter is written in the English transcriptions that you see throughout this book. (Listen to Track 1 for help with pronunciation.)

TIP

In the letter Σ, σ, you also see the symbol ς. This is the final sigma and is used only at the end of words. For example, look at the word μαθητής (ma-thee-*tees*) (*student*).

TIP

Right now you may feel like that's a lot of information, and it's difficult to learn the Greek alphabet. I have a tip that may help you. Divide the alphabet into smaller groups — let's say four groups of six — and start learning one group at a time. Write the alphabet in a notebook and at the same time pronounce each sound and repeat the name of the letter. In the end, try to say the entire alphabet.

TABLE 2-1   **The Greek Alphabet**

Capital Letter	Lowercase Letter	Name of the Letter	Pronunciation	Vowel or Consonant	Transcription
A	α	άλφα (*a*-lpha)	Pronounced like "a" in "father."	Vowel	a
B	β	βήτα (*vee*-ta)	Pronounced like "v" in "vase."	Consonant	v
Γ	γ	γάμα (*ga*-ma)	Pronounced like a soft "g" as in "good," but deeper in the throat.	Consonant	g when followed by α, o, ω, ου (*ga, go, goo*) y when followed by ε, αι; η, ι, υ, ει, οι (*ye, yee*)
Δ	δ	δέλτα (*de*-lta)	Pronounced like "th" in "this" or a soft "d."	Consonant	d
E	ε	έψιλον (*e*-psee-lon)	Pronounced like "e" in "bet."	Vowel	e
Z	ζ	ζήτα (*zee*-ta)	Pronounced like "z" in "zebra."	Consonant	z
H	η	ήτα (*ee*-ta)	Pronounced like "ee" in "see."	Vowel	ee
Θ	θ	θήτα (*thee*-ta)	Pronounced like "th" in "thing."	Consonant	th
I	ι	ιώτα (*yo*-ta)	Pronounced like "ee" in "see."	Vowel	ee, y
K	κ	κάπα (*ka*-pa)	Pronounced like "k" in "kite."	Consonant	k
Λ	λ	λάμδα (*la*-mda)	Pronounced like "l" in "lamp."	Consonant	l
M	μ	μι (mee)	Pronounced like "m" in "mother."	Consonant	m
N	ν	νι (nee)	Pronounced like "n" in "nose."	Consonant	n
Ξ	ξ	ξι (ksee)	Pronounced like "x" in "fox" or "ks."	Consonant	ks
O	ο	όμικρον (*o*-mee-kron)	Pronounced like "o" in "pot."	Vowel	o
Π	π	πι (pee)	Pronounced like "p" in "pat."	Consonant	p

(continued)

TABLE 2-1 *(continued)*

Capital Letter	Lowercase Letter	Name of the Letter	Pronunciation	Vowel or Consonant	Transcription
Ρ	ρ	ρο (ro)	Pronounced like a rolled "r" as in the Spanish word "carro."	Consonant	r
Σ	σ, ς (see Tip)	σίγμα (*see*-gma)	Pronounced like "s" in "see."	Consonant	s
Τ	τ	ταυ (taf)	Pronounced like "t" in "tap."	Consonant	t
Υ	υ	ύψιλον (*ee*-psee-lon)	Pronounced like "ee" in "see."	Vowel	ee
Φ	φ	φι (fee)	Pronounced like "f" in "fun."	Consonant	f
Χ	χ	χι (hee)	Pronounced like a soft "k" or "kh" when followed by α, ο, ω, ου (*kha, kho, khoo*), like "ch" in "Bach" and "loch." Pronounced like a strong "h" when followed by ε, αι; η, ι, υ, ει, οι (*he, hee*).	Consonant	k, kh, h
Ψ	ψ	ψι (psee)	Pronounced like "ps" in "lapse."	Consonant	ps
Ω	ω	ωμέγα (o-*me*-ga)	Pronounced like "o" in "pot."	Vowel	o

I know you! Greek letters that look and sound like English letters

As you may have noticed, some letters in the Greek alphabet look and sound like those in English. Which ones are these?

>> **Αα** is pronounced like "a."

>> **Κκ** is pronounced like "k."

>> **Οο** is pronounced like "o."

>> **Ττ** is pronounced like "t."

Greek letters that look like English letters but sound different

TIP

However, some letters may resemble those of the English alphabet, but they are pronounced completely differently. You need to get used to pronouncing them correctly!

>> **Bβ** resembles the English "B, b" but is pronounced like "v."

>> **Eε** is pronounced like a short "e," as in "pet" (not the long "e" sound).

>> **Hη** is pronounced like "ee" — be careful not to confuse it with the English "H, h."

>> **Nν** sounds like "n" — there is commonly confusion with the lowercase ν because many new learners pronounce it like the English "V, v."

>> **Pρ** is not the letter "P, p" — it is the letter **Pο** (rho) and is pronounced like "r."

>> **Υυ** is pronounced like "ee."

>> **Xχ** is pronounced like "kh" or a strong "h" — this letter isn't like the English "X, x."

Sounding More Greek

After you get a handle on the entire Greek alphabet, it's time to focus separately on vowels and consonants. The following sections explain what you need to know.

Vowels

GRAMMATICALLY SPEAKING

What is a vowel? A *vowel* is a speech sound that is produced without any significant constriction or blockage of airflow in the vocal tract. To understand what I mean, pronounce the vowels out loud:

>> **Aα** (a): Now try to read the word: **μαμά** (ma-*ma*) (*mom*)

>> **Eε** (e): Read the word: **Ελένη** (E-*le*-nee) (*Helen*)

>> **Hη, Iι, Υυ** (ee): Can you read these three words?

- **μικρή** (mee-*kree*) (*small*)

- **ηλικία** (ee-lee-*kee*-a) (*age*)

- **ύφος** (*ee*-fos) (*style*)

>> **Οο, Ωω** (o): And these two?

- **όμορφος** (*o-mo-rfos*) (*beautiful*)
- **ωκεανός** (o-ke-a-*nos*) (*ocean*)

GRAMMATICALLY
SPEAKING

As you can see, the Greek alphabet has three letters that sound like "ee" and two letters that sound like "o." And how do you know which one to use when writing? Although some basic rules guide where each "ee" and "o" are used, it's very important to also learn the spelling of words right off the bat.

Double vowels

Apart from the single vowels in the alphabet, the Greek language also has double vowels. That is, two vowels combined to create a new sound.

>> **αι:** When you see these two letters together, it sounds like "e" in "pet." For example: **παιδί** (pe-*dee*) (*child*).

>> **ει:** The epsilon and iota together create the sound "ee." For example: **ειρήνη** (ee-*ree*-nee) (*peace*).

>> **οι:** These two letters create the sound "ee." For example: **οικογένεια** (ee-ko-*ye*-nee-a) (*family*).

>> **ου:** When you see omicron and ypsilon, it sounds like "oo." For example: **Ούρσουλα** (*oo*-rsu-la) (*Ursula*).

>> **αυ:** This combination has two possible pronunciations: "af" or "av."

>> **ευ:** This combination can sound like "ef" or "ev."

TIP

What about **αυ** and **ευ**? How do we know when to pronounce them with the "f" sound and when with the "v" sound? The following rule can help you:

>> When **αυ** or **ευ** is followed by a voiced consonant (**B, Γ, Δ, Z, Λ, M, N, P**) or a vowel, it's pronounced as "av" or "ev":

- **αυγό** (av-*go*) (*egg*)
- **ευγενικός** (ev-ye-nee-*kos*) (*kind*)

>> When **αυ** or **ευ** is followed by a voiceless consonant (**Θ, K, Ξ, Π, Σ, T, Φ, X, Ψ**), it's pronounced as "af" or "ef":

- **αυτή** (af-*tee*) (*she*)
- **ευχαριστώ** (ef-kha-ree-*sto*) (*thank you*)

To better learn the double vowels, try reading these words:

>> εύκολος (*ef*-ko-los) (*easy*)

>> αιώνιος (e-*o*-nee-os) (*eternal*)

>> οικογένεια (ee-ko-*ye*-nee-a) (*family*)

>> αυτοκίνητο (af-to-*kee*-nee-to) (*car*)

>> ειρήνη (ee-*ree*-nee) (*peace*)

>> αιτία (e-*tee*-a) (*cause*)

>> αύριο (*av*-ree-o) (*tomorrow*)

>> ευκαιρία (ef-ke-*ree*-a) (*opportunity*)

Consonants

GRAMMATICALLY
SPEAKING

Let's delve into the Greek consonants! A consonant is a sound in speech that is produced by partially or completely obstructing the airflow in the vocal tract. *Voiced consonants* are the consonants in which your vocal cords vibrate when you pronounce them (**B, Γ, Δ, Z, Λ, M, N, P**). *Voiceless consonants* are the ones in which vocal cords stay relaxed, and only air flows through (**Θ, K, Ξ, Π, Σ, T, Φ, X, Ψ**).

For each consonant I provide in the following list, I also give you a word that includes it, to help you practice reading.

>> **Bβ** is pronounced like "v" as in **βιβλίο** (vee-*vlee*-o) (*book*).

>> **Γγ** is pronounced like "y" in "yes" or "g" in "go" (in front of **α, o, ω,** and **ou**) as in **γάλα** (*ga*-la) (*milk*).

>> **Δδ** is pronounced like "th" in "this" or a soft "d," as in **δάσκαλος** (*da*-ska-los) (*teacher*).

>> **Zζ** is pronounced like "z" as in **ζάχαρη** (*za*-kha-ree) (*sugar*).

>> **Θθ** is pronounced like "th" as in **θάλασσα** (*tha*-la-sa) (*sea*).

>> **Kκ** is pronounced like "k" as in **καφές** (ka-*fes*) (*coffee*).

>> **Λλ** is pronounced like "l" as in **λουλούδι** (loo-*loo*-dee) (*flower*).

>> **Mμ** is pronounced like "m" as in **μήλο** (*mee*-lo) (*apple*).

>> **Νν** is pronounced like "n" as in **νερό** (ne-*ro*) (*water*).

>> **Ξξ** is pronounced like "ks" as in **ξενοδοχείο** (kse-no-do-*hee*-o) (*hotel*).

>> **Ππ** is pronounced like "p" as in **παιδί** (pe-*dee*) (*child*).

>> **Ρρ** is pronounced like "r" (with a rolled "r") as in **ρόδι** (*ro*-dee) (*pomegranate*).

>> **Σσ/ς** is pronounced like "s" as in **σπίτι** (*spee*-tee) (*house*).

>> **Ττ** is pronounced like "t" as in **τραπέζι** (tra-*pe*-zee) (*table*).

>> **Φφ** is pronounced like "f" as in **φωτιά** (fo-*tya*) (*fire*).

>> **Χχ** is pronounced like "ch" as in **χέρι** (*he*-ree) (*hand*).

>> **Ψψ** is pronounced like "ps" as in **ψωμί** (pso-*mee*) (*bread*).

Double consonants

Double consonants are combinations of two letters that produce a single sound. These are especially useful for representing sounds like "b," "d," and "g," which don't have single-letter equivalents in the Greek alphabet.

>> **μπ** is pronounced like "b" in "bat" when it appears at the beginning of a word, or like "mb" in "thumb" when it appears in the middle of a word. For example: **μπάλα** (*ba*-la) (*ball*).

>> **ντ** is pronounced like a strong "d" in "dog" when it appears at the beginning of a word, or like "nd" in "hand" when it appears in the middle of a word. For example: **ντομάτα** (do-*ma*-ta) (*tomato*).

>> **γκ** or **γγ** is pronounced like "g" in "go" when it appears at the beginning of a word, or like "ng" in "sing" when it appears in the middle of a word. For example: **γκρίζος** (*gree*-zos) (*gray*), **φεγγάρι** (fe-*nga*-ree) (*moon*).

>> **τσ** is pronounced like "ts" in "pizza." For example: **τσάι** (*tsa*-ee) (*tea*).

>> **τζ** is pronounced like "tz" in "jeans." For example: **τζάμι** (*tza*-mee) (*glass*).

To better learn the double consonants, try reading these words:

>> **μπανάνα** (ba-*na*-na) (*banana*)

>> **ντουλάπα** (doo-*la*-pa) (*wardrobe*)

>> **γκαράζ** (ga-*ra*-z) (*garage*)

>> τσάντα (*tsa*-nda) (*bag*)

>> τζατζίκι (tza-*tzee*-kee) (*tzatziki*)

CULTURAL WISDOM

Tzatziki is a delicious Greek sauce that includes Greek yogurt and cucumber. If you've ever eaten gyros, you've most likely had it.

>> μπλούζα (*bloo*-za) (*blouse*)

>> ντομάτα (do-*ma*-ta) (*tomato*)

>> αγγούρι (a-*ngoo*-ree) (*cucumber*)

>> τσίχλα (*tsee*-khla) (*chewing gum*)

>> τζάκι (*tza*-kee) (*fireplace*)

Getting the Accent Right

The accent is a small mark you see above the vowels. Take, for example, the word πατάτα (pa–*ta*–ta) (*potato*). The accent is the line above the second alpha (ά).

What's the role of the accent? It tells us that we need to emphasize or stress the syllable that has the accent when we speak or read. By emphasizing, I mean that we say it a little louder: πα–*τά*–τα.

REMEMBER

In this book, when you see an italicized syllable in the English transcription of a word, it means that this is the syllable with the accent.

Here are some basic rules for using accents:

>> The accent goes above only vowels or double vowels. For example: φίλος (*fee*-los) (*friend*), ποτήρι (po-*tee*-ree) (*glass*).

>> In double vowels, the accent always goes on the second letter of the combination. For example: παίζω (*pe*-zo) (*I play*), εύκολος (*ef*-ko-los) (*easy*).

>> If a capitalized word starts with an accented vowel, the accent goes to the side of the letter. For example: Άμστερνταμ (*Am*-ste-rdam) (*Amsterdam*).

>> Monosyllabic words are not accented. For example: ζω (zo) (*I live*), και (ke) (*and*).

The word **ή,** which means "or," is accented because when we say it, we give it emphasis: **άσπρος ή μαύρος** (*a*-spros *ee mav*-ros) (*white or black*), **καλό ή κακό** (ka-*lo ee* ka-ko) (*good or bad*), and so on.

>> If a word is written entirely in capital letters, it does not take an accent. For example: **ΧΕΡΙ** (*he*-ree) (*hand*), **ΒΙΒΛΙΟ** (vee-*vlee*-o) (*book*).

The accent helps you a lot with reading and learning vocabulary because it shows you exactly how to emphasize and pronounce the word. So, there's no need to improvise. Just follow the symbols.

Breaking the Combinations

As I explain earlier in this chapter, Greek has double vowels, and these combinations produce certain sounds. For example, αι is pronounced as "e" and ει as "ee." However, in some cases we want to break the combination. Instead of reading αι as "e," we might want to read it as "a-ee." What do we do then? How do we indicate this in written text?

The two rules are as follows:

>> If the syllable is accented on the first of the two vowels (and not on the second, as the accentuation rule states), the combination breaks:

- τσάι (*tsa*-ee) (*tea*)
- ρολόι (ro-*lo*-ee) (*watch*)
- άυπνος (*a*-ee-pnos) (*sleepless*)
- Μάιος (*ma*-ee-os) (*May*)

>> If the combination is not accented on the first of the two vowels, then we must add two dots above the second vowel, which are called **διαλυτικά** (dya-lee-tee-*ka*) (*diaeresis*):

- φαΐ (fa-*ee*) (*food*)
- βόλεϊ (*vo*-le-ee) (*volleyball*)
- μαϊμού (ma-ee-*moo*) (*monkey*)
- θεϊκός (the-ee-*kos*) (*divine*)

Knowing the Punctuation Marks

They say the devil is in the details. And what smaller detail is there than punctuation marks! Small, but significant, as they can change the meaning of an entire sentence.

Punctuation marks in Greek do not differ from punctuation marks in English, except for two cases:

>> . This is the τελεία (te-*lee*-a) (*full stop, period*) in Greek.

>> ! This is the θαυμαστικό (thav-ma-stee-*ko*) (*exclamation mark*).

>> , This is the κόμμα (*ko*-ma) (*comma*).

>> ; This is the Greek ερωτηματικό (e-ro-tee-ma-tee-*ko*) (*question mark*), and it is always placed at the end of questions. That's right; Greek doesn't use "?" as a question mark.

>> «. . .» These are the εισαγωγικά (ee-sa-go-yee-*ka*) (*quotation marks*). They are used when we want to quote someone's words verbatim, when we cite proverbs or sayings, and when we talk about titles of books, works, and the like.

FUN & GAMES

Now that you've learned the letters and can read in Greek, I want to give you some very basic words to read out loud. (And . . . if you memorize what they mean, then you're a star!)

>> ναι (ne) (*yes*)

>> όχι (o-hee) (*no*)

>> ευχαριστώ (ef-kha-ree-*sto*) (*thank you*)

>> παρακαλώ (pa-ra-ka-*lo*) (*please, you're welcome*)

>> γεια (ya) (*hello, hi*)

>> καλημέρα (ka-lee-*me*-ra) (*good morning*)

>> καληνύχτα (ka-lee-*nee*-khta) (*good night*)

>> συγγνώμη (see-*gno*-mee) (*sorry, excuse me*)

>> αγάπη (a-*ga*-pee) (*love*)

>> χαρά (cha-*ra*) (*joy*)

>> ειρήνη (ee-*ree*-nee) (*peace*)

>> νερό (ne-*ro*) (*water*)

>> φαγητό (fa-yee-*to*) (*food*)

>> οικογένεια (ee-ko-*ye*-nee-a) (*family*)

>> σπίτι (*spee*-tee) (*house, home*)

Chapter **3**

Tackling Basic Grammar

G rammar is the misunderstood power of every language! Often, prospective students come to me and say, "I don't want to learn grammar; I just want to learn how to speak Greek!" My friend, you're making your life difficult. Grammar is here to help you speak Greek (or any other language) more correctly and quickly. The logic upon which every language is based also reveals a small part of how its speakers think. Love grammar because it's your ally.

In this chapter, I ease you into your Greek grammar journey with the use of nouns. They are one of the fundamental categories of words in grammar. We use nouns to name people, animals, things, places, ideas, and emotions. In Greek, nouns have genders, singular and plural forms, and cases. Are you ready to unlock this system of the Greek language?

TIP

There's more to grammar than just nouns, of course. Flip to Chapter 4 for details on verbs, adjectives, and more.

Familiarizing Yourself with a Few Basic Nouns

Here I want to give you some basic Greek nouns that I use as examples to talk to you about genders and cases in the rest of this chapter. When learning a language, it's important to start building your vocabulary early so that you can gradually express yourself.

>> άνθρωπος (*an*-thro-pos) (*person*)

>> σπίτι (*spee*-tee) (*house*)

>> θάλασσα (*tha*-la-sa) (*sea*)

>> γάτα (*ga*-ta) (*cat*)

>> δέντρο (*de*-ndro) (*tree*)

>> σκύλος (*skee*-los) (*dog*)

>> ήλιος (*ee*-lyos) (*sun*)

>> νερό (ne-*ro*) (*water*)

>> καρέκλα (ka-*re*-kla) (*chair*)

>> παιδί (pe-*dee*) (*child*)

>> αθλητής (a-thlee-*tees*) (*athlete*)

>> αυτοκίνητο (af-to-*kee*-nee-to) (*car*)

>> βιβλίο (vee-*vlee*-o) (*book*)

>> δουλειά (doo-*lya*) (*work*)

>> δρόμος (*dro*-mos) (*road*)

>> όνομα (*o*-no-ma) (*name*)

>> αγάπη (a-*ga*-pee) (*love*)

>> μαγαζί (ma-ga-*zee*) (*shop*)

>> άνδρας (*an*-dras) (*man*)

TIP

Here are a few tips to start working with Greek nouns (and all Greek vocabulary in general):

>> If you want to practice the genders you read about in the next section, you can look at these words and think about their gender based on their endings.

>> A good way to learn vocabulary is to start by reading this list out loud a few times. If it helps, you can even write down these words a few times or make flashcards to play with in your free time.

>> It will help you if you study a little every day. Instead of working on Greek once a week for many hours, it's better to break your studying into 10–15 minutes a day and learn some vocabulary and grammar. You'll be able to progress continuously without feeling overwhelmed!

Understanding the Genders of Nouns

Greek grammar has three genders of nouns: masculine, feminine, and neuter.

GRAMMATICALLY SPEAKING

Grammatical genders have no relation to the genders of humans and are not based on human logic. For example, in Greek, the word καρέκλα (ka-re-kla) (*chair*) is feminine, and the word λουλούδι (loo-*loo*-dee) (*flower*) is neuter. Each noun has only one gender.

REMEMBER

So, how do we distinguish genders? I promised we'd ease into grammar! And we will. Identifying a word's gender is easy. You need to look at two features:

>> **The ending:** The ending is the group of letters with which a word finishes. Every word has a base part that doesn't change easily, called the *stem,* and an ending, which consists of the final letters that change depending on the word's form.

In the word μπαμπάς (ba-*bas*) (*father*), the stem is μπαμπ- and the ending is -ας. So, if we want to determine the gender of the word μπαμπάς, we look at the ending -ας.

>> **The article:** The article is a small word that comes before every noun. This word changes depending on the noun's gender.

Noun endings

The masculine nouns have three main endings (plus a few less common ones):

>> **-ος:** For example, άνθρωπος (*an*-thro-pos) (*person*), κήπος (*kee*-pos) (*garden*), δρόμος (*dro*-mos) (*road*)

>> **-ας:** For example, αγκώνας (a-*go*-nas) (*elbow*), κανόνας (ka-*no*-nas) (*rule*), άντρας (*an*-dras) (*man*)

>> **-ης:** For example, **καθρέφτης** (ka-*thre*-ftees) (*mirror*), **δυναμίτης** (dee-na-*mee*-tees) (*dynamite*), **φορτιστής** (for-tee-*stees*) (*charger*)

Next, we have feminine nouns, which have two main endings:

>> **-α:** For example, **γάτα** (*ga*-ta) (*cat*), **δουλειά** (doo-*lya*) (*work*), **ημέρα** (ee-*me*-ra) (*day*)

>> **-η:** For example, **αυλή** (av-*lee*) (*yard*), **ζωή** (zo-*ee*) (*life*), **δύναμη** (*dee*-na-mee) (*strength*)

Finally, we have neuter nouns with the following three endings:

>> **-ο:** For example, **νερό** (ne-*ro*) (*water*), **αυτοκίνητο** (af-to-*kee*-nee-to) (*car*), **κινητό** (kee-nee-*to*) (*mobile phone*)

>> **-ι:** Here we have all words ending in **-ι,** such as **παιδί** (pe-*dee*) (*child*), **σπίτι** (*spee*-tee) (*house*), and **μολύβι** (mo-*lee*-vee) (*pencil*)

>> **-μα:** Words ending in **-μα** include **όνομα** (*o*-no-ma) (*name*), **πρόγραμμα** (*pro*-gra-ma) (*program*), and **στόμα** (*sto*-ma) (*mouth*)

TIP

Pay close attention to spelling! In Greek, words ending in **-η** are always feminine, while words ending in **-ι** are always neuter. While both endings may have a similar sound (like "ee"), they shouldn't be confused. Always observe the spelling carefully.

TIP

Also, take note of feminine words ending in **-α** and neuter words ending in **-μα.** If you notice a **μ** before the **-α,** then you can be sure that the word is neuter!

GRAMMATICALLY SPEAKING

There are quite a few foreign words that we use in Modern Greek. Some of them have been fully adopted into the Greek language and have acquired Greek endings — for example, the word **ντουλάπα,** which comes from the Turkish dolap and means wardrobe. Other words, however, still retain their foreign endings, like the word **γκαράζ** (garage). All foreign words that have Greek endings are assigned a grammatical gender, as we've learned (**η ντουλάπα** — feminine) based on their ending. Words with foreign endings are always neuter: **το κομπιούτερ** (the computer), **το γκαράζ** (the garage), **το προφίλ** (the profile).

The articles

Earlier in this chapter, I explain that you can determine the gender of a word by looking at its ending and its article. After you know all about endings, let me tell you about the articles and how they are used!

GRAMMATICALLY SPEAKING

An article is a grammatical word used to define a noun; in English, articles include *a, an,* and *the.* In Greek, the article adjusts to the gender, number, and case of the noun it accompanies. (Find out more about cases later in this chapter.)

The article ο always accompanies masculine nouns:

>> ο αγώνας (o a-*go*-nas) (*the elbow*)

>> ο δρόμος (o *dro*-mos) (*the road*)

>> ο δυναμίτης (o dee-na-*mee*-tees) (*the dynamite*)

The article η accompanies feminine nouns:

>> η καρέκλα (ee ka-*re*-kla) (*the chair*)

>> η αυλή (ee av-*lee*) (*the yard*)

Finally, the article το accompanies neuter nouns:

>> το πρόγραμμα (to *pro*-gra-ma) (*the program*)

>> το παιδί (to pe-*dee*) (*the child*)

>> το δέντρο (to *de*-ndro) (*the tree*)

Breaking Down the Cases

You may have never heard about grammatical cases, especially if you haven't delved into the structure of a language. Here I'll explain cases to you as simply as possible and try to introduce you smoothly to this grammatical concept.

Cases refer to the changes made to nouns, adjectives, pronouns, articles, and passive participles to express different things in a sentence. In other words, depending on what you want to say, you use the corresponding case.

In modern Greek, we have four cases: nominative, genitive, accusative, and vocative. In the following sections I focus on the first three in detail and provide plenty of examples to make your life easier. Just trust the process! (*Note:* I don't cover the vocative case because this chapter is only an introduction to Greek grammar, and I explain only the most important things you need to know as a beginner.)

Nominative case

The nominative is the first case, and it's used when you want to introduce some-one or something. The following sections explain what you need to know.

REMEMBER

The nominative is the basic form of a noun, adjective, or pronoun — that is, the form you'd use if you were to write that word in a dictionary or a vocabulary list.

Articles in the nominative case

As I explain earlier in this chapter, the articles associated with the nominative case are o for masculine nouns, η for feminine nouns, and το for neuter nouns. Examples of nouns in the nominative case include the following:

>> ο Γιάννης (o *ya*-nees) (a Greek name that roughly translates to John in English)

>> ο αθλητής (o a-thlee-*tees*) (*the athlete*)

>> η δουλειά (ee doo-*lya*) (*the job*)

>> η αγάπη (ee a-*ga*-pee) (*the love*)

>> το όνομα (to *o*-no-ma) (*the name*)

>> το μαγαζί (to ma-ga-*zee*) (*the shop*)

The nominative case, like all cases, has both singular and plural forms (see the next section). The articles also have a plural form in the nominative:

>> The masculine article o (o) becomes οι (ee) in the plural.

>> The feminine article η (ee) also becomes οι (ee) in the plural.

>> And the neuter article, which in the singular is το (to), changes to τα (ta) in the plural.

Table 3-1 summarizes singular and plural articles in the nominative case.

TABLE 3-1

Articles in the Nominative Case

Gender	Singular Article	Plural Article
Masculine	o	οι
Feminine	η	οι
Neuter	το	τα

Singular and plural nouns in the nominative case

Let me show you how nouns in the nominative case, depending on their endings and gender, form the plural.

All masculine nouns, depending on which of the three endings they have, form their plural with the corresponding ending. Table 3-2 shows you the details.

TABLE 3-2   **Masculine Nouns in the Nominative Case**

Masculine Noun Ending	Singular Form	Plural Form
-ας	ο άντρας (o *an*-dras) (*the man*)	οι άντρες (ee *an*-dres) (*the men*)
-ος	ο δρόμος (o *dro*-mos) (*the road*)	οι δρόμοι (ee *dro*-mee) (*the roads*)
-ης	ο αθλητής (o a-thlee-*tees*) (*the athlete*)	οι αθλητές (ee a-thlee-*tes*) (*the athletes*)

All feminine nouns, depending on which of the two endings they have, form their plural as shown in Table 3-3.

TABLE 3-3   **Feminine Nouns in the Nominative Case**

Feminine Noun Ending	Singular Form	Plural Form
-α	η δουλειά (ee doo-*lya*) (*the job*)	οι δουλειές (ee doo-*lyes*) (*the jobs*)
-η	η αυλή (ee av-*lee*) (*the yard*)	οι αυλές (ee av-*les*) (*the yards*)

All neuter nouns, depending on which of the three endings they have, form their plural as shown in Table 3-4.

TABLE 3-4   **Neuter Nouns in the Nominative Case**

Neuter Noun Ending	Singular Form	Plural Form
-ο	το νερό (to ne-*ro*) (*the water*)	τα νερά (ta ne-*ra*) (*the waters*)
-ι	το παιδί (to pe-*dee*) (*the child*)	τα παιδιά (ta pe-*dya*) (*the children*)
-μα	το όνομα (to *o*-no-ma) (*the name*)	τα ονόματα (ta o-*no*-ma-ta) (*the names*)

Uses of the nominative case

REMEMBER

In a sentence, the word in the nominative answers the question "who?" or "what?" — it acts as the subject of the sentence. Look at the following examples to understand this better:

» **Ο αθλητής τρέχει.** (o a-thlee-*tees* tre-hee) (*The athlete is running.*)

If I ask "Who is running?" the answer is "the athlete."

» **Το μαγαζί κλείνει.** (to ma-ga-*zee klee*-nee) (*The shop is closing.*)

Here, if I ask "What is closing?" the answer is "the shop."

» **Η Μαρία και ο Γιώργος πηγαίνουν διακοπές.** (ee ma-*ree*-a ke o *yor*-gos pee-*ge*-noon dya-ko-*pes*) (*Maria and George are going on vacation.*)

Again, if I ask "Who is going?" the answer is "Maria and George." These two words are the subjects of the sentence and are in the nominative case.

Accusative case

The accusative is the second grammatical case to examine. However, before I tell you when we use it, we need to look at the changes that occur to nouns when they are in the accusative case. I discuss both the singular and plural forms of the accusative as well as articles and uses in the following sections.

Articles in the accusative case

First of all, let me tell you that the article changes in the accusative. The articles in the accusative are τον (ton), τη(ν) (tee[n]) and το (to). Here are the following rules:

» The masculine article **ο** in the nominative becomes **τον** in the accusative. In the plural, the article **τον** changes to **τους.**

» The feminine article **η** in the nominative becomes **τη(ν)** in the accusative and in the plural becomes **τις.**

GRAMMATICALLY SPEAKING

The feminine article in the accusative has a peculiarity: the **-ν** at the end of the article isn't stable. We keep the **-ν** when the next word starts with

● Any vowel: For example, **την αγάπη** (teen a-*ga*-pee) (*the love*)

● The consonants κ, ξ, π, τ, ψ, μπ, ντ, γκ, τσ, τζ: For example, **την καρέκλα** (teen ka-*re*-kla) (*the chair*)

We drop the **-ν** when the next word starts with the remaining consonants (except those mentioned earlier): For example, **τη δουλειά** (tee doo-*lya*) (*the day*).

>> In the nominative, the neuter article **το** in the plural is **τα,** and it remains exactly the same in the accusative: **το** and **τα.** One less thing for you to remember!

Singular and plural nouns in the accusative case

Get ready to see how nouns change according to their gender in the accusative.

In the nominative, singular masculine nouns have one of three endings: **-ας, -ος,** or **-ης.** Table 3-5 shows you how those endings change in the singular accusative and the plural accusative.

TABLE 3-5   **Masculine Nouns in the Accusative Case**

Masculine Noun Ending	Singular Form	Plural Form
-ας	τον άντρα (ton *an*-dra)	τους άντρες (toos *an*-dres)
-ος	τον δρόμο (ton *dro*-mo)	τους δρόμους (toos *dro*-moos)
-ης	τον αθλητή (ton a-thlee-*tee*)	τους αθλητές (toos a-thlee-*tes*)

In the nominative, singular feminine nouns end in **-α** or **-η.** Table 3-6 shows you how those endings change in the singular accusative and the plural accusative.

TABLE 3-6   **Feminine Nouns in the Accusative Case**

Feminine Noun Ending	Singular Form	Plural Form
-α	τη δουλειά (tee doo-*lya*)	τις δουλειές (tees doo-*lyes*)
-η	την αυλή (teen av-*lee*)	τις αυλές (tees av-*les*)

In the nominative, neuter nouns end in **-ο, -ι** or **-μα.** Table 3-7 shows you how those endings change in the singular accusative and the plural accusative.

TABLE 3-7 **Neuter Nouns in the Accusative Case**

Neuter Noun Ending	Singular Form	Plural Form
-o	το νερό (to ne-*ro*)	τα νερά (ta ne-*ra*)
-ι	το παιδί (to pe-*dee*)	τα παιδιά (ta pe-*dya*)
-μα	το όνομα (to *o*-no-ma)	τα ονόματα (ta o-*no*-ma-ta)

Uses of the accusative case

You may be wondering about the use of the accusative case in the Greek language. Let's take a look at some basic uses in this section.

REMEMBER

The accusative is used as the object of a verb. To identify it, you simply ask "whom" or "what." Look at the following examples to understand practically what I'm explaining:

>> **Η Μαρία ταΐζει τον σκύλο.** (ee ma-*ree*-a ta-*ee*-zee ton *skee*-lo) (*Maria feeds the dog.*)

Here, if I ask, "Whom does Maria feed?" the answer is "the dog." This is the object of the sentence and is in the accusative case. (It's a masculine noun.)

>> **Ο Γιώργος παντρεύεται την Ειρήνη.** (o *yor*-gos pa-*ndre*-ve-te teen ee-*ree*-nee) (*George marries Irene.*)

To the question "Whom does George marry?" the answer is "Irene," so again we see the word in the accusative. (It's a feminine noun.)

>> **Οι γονείς φροντίζουν τα παιδιά.** (ee go-*nees* fro-*ndee*-zoon ta pe-*dya*) (*The parents take care of the children.*)

If I ask, "Whom do the parents take care of?" your answer is "the children." Again, as you see, this is the object and is in the accusative. (It's a neuter noun.)

Additionally, the accusative is used when a noun follows one of the following prepositions:

>> με (me) (*with*): Example: **Πηγαίνω με το αυτοκίνητο.** (pee-*ye*-no me to af-to-*kee*-nee-to) (*I go with the car.*) You can tell this noun in the accusative is neuter.

>> για (ya) (*for*): Example: **Αγόρασα ένα αυτοκίνητο για την κόρη μου.** (a-*go*-ra-sa *e*-na af-to-*kee*-nee-to ya teen *ko*-ree moo) (*I bought a car for my daughter.*) You can tell this noun in the accusative is feminine.

>> πρoς (pros) (*toward*): Example: **Πηγαίνω πρoς τo κέντρo.** (pee-*ye*-no pros to *ke*-ndro) (*I go toward the center.*) You can tell this noun in the accusative is neuter.

>> σε (se) (*to, in, at*): Example: **Πάω στo εστιατόριo.** (*pa*-o sto e-stee-a-*to*-ree-o) (*I'm going to the restaurant.*)

This particular preposition has a peculiarity. When it's next to the articles of the accusative — **τoν, τη(ν), τo** — it merges with them to form the articles **στoν, στη(ν), στo.** Examples:

● **Τηλεφωνώ στη γιαγιά μoυ.** (tee-le-fo-*no* stee ya-*ya* moo) (*I call my grand-mother.*) You can tell this noun in the accusative is feminine.

● **Ο Νίκoς πηγαίνει στo γυμναστήριo.** (o *nee*-kos pee-*ye*-nee sto yee-mna-*stee*-ree-o) (*Nikos goes to the gym.*) You can tell this noun in the accusative is neuter.

Genitive case

The third case I explain to you is the genitive. As with the previous two cases, changes occur in the articles and nouns.

Articles in the genitive case

Let's start with the articles in the genitive case:

>> The masculine article **o** (o) in the singular becomes **τoυ** (too) and in the plural **των** (ton).

>> The feminine article **η** (ee) becomes **της** (tees) in the singular and **των** (ton) in the plural.

>> The neuter article **τo** (to) becomes **τoυ** (too) in the singular and **των** (ton) in the plural.

Singular and plural nouns in the genitive case

The endings of nouns change in the genitive. I show you how to adapt them according to their endings.

In the nominative, singular masculine nouns have one of three endings: -ας, -oς, or -ης. Table 3-8 shows you how those endings change in the singular genitive and the plural genitive.

TABLE 3-8 **Masculine Nouns in the Genitive Case**

Masculine Noun Ending	Singular Form	Plural Form
-ας	του άντρα (too *an*-dra)	των αντρών (ton an-*dron*)
-ος	του δρόμου (too *dro*-moo)	των δρόμων (ton *dro*-mon)
-ης	του αθλητή (too a-thlee-*tee*)	των αθλητών (ton a-thlee-*ton*)

In the nominative, singular feminine nouns end in -α or -η. Table 3-9 shows you how those endings change in the singular genitive and the plural genitive.

TABLE 3-9 **Feminine Nouns in the Genitive Case**

Feminine Noun Ending	Singular Form	Plural Form
-α	της δουλειάς (tees doo-*lyas*)	των δουλειών (ton doo-*lyon*)
-η	της αυλής (tees av-*lees*)	των αυλών (ton av-*lon*)

In the nominative, neuter nouns end in -ο, -ι, or -μα. Table 3-10 shows you how those endings change in the singular genitive and the plural genitive.

TABLE 3-10 **Neuter Nouns in the Genitive Case**

Neuter Noun Ending	Singular Form	Plural Form
-ο	του νερού (too ne-*roo*)	των νερών (ton ne-*ron*)
-ι	του παιδιού (too pe-*dyoo*)	των παιδιών (ton pe-*dyon*)
-μα	του ονόματος (too o-*no*-ma-tos)	των ονομάτων (ton o-no-*ma*-ton)

Uses of the genitive case

When do you use the genitive, and how is it different from the other two cases we've discussed?

REMEMBER

With the genitive, you can express ownership or to whom something belongs. For example: Αυτό είναι το καπέλο του άντρα. (af-*to ee*-ne to ka-*pe*-lo too *an*-dra) (*This is the man's hat.*) The hat belongs to the man, so the word for "man" is in the genitive.

Similarly, notice these phrases:

» ο γιος της Μαρίας (o yos tees ma-*ree*-as) (*Maria's son*)

» το σπίτι του Νίκου (to *spee*-tee too *nee*-koo) (*Nikos's house*)

Additionally, we can use the genitive to explain something in more detail by providing extra information about it. Example: Ο Μάριος πήρε το πτυχίο της ιατρικής. (o *ma*-ree-os *pee*-re to ptee-*hee*-o tees ee-a-tree-*kees*) (*Marios got a medicine degree.*) In this sentence, the word for medicine (ιατρικής), which is in the genitive, explains the kind of degree Marios got.

What does the genitive explain in the following sentences?

» Έχω μία κρέμα προσώπου. (*e*-kho *mee*-a *kre*-ma pro-*so*-poo) (*I have a face cream.*)

» Κρατάω ένα μπολ παγωτού. (kra-*ta*-o *e*-na bol pa-go-*too*) (*I'm holding an ice cream bowl.*)

» Πίνω καφέ Κολομβίας. (*pee*-no ka-*fe* ko-lo-*mvee*-as) (*I drink Colombian coffee.*)

You're correct if you answered that all the descriptive words (face, ice cream, and Colombian) are in the genitive case.

The genitive is also related to certain prepositions:

» εναντίον (e-na-*dee*-on) (*against*): Example: Ο άντρας επιτέθηκε εναντίον του λιονταριού. (o *a*-ndras e-pee-*te*-thee-ke e-na-*dee*-on too lyo-da-*ryoo*) (*The man attacked the lion.*) The word for "lion" is in the genitive.

» εξαιτίας (e-kse-*tee*-as) (*because of*): Example: Εξαιτίας της βροχής δεν πήγαμε στο βουνό. (e-kse-*tee*-as tees vro-*hees* den *pee*-ga-me sto voo-*no*) (*Because of the rain, we didn't go to the mountain.*) The word for "rain" is in the genitive.

» μεταξύ (me-ta-*ksee*) (*between*): Example: Μεταξύ της φράουλας και της μπανάνας προτιμώ τη φράουλα. (me-ta-*ksee* tees *fra*-oo-las ke tees ba-*na*-nas pro-tee-*mo* tee *fra*-oo-la) (*Between the strawberry and the banana, I prefer the strawberry.*) The words for "strawberry" and "banana" are in the genitive.

You also encounter the genitive in Greek when talking about dates. For instance, when you see March 15, you read it as δεκαπέντε Μαρτίου (de-ka-*pe*-nde Ma-*rtee*-oo), putting the month in the genitive.

Here are some more examples to help you understand (see Chapter 6 for more details on dates and numbers):

>> January 29 is **είκοσι εννιά Ιανουαρίου** (*ee*-ko-see e-*nya* ee-a-noo-a-*ree*-oo).

>> July 7 is **επτά Ιουλίου** (e-*pta* ee-oo-*lee*-oo).

Putting it all together: An overview of the cases

In the preceding sections, I explain each case in detail and how nouns change. In this section I consolidate all this information into three tables — one for each gender — so that you can have a comprehensive overview.

Masculine nouns in the nominative case end in -ας, -ος, or -ης. Table 3-11 shows the articles and endings for masculine nouns in the nominative, accusative, and genitive cases.

TABLE 3-11   **Masculine Nouns in Three Cases**

Masculine Noun Ending	Singular Nominative	Plural Nominative	Singular Accusative	Plural Accusative	Singular Genitive	Plural Genitive
-ας	ο άντρας	οι άντρες	τον άντρα	τους άντρες	του άντρα	των αντρών
-ος	ο δρόμος	οι δρόμοι	τον δρόμο	τους δρόμους	του δρόμου	των δρόμων
-ης	ο αθλητής	οι αθλητές	τον αθλητή	τους αθλητές	του αθλητή	των αθλητών

Feminine nouns in the nominative case end in -α or -η. Table 3-12 shows the articles and endings for feminine nouns in the nominative, accusative, and genitive cases.

TABLE 3-12   **Feminine Nouns in Three Cases**

Feminine Noun Ending	Singular Nominative	Plural Nominative	Singular Accusative	Plural Accusative	Singular Genitive	Plural Genitive
-α	η δουλειά	οι δουλειές	την δουλειά	τις δουλειές	της δουλειάς	των δουλειών
-η	η αυλή	οι αυλές	την αυλή	τις αυλές	της αυλής	των αυλών

Neuter nouns in the nominative case end in -o, -ι or -μα. Table 3-13 shows the articles and endings for neuter nouns in the nominative, accusative, and genitive cases.

TABLE 3-13   **Neuter Nouns in Three Cases**

Neuter Noun Ending	Singular Nominative	Plural Nominative	Singular Accusative	Plural Accusative	Singular Genitive	Plural Genitive
-o	το νερό	τα νερά	το νερό	τα νερά	του νερού	των νερών
-ι	το παιδί	τα παιδιά	το παιδί	τα παιδιά	του παιδιού	των παιδιών
-μα	το όνομα	τα ονόματα	το όνομα	τα ονόματα	του ονόματος	των ονομάτων

What's Mine and What's Yours: Possessive Pronouns

I want to introduce you to possessive pronouns, which are especially helpful when talking about things that belong to you in Greek. These pronouns accompany nouns, as in this example: η τσάντα μου (ee *tsa*-nda moo) (*my bag*). Here, μου is the pronoun indicating that the bag belongs to me.

REMEMBER

Possessive pronouns change depending on the person to whom something belongs. Let's look at these changes:

>> μου (moo) (*my*): Used for something that belongs to me

Example: το παιδί μου (to pe-*dee* moo) (*my child*)

>> σου (soo) (*your* [singular]): Used for something that belongs to you

Example: η φίλη σου (ee *fee*-lee soo) (*your friend*)

>> του (too) (*his/its*): Refers to something belonging to a masculine or neuter noun

Example: ο φίλος του (o *fee*-los too) (*his friend*), το χρώμα του (to *khro*-ma too) (*its color*)

>> της (tees) (*her*): Refers to something belonging to a feminine noun

Example: το σπίτι της (to *spee*-tee tees) (*her house*)

>> **μας** (mas) (*our*): For something belonging to us

Example: **το τραπέζι μας** (to tra-*pe*-zee mas) (*our table*)

>> **σας** (sas) (*your* [plural]): The plural or polite form of "your"

Example: **η παρέα σας** (ee pa-*re*-a sas) (*your company*)

>> **τους** (toos) (*their*): Used for something that belongs to them

Example: **οι ιδέες τους** (ee ee-*de*-es toos) (*their ideas*)

How could you say that the cat is yours? You would say: **η γάτα μου** (ee *ga*-ta moo) (*my cat*). And if the cat belongs to Maria? Then you would say: **η γάτα της** (ee *ga*-ta tees) (*her cat*).

How would you say that the book is yours (plural)? You would say: **το βιβλίο σας** (to vee-*vlee*-o sas) (*your book*). And if it is ours? You would say: **το βιβλίο μας** (to vee-*vlee*-o mas) (*our book*).

FUN & GAMES

Here is a list of country names, and I want you to place each word into the correct box based on its grammatical gender. (Find out more about different countries and nationalities in Chapter 5.)

» Μεξικό

» Λίβανος

» Βέλγιο

» Ιράκ

» Αγγλία

» Καναδάς

» Αμερική

» Γερμανία

» Μαυρίκιος

» Περού

» Ταϊλάνδη

» Παναμάς

» Πουέρτο Ρίκο

Masculine	Feminine	Neuter

Chapter **4**

Grammar Beyond the Basics

This chapter is the most technical chapter of the book, as here you discover many things related to verb tenses and conjugations. You may say that it's also the most demanding chapter because it requires a careful approach to absorb all the information provided. At the same time, however, it's one of the most important chapters, as you find out how to talk about the present, past, and future in Greek and how to use adjectives to enrich your speech. Are you ready?

Introducing a Few Basic Greek Verbs

What are verbs? Verbs are words that express an action or a state. They are one of the basic parts of speech because they help you explain what a noun does, feels, or what state it is in.

For example, look at the following sentence: Η Μαρία τρέχει. (ee ma-*ree*-a *tre*-hee) (*Maria runs.*) The verb τρέχει, which means "to run," shows Maria's action. Similarly, in the sentence Το παιδί κλαίει (to pe-*dee kle*-ee) (*The child cries*), the verb κλαίει indicates the state the child is in.

Before I dive deep into analyzing verbs, I would like to give you some basic verbs in the Greek language that will help you form your first sentences in Greek. So, let's begin:

>> είμαι (*ee*-me) (*to be*)

>> έχω (*e*-kho) (*to have*)

>> κάνω (*ka*-no) (*to do*)

>> πηγαίνω (pee-*ye*-no) (*to go*)

>> μένω (*me*-no) (*to live, to stay*)

>> πίνω (*pee*-no) (*to drink*)

>> βλέπω (*vle*-po) (*to see*)

>> διαβάζω (dya-*va*-zo) (*to read*)

>> γράφω (*gra*-fo) (*to write*)

>> δουλεύω (doo-*lev*-o) (*to work*)

>> πληρώνω (plee-*ro*-no) (*to pay*)

>> μαθαίνω (ma-*the*-no) (*to learn*)

>> δίνω (*dee*-no) (*to give*)

>> παίρνω (*pe*-rno) (*to take*)

>> παίζω (*pe*-zo) (*to play*)

>> ανοίγω (a-*nee*-go) (*to open*)

>> κλείνω (*klee*-no) (*to close*)

>> μιλάω (mee-*la*-o) (*to speak*)

>> αγαπάω (a-ga-*pa*-o) (*to love*)

>> φοράω (fo-*ra*-o) (*to wear*)

>> ρωτάω (ro-*ta*-o) (*to ask*)

>> έρχομαι (*e*-rkho-me) (*to come*)

>> χρειάζομαι (khree-*a*-zo-me) (*to need*)

>> κάθομαι (*ka*-tho-me) (*to sit*)

>> σηκώνομαι (see-*ko*-no-me) (*to get up*)

>> λυπάμαι (lee-*pa*-me) (*to be sad*)

>> κοιμάμαι (kee-*ma*-me) (*to sleep*)

- » φοβάμαι (fo-*va*-me) (*to be afraid*)

- » τρώω (*tro*-o) (*to eat*)

- » ακούω (a-*koo*-o) (*to listen*)

- » οδηγώ (o-dee-*go*) (*to drive*)

- » τηλεφωνώ (tee-le-fo-*no*) (*to call*)

- » μπορώ (bo-*ro*) (*to be able*)

By learning these verbs, you build a good foundation and move forward with the Greek language.

TIP

A good idea for organizing the list of verbs you've learned is to categorize them based on their topic. For example, you can group together verbs related to emotions such as λυπάμαι (lee-*pa*-me) (*to be sad*), αγαπώ (a-ga-*po*) (*to love*), φοβάμαι (fo-*va*-me) (*to be afraid*), and so on, or verbs related to daily habits such as δουλεύω (doo-*lev*-o) (*to work*), κοιμάμαι (kee-*ma*-me) (*to sleep*), τηλεφωνώ (tee-le-fo-*no*) (*to call*), οδηγώ (o-dee-*go*) (*to drive*), and the like. This way, you not only strengthen your vocabulary in various topics but also create mental connections between the words, making it easier to remember them. Of course, you probably can think of other ways of categorizing them that may work better for you.

Who Does What? The Persons of Greek Verbs

Verbs in Greek, just like in English, have persons (that is, first person, second person, third person), and they change and adapt depending on the person with whom they are used. Therefore, I cannot discuss verbs without first understanding the persons.

Singular persons include the following:

- » εγώ (e-*go*) (*I*): This is the first person. I use it when I want to talk about myself. Examples: εγώ τρέχω (e-*go* tre-kho) (*I run*), εγώ παίζω (e-*go* pe-zo) (*I play*), εγώ κάνω (e-*go* ka-no) (*I do*).

- » εσύ (e-*see*) (*you, singular*): This is the second person. I use it when I want to talk about what you (singular) do. Examples: εσύ κάνεις (e-*see* ka-nees) (*you do*), εσύ μπορείς (e-*see* bo-*rees*) (*you can*).

>> **αυτός** (af-*tos*) (*he*): This is the masculine third person, as in "he" in English. Examples: **αυτός διαβάζει** (af-*tos* dya-*va*-zee) (*he reads*), **αυτός ακούει** (af-*tos* a-*koo*-ee) (*he listens*).

>> **αυτή** (af-*tee*) (*she*): The third person for feminine nouns. It's used when we talk about actions performed by a feminine noun. Examples: **αυτή τρέχει** (af-*tee* *tre*-hee) (*she runs*), **αυτή οδηγεί** (af-*tee* o-dee-*yee*) (*she drives*).

>> **αυτό** (af-*to*) (*it*): The third person also has a neuter form, used for actions performed by neuter nouns. Examples: **αυτό περπατάει** (af-*to* pe-rpa-*ta*-ee) (*it walks*), **αυτό οδηγεί** (af-*to* o-dee-*yee*) (*it drives*).

TIP

Confused by the mention of masculine, feminine, and neuter nouns? Head to Chapter 3 for the basics.

Plural persons include the following:

>> **εμείς** (e-*mees*) (*we*): This is the first person of the plural. Examples: **εμείς είμαστε** (e-*mees* ee-ma-ste) (*we are*), **εμείς μπορούμε** (e-*mees* bo-*roo*-me) (*we can*).

>> **εσείς** (e-*sees*) (*you,* plural): This is the second person of the plural.

REMEMBER

In English, the second person ("you") is the same for both singular and plural, whereas in Greek, the singular is **εσύ** and the plural is **εσείς.**

>> **Third person (plural):** In English, the third person plural is "they" and is the same for all three genders. However, in Greek, there are three different plural forms, depending on the gender:

- **αυτοί** (af-*tee*) (*they,* masculine): Used for masculine plural nouns

- **αυτές** (af-*tes*) (*they,* feminine): Used for plural feminine nouns

- **αυτά** (af-*ta*) (*they,* neuter): Used for plural neuter nouns

GRAMMATICALLY SPEAKING

The masculine plural form doesn't only refer to a group of masculine nouns. For example: **ο Γιώργος και ο Νίκος τρέχουν** (o *yo*-rgos ke o *nee*-kos *tre*-khoon) (*George and Nikos run*) can be **αυτοί τρέχουν** (af-*tee tre*-khoon) (*they run*). But the masculine plural form can also refer to a mixed group of genders. For example: **ο Νίκος, η Έλσα, και η Γεωργία περπατούν** (o *nee*-kos, ee *e*-lsa, ke ee ye-o-*ryee*-a pe-rpa-*toon*) (*Nikos, Elsa, and Georgia walk*) is also **αυτοί περπατούν** (af-*tee* pe-rpa-*toon*) (*they walk*). So, when referring to mixed groups of masculine, feminine, and neuter nouns, use the masculine plural form **αυτοί.**

The Verb "Είμαι" (To Be)

After you understand the persons of verbs (see the previous section), it's time to talk about the most basic verb in Greek, the auxiliary verb είμαι (*ee*-me) (*to be*). Table 4-1 shows the conjugation of this useful verb.

TABLE 4-1

The Verb Είμαι

Person	Conjugation	Translation
εγώ	είμαι (*ee*-me)	I am
εσύ	είσαι (*ee*-se)	You are
αυτός/αυτή/αυτό	είναι (*ee*-ne)	He/she/it is
εμείς	είμαστε (*ee*-ma-ste)	We are
εσείς	είστε/είσαστε (*ee*-ste/*ee*-sa-ste)	You are
αυτοί/αυτές/αυτά	είναι (*ee*-ne)	They are

To better understand the use of the verb είμαι and to be able to use it yourself when speaking, take a look at the following examples:

Εγώ είμαι η Ειρήνη. (e-*go ee*-me ee ee-*ree*-nee) (*I am Eirini.*)

Η δασκάλα είναι 29 χρονών. (ee da-*ska*-la *ee*-ne ee-ko-see e-*nya* khro-*non*) (*The teacher is 29 years old.*)

Ο Γιώργος και ο Γιάννης είναι φίλοι. (o *yo*-rgos ke o *ya*-nees *ee*-ne *fee*-lee) (*George and John are friends.*)

Breaking Down Verb Types

Beyond the auxiliary verb είμαι (*to be*), which I conjugate in the previous section, the rest of the verbs in the Greek language are categorized based on their type. Verbs in each category function the same way and are conjugated in the same manner, meaning they have the same endings.

REMEMBER

Every verb has two parts: the stem and the ending.

>> The stem of a verb is its core part that remains constant in all conjugations and from which its various forms are derived.

>> The different endings added to the stem indicate person, number, tense, and so on.

For example, in the verb δουλεύω (doo-*lev*-o) (*I work*), in the first-person singular, the stem is δουλεύ- and the ending is -ω. The ending that a verb has in the first-person singular determines the category (type) to which the verb belongs.

So, in the verb δουλεύω, the ending is -ω (omega without an accent), and it belongs to Type A. Similarly, the verb αγαπάω (*I love*) ends in -άω and belongs to Type B1. Of course, I explain each type individually in the following sections. And if all this theory feels overwhelming, don't worry! I'm here to help you untangle the web of Greek verbs step by step. Let's go!

REMEMBER

You may be thinking, "Why should I bother with endings, theory, and grammar?" Being able to use verbs correctly in a language is crucial for expressing yourself and for native speakers to understand what you're saying.

Type A verbs

Type A verbs include verbs that, in the first-person singular, end in -ω (the omega without an accent). Here are some examples:

>> πηγαίνω (pee-*ye*-no) (*to go*)

>> πίνω (*pee*-no) (*to drink*)

>> διαβάζω (dya-*va*-zo) (*to read, to study*)

Table 4-2 shows you how a verb of this type is conjugated across all persons. This conjugation is in ενεστώτας (e-ne-*sto*-tas) (*present tense*).

GRAMMATICALLY
SPEAKING

In the third-person plural, you see the endings -ουν or -ουνε. The first is common in written language, mainly in a formal and neutral style, while the second is very common in spoken language and in children's literature texts.

All right, let's also look at some example sentences:

Η Μάρθα πηγαίνει στην εκκλησία. (ee *ma*-rtha pee-*ye*-nee steen e-klee-*see*-a) (*Martha is going to church.*)

Διαβάζουμε μαθηματικά γιατί έχουμε διαγώνισμα. (dya-*va*-zoo-me ma-thee-ma-tee-*ka* ya-*tee* e-khoo-me dee-a-*go*-nee-sma) (*We are studying math because we have a test.*)

TABLE 4-2 **Type A Verb Conjugation**

Person	The Verb Διαβάζω	The Verb Πίνω	Ending
εγώ	διαβάζω (dya-*va*-zo) (*I read*)	πίνω (*pee*-no) (*I drink*)	-ω
εσύ	διαβάζεις (dya-*va*-zees) (*you read*)	πίνεις (*pee*-nees) (*you drink*)	-εις
αυτός/αυτή/αυτό	διαβάζει (dya-*va*-zee) (*he/she/it reads*)	πίνει (*pee*-nee) (*he/she/it drinks*)	-ει
εμείς	διαβάζουμε (dya-*va*-zoo-me) (*we read*)	πίνουμε (*pee*-noo-me) (*we drink*)	-ουμε
εσείς	διαβάζετε (dya-*va*-ze-te) (*you read*)	πίνετε (*pee*-ne-te) (*you drink*)	-είτε
αυτοί/αυτές/αυτά	διαβάζουν(ε) (dya-*va*-zoon[e]) (*they read*)	πίνουν(ε) (*pee*-noon[e]) (*they drink*)	-ουν(ε)

Type B1 and B2 verbs

The second type of verbs is Type B, which has two subgroups, B1 and B2.

» The first group (B1) includes verbs that end in **-άω.** Take, for example, the verb **μιλάω** (mee-*la*-o) (*to speak*). These verbs also have a shorter form ending in **-ώ.** This means you can choose to say either **μιλάω** or **μιλώ** (mee-*lo*). Both forms are equivalent, so it's up to you to decide which one you prefer to use.

» Type B2, on the other hand, includes verbs that end in **-ώ** (omega with an accent) — for example, the verb **μπορώ** (bo-*ro*) (*to be able to*).

Table 4-3 conjugates the verbs from Type B1 so you can see the endings.

TABLE 4-3 **Type B1 Verb Conjugation**

Person	The Verb Μιλάω/Μιλώ	Ending
εγώ	μιλάω/μιλώ (mee-*la*-o/mee-*lo*) (*I speak*)	-άω/-ώ
εσύ	μιλάς (mee-*las*) (*you speak*)	-άς
αυτός/αυτή/αυτό	μιλάει/μιλά (mee-*la*-ee/mee-*la*) (*he/she/it speaks*)	-άει/-ά
εμείς	μιλάμε (mee-*la*-me) (*we speak*)	-άμε
εσείς	μιλάτε (mee-*la*-te) (*you speak*)	-άτε
αυτοί/αυτές/αυτά	μιλάν(ε)/μιλούν(ε) (mee-*la*-n[e]/mee–*loo*-n[e]) (*they speak*)	-άν(ε)/-ούν(ε)

Table 4-4 shows you how to conjugate Type B2 verbs.

TABLE 4-4

Type B2 Verb Conjugation

Person	The Verb Μπορώ	Ending
εγώ	μπορώ (bo-*ro*) (*I can*)	-ώ
εσύ	μπορείς (bo-*rees*) (*you can*)	-είς
αυτός/αυτή/αυτό	μπορεί (bo-*ree*) (*he/she/it can*)	-εί
εμείς	μπορούμε (bo-*roo*-me) (*we can*)	-ούμε
εσείς	μπορείτε (bo-*ree*-te) (*you can*)	-είτε
αυτοί/αυτές/αυτά	μπορούν(ε) (bo-*roo*-n[e]) (*they can*)	-ούν(ε)

Here are two simple examples with B1 and B2 verbs:

Η Νίκη μιλάει με την Μαρίνα. (ee *nee*-kee mee-*la*-ee me teen ma-*ree*-na) (*Niki talks with Marina.*)

Εμείς χρησιμοποιούμε το αυτοκίνητο. (e-mees khree-see-mo-pee-*oo*-me to af-to-*kee*-nee-to) (*We use the car.*)

Type AB verbs

Type AB verbs have stems that end in a vowel. In this case, the combination of a vowel and an ending — for example, the verb ακούω (a-*koo*-o) (*to hear*). The stem is ακού-, which ends in the vowel -ου, and the ending is -ω.

Table 4-5 looks at the conjugation of the verbs in this category.

Here are a few examples to help you see how such verbs are used in sentences:

Εσείς ακούτε κλασσική μουσική; (e-*sees* a-*koo*-te kla-see-*kee* moo-see-*kee*) (*Do you listen to classical music?*)

Ο Νίκος και η Βίκυ τρώνε πολλές σαλάτες. (o *nee*-kos ke ee *vee*-kee *tro*-ne po-*les* sa-*la*-tes) (*Nikos and Vicky eat a lot of salads.*)

Το μωρό κλαίει δυνατά. (to mo-*ro* *kle*-ee dee-na-*ta*) (*The baby cries loudly.*)

TABLE 4-5

Type AB Verb Conjugation

Person	The Verb Ακούω	Endings
εγώ	ακούω (a-*koo*-o) (*I listen*)	-ω
εσύ	ακούς (a-*koos*) (*you listen*)	-ς
αυτός/αυτή/αυτό	ακούει (a-*koo*-ee) (*he/she/it listens*)	-ει
εμείς	ακούμε (a-*koo*-me) (*we listen*)	-με
εσείς	ακούτε (a-*koo*-te) (*you listen*)	-τε
αυτοί/αυτές/αυτά	ακούν(ε) (a-*koo*-n[e]) (*they listen*)	-ν(ε)

Type Γ1 and Γ2 verbs

This is the last category of verbs. Verbs that end in -oμαι belong to type Γ1, and verbs that end in -αμαι belong to type Γ2.

An example of a type Γ1 verb is έρχομαι (*e*-rkho-me) (*I come*). Its root is έρχ-, and its suffix is -oμαι. Similarly, an example of a type Γ2 verb is κοιμάμαι (kee-*ma*-me) (*I sleep*), with the root κοιμ- and the suffix -άμαι. Table 4-6 shows how to conjugate a Γ1 verb.

TABLE 4-6

Type Γ1 Verb Conjugation

Person	The Verb Έρχομαι	Ending
εγώ	έρχομαι (*e*-rkho-me) (*I come*)	-ομαι
εσύ	έρχεσαι (*e*-rkhe-se) (*you come*)	-εσαι
αυτός/αυτή/αυτό	έρχεται (*e*-rkhe-te) (*se/she/it comes*)	-εται
εμείς	ερχόμαστε (e-*rkho*-ma-ste) (*we come*)	-όμαστε
εσείς	έρχεστε/ερχόσαστε (*e*-rkhe-ste/e-rkho-sa-ste) (*you come*)	-εστε/-οσαστε
αυτοί/αυτές/αυτά	έρχονται (*e*-rkho-de) (*they come*)	-ονται

Table 4-7 shows how to conjugate a Γ2 verb.

TABLE 4-7

Type Γ1 Verb Conjugation

Person	The Verb Κοιμάμαι	Ending
εγώ	**κοιμάμαι** (kee-*ma*-me) (*I sleep*)	**-άμαι**
εσύ	**κοιμάσαι** (kee-*ma*-se) (*you sleep*)	**-άσαι**
αυτός/αυτή/αυτό	**κοιμάται** (kee-*ma*-te) (*he/she/it sleeps*)	**-άται**
εμείς	**κοιμόμαστε** (kee-*mo*-ma-ste) (*we sleep*)	**-όμαστε**
εσείς	**κοιμάστε/κοιμόσαστε** (kee-*ma*-ste/kee-*mo*-sa-ste) (*you sleep*)	**-άστε/-όσαστε**
αυτοί/αυτές/αυτά	**κοιμούνται** (kee-*moo*-de) (*they sleep*)	**-ούνται**

Here are some examples of these verb types in action:

> **Η Μαρία κοιμάται.** (ee ma-*ree*-a kee-*ma*-te) (*Maria goes to sleep.*)

> **Ο πατέρας έρχεται από τη δουλειά το απόγευμα.** (o pa-*te*-ras *e*-rkhe-te a-*po* tee doo-*lya* to a-*po*-yev-ma) (*The father comes home from work in the evening.*)

Nouns and Verbs in the Mix: Forming Sentences

In Chapter 3, I explain how to conjugate and use nouns, and earlier in this chapter, I introduce you to verbs. After you have this foundational knowledge, it's a good time to show you how to mix these to create sentences in Greek.

REMEMBER

You need to know three main principles in forming sentences:

» **Basic sentence structure:** Let's start with the basics. The typical word order in Greek is **subject–verb–object**. For example:

- **Η Μαρία τρώει το μήλο.** (ee ma-*ree*-a *tro*-ee to *mee*-lo) (*Maria eats the apple.*)

Here, **Η Μαρία** is the subject, **τρώει** is the verb, and **το μήλο** is the object.

» **Agreement between words:** It's important to remember that in Greek, words (nouns, adjectives, verbs) must agree in gender, number, and case (see Chapter 3 for details). For example:

- **Ο Νίκος κοιμάται.** (o *nee*-kos kee-*ma*-te) (*Nikos is sleeping.*)

Ο Νίκος is the subject; it's masculine, singular. The verb is conjugated to match the subject, so here it is in the third person singular: **κοιμάται.**

>> **Combining nouns and verbs:** We use the correct case for nouns based on their role in the sentence (for example, nominative for the subject, accusative for the object). For instance:

● **Το παιδί διαβάζει το βιβλίο.** (to pe-*dee* dya-*va*-zee to vee-*vlee*-o) (*The child reads the book.*)

Το παιδί is the subject in the nominative case, and **το βιβλίο** is the object in the accusative case.

Here Come the Adjectives

You can find out about nouns in Chapter 3 and verbs earlier in this chapter. Great! With that knowledge, you can create simple sentences in Greek. But wouldn't it be nice to describe the things you're talking about? Absolutely! And to do that, you need adjectives.

Adjectives are words used to describe or give characteristics to nouns, helping to define them better. Let's look at the following examples:

>> **ο καλός άνθρωπος** (o ka-*los* a-nthro-pos) (*the good person*): Here, we gain information about the quality of the person.

>> **η μεγάλη αυλή** (ee me-*ga*-lee av-lee) (*the big yard*): The adjective helps us understand the size of the yard.

>> **το μικρό παιδί** (to mee-*kro* pe-dee) (*the young kid*): The adjective **μικρό** gives us information about the age of the child.

REMEMBER

Wonderful! It seems simple, but since you're learning Greek, there's always a twist. Adjectives have gender, declensions, and number.

>> **Gender:** In Chapter 3, you see that nouns have gender, meaning they can be masculine, feminine, or neuter. Adjectives, however, have all three genders. Let's look at the adjective **καλός** (*good*):

● Masculine: **ο καλός φίλος** (o ka-*los* fee-los) (*the good friend*)

● Feminine: **η καλή φίλη** (ee ka-*lee* fee-lee) (*the good friend*)

● Neuter: **το καλό βιβλίο** (to ka-*lo* vee-*vlee*-o) (*the good book*)

>> **Number:** Similarly, adjectives have different forms for the singular and plural:

- Singular: **το ψηλό δέντρο** (to psee-*lo* de-dro) (*the tall tree*)

- Plural: **τα ψηλά δέντρα** (ta psee-*la* de-dra) (*the tall trees*)

>> **Case:** Adjectives are declined just like nouns and always agree with them in case (see Chapter 3). For example:

- Nominative: **ο όμορφος κήπος** (o o-mo-rfos *kee*-pos) (*the beautiful garden*)

- Genitive: **του όμορφου κήπου** (too o-mo-rfoo *kee*-poo) (*of the beautiful garden*)

- Accusative: **τον όμορφο κήπο** (ton o-mo-rfo *kee*-po) (*the beautiful garden*)

Checking out some basic adjectives

In this section, I'd like to give you a list of the most basic adjectives in Greek. When I say basic, I mean those most frequently used in daily conversations and the ones that will help you when speaking:

>> **καλός/καλή/καλό** (ka-*los*/ka-*lee*/ka-*lo*) (*good*)

>> **κακός/κακή/κακό** (ka-*kos*/ka-*kee*/ka-*ko*) (*bad*)

>> **μεγάλος/μεγάλη/μεγάλο** (me-*ga*-los/me-*ga*-lee/me-*ga*-lo) (*big, large*)

>> **μικρός/μικρή/μικρό** (mee-*kros*/mee-*kree*/mee-*kro*) (*small*)

>> **όμορφος/όμορφη/όμορφο** (o-mo-rfos/o-mo-rfee/o-mo-rfo) (*beautiful*)

>> **άσχημος/άσχημη/άσχημο** (*a*-skhee-mos/*a*-skhee-mee/*a*-skhee-mo) (*ugly*)

>> **νέος/νέα/νέο** (*ne*-os/*ne*-a/*ne*-o) (*young*)

>> **παλιός/παλιά/παλιό** (pa-*lyos*/pa-*lya*/pa-*lyo*) (*old*)

>> **φθηνός/φθηνή/φθηνό** (fthee-*nos*/fthee-*nee*/fthee-*no*) (*cheap*)

>> **ακριβός/ακριβή/ακριβό** (a-kree-*vos*/a-kree-*vee*/a-kree-*vo*) (*expensive*)

>> **δυνατός/δυνατή/δυνατό** (dee-na-*tos*/dee-na-*tee*/dee-na-*to*) (*strong*)

>> **αδύναμος/αδύναμη/αδύναμο** (a-*dee*-na-mos/a-*dee*-na-mee/a-*dee*-na-mo) (*weak*)

>> **ζεστός/ζεστή/ζεστό** (ze-*stos*/ze-*stee*/ze-*sto*) (*warm/hot*)

>> **κρύος/κρύα/κρύο** (*kree*-os/*kree*-a/*kree*-o) (*cold*)

>> **ψηλός/ψηλή/ψηλό** (psee-*los*/pse-*lee*/psee-*lo*) (*tall*)

>> **κοντός/κοντή/κοντό** (ko-*dos*/ko-*dee*/ko-*do*) (*short*)

>> **γρήγορος/γρήγορη/γρήγορο** (*gree*-go-ros/*gree*-go-ree/*gree*-go-ro) (*fast*)

>> **αργός/αργή/αργό** (a-*rgos*/a-*ryee*/a-*rgo*) (*slow*)

>> **έξυπνος/έξυπνη/έξυπνο** (*e*-ksee-pnos/*e*-ksee-pnee/*e*-ksee-pno) (*smart*)

>> **χαζός/χαζή/χαζό** (kha-*zos*/kha-*zee*/kha-*zo*) (*foolish, silly*)

Conjugating adjectives

Before I give you examples of using adjectives and nouns together, it's important to understand how basic adjectives are declined. I could dedicate many pages to cover all categories of adjectives in the Greek language, but it's better to focus on the two most fundamental ones:

>> Adjectives ending in **-ος, -η, -ο** such as **ο καλός, η καλή, το καλό** (o ka-*los*, ee ka-*lee*, to ka-*lo*) (*good*)

>> Adjectives ending in **-ος, -α, -ο** such as **ο νέος, η νέα, το νέο** (o *ne*-os, ee *ne*-a, to *ne*-o) (*young, new*)

GRAMMATICALLY SPEAKING

As you can see, the masculine and neuter forms don't change endings, but the feminine form ends in –η in the first case and –α in the second case.

Let's now look at how these adjectives are declined in the singular and plural for all three genders. Table 4-8 shows how to decline adjectives ending in -ος, -η, -ο.

TABLE 4-8   Conjugating Adjectives in -ος, -η, -ο

Cases	Masculine	Feminine	Neutral
Singular nominative	**ο καλός** (o ka-*los*)	**η καλή** (ee ka-*lee*)	**το καλό** (to ka-*lo*)
Singular accusative	**τον καλό** (ton ka-*lo*)	**την καλή** (teen ka-*lee*)	**το καλό** (to ka-*lo*)
Singular genitive	**του καλού** (tou ka-*loo*)	**της καλής** (tees ka-*lees*)	**του καλού** (too ka-*loo*)
Plural nominative	**οι καλοί** (ee ka-*lee*)	**οι καλές** (ee ka-*les*)	**τα καλά** (ta ka-*la*)
Plural accusative	**τους καλούς** (toos ka-*loos*)	**τις καλές** (tees ka-*les*)	**τα καλά** (ta ka-*la*)
Plural genitive	**των καλών** (ton ka-*lon*)	**των καλών** (ton ka-*lon*)	**των καλών** (ton ka-*lon*)

Table 4-9 shows how to decline adjectives ending in -ος, -α, -ο.

TABLE 4-9 Conjugating Adjectives in -ος, -α, -ο

Cases	Masculine	Feminine	Neutral
Singular nominative	ο νέος (o *ne*-os)	η νέα (ee *ne*-a)	το νέο (to *ne*-o)
Singular accusative	τον νέο (ton *ne*-o)	την νέα (teen *ne*-a)	το νέο (to *ne*-o)
Singular genitive	του νέου (too *ne*-oo)	της νέας (tees *ne*-as)	του νέου (too *ne*-oo)
Plural nominative	οι νέοι (ee *ne*-ee)	οι νέες (ee *ne*-es)	τα νέα (ta *ne*-a)
Plural accusative	τους νέους (toos *ne*-oos)	τις νέες (tees *ne*-es)	τα νέα (ta *ne*-a)
Plural genitive	των νέων (ton *ne*-on)	των νέων (ton *ne*-on)	των νέων (ton *ne*-on)

Combining nouns and adjectives

When you combine an adjective with a noun, you need to ensure that they agree in gender, number, and case. For example, look at this sentence:

Η όμορφη γυναίκα φοράει ένα λουλουδάτο φόρεμα. (ee *o*-mo-rfee yee-*ne*-ka fo-*ra*-ee e-na loo-loo-*da*-to fo-re-ma) (*The beautiful woman wears a flowery dress.*)

The word γυναίκα is feminine, singular, and nominative. Therefore, the adjective όμορφη is also feminine, singular, and nominative. Similarly, there's agreement between the words λουλουδάτο and φόρεμα. They are both neutral gender, singular, and accusative case.

Now observe the following sentences and see how the adjectives adapt to the nouns:

Οι γρήγοροι αθλητές τρέχουν στον μεγάλο δρόμο. (ee *gree*-go-ree a-thlee-*tes* tre-khoon ston me-*ga*-lo *dro*-mo) (*The fast athletes run on the big road.*)

Οι μητέρες των ήσυχων παιδιών είναι χαρούμενες. (ee mee-*te*-res ton *ee*-see-khon pe-*dyon* ee-ne kha-*roo*-me-nes) (*The mothers of the quiet children are happy.*)

Τα ωραία μάτια της Ελένης είναι καστανά. (ta o-*re*-a *ma*-tya tees e-*le*-nees ee-ne ka-sta-*na*) (*The beautiful eyes of Helen are brown.*)

Talking About the Past

Suppose that yesterday you had a lovely evening at the cinema with your partner, and you want to talk about it with your Greek friend. Since it happened yesterday, you need to use a past tense. In this section, I discuss the simple past tense in Greek known as the aorist (αόριστος).

The aorist is a past tense used to describe actions that are completed or viewed as a single event in the past. You can better understand what I mean when you see some examples, but before I give you examples, I need to explain how to transform a verb from the present tense to the aorist.

Type A and AB verbs

The secret for putting Type A and AB verbs in the simple past tense is to follow three steps. First, change the stem ending according to the following rules.

>> Any vowel, ν, ζ, τ, δ, θ, σ: These letters change to -σ. For example:

πληρώνω → πλήρωσα (plee-*ro*-no → *plee*-ro-sa) (*I pay* → *I paid*)

>> κ, γ, χ, χν, ζ: These letters change to -ξ. For example:

κοιτάζω → κοίταξα (kee-*ta*-zo → *kee*-ta-ksa) (*I look* → *I looked*)

>> π, β, φ, πτ, φτ, αυ, ευ: These change to -ψ. For example:

δουλεύω → δούλεψα (doo-*lev*-o → *doo*-le-psa) (*I work* → *I worked*)

>> μ, ν, λ, ρ: These consonants are typically *retained* in the aorist form, especially in verbs with ancient roots. For example:

μένω → έμεινα (*me*-no → *e*-mee-na) (*I stay* → *I stayed*)

>> ξ, ψ: These two consonants don't change in the simple past tense. You just need to add the ending of the tense, with no stem change.

GRAMMATICALLY
SPEAKING

Why do you encounter the letter ζ in two of the preceding categories? Because this letter has a dual behavior. So, the double listing isn't a mistake — it's a reflection of how ζ straddles two transformation patterns, depending on the verb's structure.

>> ζ behaves like a soft consonant when it follows or is preceded by a vowel or is part of a stem that ends in a vowel + ζ. For example: καθαρίζω → καθάρισα (ka-tha-*ree*-zo → ka-*tha*-ree-sa) (*I clean* → *I cleaned*).

>> ζ behaves like a hard consonant when it's part of a stem where ζ acts as a strong consonant, often in monosyllabic or compound verbs. For example: αλλάζω → άλλαξα (a-*la*-zo → *a*-la-ksa) (*I change* → *I changed*).

Next, remove the present tense ending and add the aorist endings. What are the endings? Here they are in Table 4-10.

TABLE 4-10

Type A and AB Verbs: Simple Past Conjugation

Ending	Πληρώνω (plee-*ro*-no) (*I pay*)	Δουλεύω (doo-*lev*-o) (*I work*)
-α	πλήρωσα (*plee*-ro-sa) (*I paid*)	δούλεψα (*doo*-le-psa) (*I worked*)
-ες	πλήρωσες (*plee*-ro-ses) (*you paid* [singular])	δούλεψες (*doo*-le-pses) (*you worked* [singular])
-ε	πλήρωσε (*plee*-ro-se) (*he/she/it paid*)	δούλεψε (*doo*-le-pse) (*he/she/it worked*)
-αμε	πληρώσαμε (plee-*ro*-sa-me) (*we paid*)	δουλέψαμε (doo-*le*-psa-me) (*we worked*)
-ατε	πληρώσατε (plee-*ro*-sa-te) (*you paid* [plural])	δουλέψατε (doo-*le*-psa-te) (*you worked* [plural])
-αν/-ανε	πλήρωσαν/πληρώσανε (*plee*-ro-san/plee-*ro*-sa-ne) (*they paid*)	δούλεψαν/δουλέψανε (doo-le-psan/doo-*le*-psa-ne) (*they worked*)

TIP

As you can see, the verbs have two types in the third person plural — for example, πλήρωσαν/πληρώσανε, δούλεψαν/δουλέψανε. The first is common in written language, mainly in a formal and neutral style, while the second is very common in spoken language and in children's literature texts.

Finally, adjust the stress mark. In the aorist tense, the stress must always be placed on the third syllable (counting from the end). For example:

>> α-γο-ρά-ζω becomes α-γό-ρα-σα.

>> δου-λεύ-ω becomes δού-λε-ψα.

GRAMMATICALLY
SPEAKING

What happens with words that have only two syllables? Where does the stress go? You must add an extra syllable. For example, the verb παίζω (*pe*-zo) (*I play*) has only two syllables, so you add ε- to the beginning of the word and say έπαιξα. Examples include the following:

>> εγώ έπαιξα (e-*go* e-pe-ksa) (*I played*)

>> εσύ έπαιξες (e-*see* e-pe-kses) (*You played*)

>> αυτός/αυτή/αυτό έπαιξε (af-*tos*/af-*tee*/af-*to* e-pe-kse) (*he/she/it played*)

But in the following examples, no extra syllable is needed because the word already has three syllables, leaving enough space for the stress.

>> εμείς παίξαμε (e-*mees* pe-ksa-me) (*we played*)

>> εσείς παίξατε (e-*sees* pe-ksa-te) (*You* [plural] *played*)

Examples of other such verbs include these:

>> μένω (*me*-no) (*I stay*) → έμεινα (*e*-mee-na) (*I stayed*)

>> τρέχω (*tre*-kho) (*I run*) → έτρεξα (*e*-tre-ksa) (*I ran*)

Negation in the aorist, as in the present tense, is formed with δε(ν) (de[n]): for example, δεν έπαιξα (den *e*-pe-ksa) (*I did not play*), δεν αγόρασα (den a-*go*-ra-sa) (*I did not buy*), δεν έμεινα (den *e*-mee-na) (*I did not stay*), and so on.

Type B1 and B2 verbs

In putting Types B1 and B2 into the simple past tense, the main characteristic is that we add an -η- (and less commonly -ε- or -α-) to the end of the verb stem. For example:

>> The verb μιλάω (mee-*la*-o) (*to speak*) becomes μίλησα (*mee*-lee-sa) (*I spoke*).

>> The verb ρωτάω (ro-*ta*-o) (*to ask*) becomes ρώτησα (*ro*-tee-sa) (*I asked*).

Some verbs, instead of adding -η- to the end of their stem (like μίλησα), add -α-. For example:

>> The verb γελάω (ye-*la*-o) (*to laugh*) becomes γέλασα (*ye*-la-sa) (*I laughed*).

>> The verb πεινάω (pee-*na*-o) (*to be hungry*) becomes πείνασα (*pee*-na-sa) (*I was hungry*).

Far fewer verbs have -ε- added to the end of their stem. For instance:

>> The verb μπορώ (bo-*ro*) (*to be able*) becomes μπόρεσα (*bo*-re-sa) (*I was able*).

>> The verb φορώ (fo-*ro*) (*to wear*) becomes φόρεσα (*fo*-re-sa) (*I wore*).

No strict rule dictates which of the Type B verbs end their stem in -η-, -α-, or -ε- in the simple past tense. It's something you learn as you expand your vocabulary and study various verbs in the aorist tense.

The good news is that the endings remain the same in the aorist tense of Type B verbs as they do in Type A. Check out Table 4-11.

TABLE 4-11 Type B Verbs: Simple Past Conjugation

Verbs Ending in -ησα	Verbs Ending in -ασα	Verbs Ending in -εσα
μιλάω/ώ (mee-*la*-o) (*I speak*)	γελάω/ώ (ye-*la*-o) (*I laugh*)	μπορώ (bo-*ro*) (*I can, I am able to*)
μίλησα (*mee*-lee-sa) (*I spoke*)	γέλασα (*ye*-la-sa) (*I laughed*)	μπόρεσα (*bo*-re-sa) (*I was able to*)
μίλησες (*mee*-lee-ses) (*you spoke*, singular)	γέλασες (*ye*-la-ses) (*you laughed*, singular)	μπόρεσες (*bo*-re-ses) (*you were able to*, singular)
μίλησε (*mee*-lee-se) (*he/she/it spoke*)	γέλασε (*ye*-la-se) (*he/she/it laughed*)	μπόρεσε (*bo*-re-se) (*he/she/it was able to*)
μιλήσαμε (mee-*lee*-sa-me) (*we spoke*)	γελάσαμε (ye-*la*-sa-me) (*we laughed*)	μπορέσαμε (bo-*re*-sa-me) (*we were able to*)
μιλήσατε (mee-*lee*-sa-te) (*you spoke*, plural)	γελάσατε (ye-*la*-sa-te) (*you laughed*, plural)	μπορέσατε (bo-*re*-sa-te) (*you were able to*, plural)
μίλησαν/μιλήσανε (*mee*-lee-san/ mee-*lee*-sa-ne) (*they spoke*)	γέλασαν/γελάσανε (*ye*-la-san/ ye-*la*-sa-ne) (*they laughed*)	μπόρεσαν/μπορέσανε (*bo*-re-san/ bo-*re*-sa-ne) (*they were able to*)

In the same way you conjugate μιλάω/ω, you conjugate the following:

>> ρωτάω (ro-*ta*-o) (*to ask*)

>> απαντάω (a-pa-*da*-o) (*to answer*)

>> ξυπνάω (ksee-*pna*-o) (*to wake up*)

>> περπατάω (pe-rpa-*ta*-o) (*to walk*)

>> σταματάω (sta-ma-*ta*-o) (*to stop*)

>> αργώ (a-*rgo*) (*to be late*)

>> τηλεφωνώ (tee-le-fo-*no*) (*to call*)

In the same way you conjugate γελάω/ώ, you conjugate the following:

>> διψάω (dee-*psa*-o) (*to be thirsty*)

>> πεινάω (pee-*na*-o) (*to be hungry*)

>> χαλάω (kha-*la*-o) (*to break*)

In the same way you conjugate μπορώ, you conjugate the following:

>> φοράω (fo-*ra*-o) (*to wear*)

>> πονάω (po-*na*-o) (*to be in pain*)

>> καλώ (ka-*lo*) (*to invite*)

Type Γ1 and Γ2 verbs

TIP

Type Γ1 and Γ2 verbs also have an aorist tense. However, since that formation is more complex, I prefer not to include it in this book, which is intended for those of you who are just taking your first steps in the Greek language. If, nevertheless, you wish to learn more grammar, you can join our online school, Greek Learning Hub, at https://greeklearninghub.com/.

Some irregular verbs in the simple past tense

Now, I don't want to scare you, but there are also verbs that don't follow the rules to form the aorist tense. These are the irregular verbs. I would love to give you a trick to help you form them, but unfortunately, the only thing you can do is learn them as they are. Table 4-12 has a few.

TABLE 4-12 **Some Irregular Verbs in the Simple Past Tense**

Verb (Present Tense)	Past Tense (Aorist)
λέω (*le*-o) (*to say*)	είπα (*ee*-pa) (*I said*)
τρώω (*tro*-o) (*to eat*)	έφαγα (*e*-fa-ga) (*I ate*)
βλέπω (*vle*-po) (*to see*)	είδα (*ee*-da) (*I saw*)
πηγαίνω (pee-*ye*-no) (*to go*)	πήγα (*pee*-ga) (*I went*)
φέρνω (*fe*-rno) (*to bring*)	έφερα (*e*-fe-ra) (*I brought*)
δίνω (*dee*-no) (*to give*)	έδωσα (*e*-do-sa) (*I gave*)
παίρνω (*pe*-rno) (*to take*)	πήρα (*pee*-ra) (*I took*)
μένω (*me*-no) (*to stay*)	έμεινα (*e*-mee-na) (*I stayed*)
έρχομαι (e-*rkho*-me) (*to come*)	ήρθα (*ee*-rtha) (*I came*)

(continued)

TABLE 4-12 *(continued)*

Verb (Present Tense)	Past Tense (Aorist)
πίνω (*pee*-no) (*to drink*)	ήπια (*ee*-pya) (*I drank*)
μαθαίνω (ma-*the*-no) (*to learn*)	έμαθα (*e*-ma-tha) (*I learned*)
ανεβαίνω (a-ne-*ve*-no) (*to climb, to go up*)	ανέβηκα (a-*ne*-vee-ka) (*I climbed, I went up*)

Talkin' the Talk

PLAY THIS

Maria explains to her father how she spent the previous evening out with her friends. (Track 2)

Dad: Πώς πέρασες εχθές;
pos *pe*-ra-ses e-*khthes*;
How did you enjoy yesterday?

Maria: Πολύ ωραία! Πήγαμε στο σινεμά. Είδαμε μία ρομαντική ταινία. Μετά περπατήσαμε στο κέντρο. Μπήκαμε σε ένα μπαρ και ήπιαμε ένα ποτό. Κατά τις δώδεκά πήρα ένα ταξί και γύρισα στο σπίτι.
po-*lee* o-*re*-a! *pee*-ga-me sto see-ne-*ma*. ee-da-me *mee*-a ro-ma-dee-*kee* te-*nee*-a. me-*ta* pe-rpa-*tee*-sa-me sto *ke*-dro. *bee*-ka-me se *e*-na bar ke *ee*-pya-me *e*-na po-*to*. ka-*ta* tees *do*-de-ka *pee*-ra *e*-na ta-*ksee* ke *yee*-ree-sa sto *spee*-tee.
It was very nice! We went to the cinema. We watched a romantic movie. Afterward, we walked in the city center. We went into a bar and had a drink. Around twelve o'clock, I took a taxi and came home.

Dad: Ήρθε και η Νίκη;
ee-rthe ke ee *nee*-kee;
Did Niki come, too?

Maria: Όχι, δεν ήρθε γιατί ήταν άρρωστη. Ήρθε η Μαρίνα και η Βίκυ.
o-hee, den *ee*-rthe ya-*tee* ee-tan *a*-ro-stee. ee-rthe ee ma-*ree*-na ke ee *vee*-kee.
No, she didn't come because she was sick. Marina and Vicky came instead.

WORDS TO KNOW		
Πώς πέρασες;	pos *pe*-ra-ses	*How did you enjoy your time?*
εχθές	e-*khthes*	*yesterday*
Πολύ ωραία!	po-*lee* o-*re*-a	*It was very nice!*
το σπίτι	to spee-tee	*home*

Talking About the Future

They say that "the best way to predict the future is to create it." Yes, and if you can create the future in Greek, you're truly a pro! I'm talking about the future tense, of course. Let's dive into the Greek future tense in more detail!

Similar to English, we use the simple future (steegmieos melodas) tense to talk about an action that will happen in the future without concerning ourselves with its duration. The simple future describes an action or event that will take place in the future without being interested in its duration. For example:

> **Θα παίξω τένις αύριο.** (tha *pe*-kso *te*-nees *av*-ree-o) (*I will play tennis tomorrow.*)

Here, we see a plan for tomorrow, but we're not concerned about when or for how long the game will last. What matters is mentioning the future plan, so we place the verb in the simple future tense. The following sections show you how to form this tense.

Type A and AB Verbs

To put Type A and Type AB verbs into the future simple tense, you need to follow a couple of rules. If you've already learned these changes while studying the simple past tense (as I explain earlier in this chapter), you're almost ready to learn the future tense as well.

First change the stem ending. Similar to the past simple tense, in the simple future tense, we also need to change the last letter of the verb stem.

>> Any vowel, **ν, ζ, τ, δ, θ, σ:** These letters change to **-σ.** For example:

πληρώνω → πληρώσω (plee-*ro*-no → ple-*ro*-so) (*I pay → I will pay*)

>> **κ, γ, χ, χν, ζ:** These letters change to **-ξ.** For example:

κοιτάζω → κοιτάξω (kee-*ta*-zo → kee-*ta*-kso) (*I look → I will look*)

>> π, β, φ, πτ, φτ, αυ, ευ: These change to -ψ. For example:

δουλεύω → δουλέψω (doo-*lev*-o → doo-*le*-pso) (*I work* → *I will work*)

>> μ, ν, λ, ρ: These consonants are typically *retained* in the aorist form, especially in verbs with ancient roots. For example:

μένω → μείνω (*me*-no → *mee*-no) (*I stay* → *I will stay*)

>> ξ, ψ: These two consonants don't change in the future simple tense. You just need to add the ending of the tense with no stem change.

GRAMMATICALLY
SPEAKING

Why does the letter ζ appear in two separate categories? This is due to its flexible phonetic nature. Rather than being an error, its double listing highlights the fact that ζ can behave in more than one way, depending on the verb's form.

>> In some verbs, especially those where ζ follows or is near a vowel, it acts like a soft consonant and shifts to -σ in the future simple. For example: **καθαρίζω** (ka-tha-*ree*-zo) (*I clean*) becomes **καθαρίσω** (ka-tha-*ree*-so) (*I will clean*).

>> In other cases, particularly with shorter or compound verbs, ζ functions more like a hard consonant and transforms into -ξ. For example: **αλλάζω** (a-*la*-zo) (*I change*) becomes **αλλάξω** (a-*la*-kso) (*I will change*).

Next, add θα (tha) and the endings of simple future as shown in Table 4-13. For example: θα πληρώσω (tha plee-*ro*-so), θα ξεχάσω (tha kse-*kha*-so), and θα δουλέψω (tha doo-*le*-pso).

TABLE 4-13 **Type A and AB Verbs: Simple Future Conjugation**

Θα & Ending	Πληρώνω (plee-*ro*-no) (*I pay*)	Γράφω (*gra*-fo) (*I write*)
θα -ω	θα πληρώσω (tha plee-*ro*-so) (*I will pay*)	θα γράψω (tha *gra*-pso) (*I will write*)
θα -εις	θα πληρώσεις (tha plee-*ro*-sees) (*you will pay*, singular)	θα γράψεις (tha *gra*-psees) (*you will write*, singular)
θα -ει	θα πληρώσει (tha plee-*ro*-see) (*he/she/it will pay*)	θα γράψει (tha *gra*-psee) (*he/she/it will write*)
θα -ουμε	θα πληρώσουμε (tha plee-*ro*-soo-me) (*we will pay*)	θα γράψουμε (tha *gra*-psoo-me) (*we will write*)
θα -ετε	θα πληρώσετε (tha plee-*ro*-se-te) (*you will pay*, plural)	θα γράψετε (tha *gra*-pse-te) (*you will write*, plural)
θα -ουν/ουνε	θα πληρώσουν/πληρώσουνε (tha plee-*ro*-soon/plee-*ro*-soo-ne) (*they will pay*)	θα γράψουν/γράψουνε (tha *gra*-psoon/*gra*-psoo-ne) (*they will write*)

When we want to use negation, we can say δεν + θα + verb. For example: Δεν θα αγοράσω την τσάντα. (den tha a-go-*ra*-so teen *tsa*-da) (*I will not buy the bag.*)

Type B1 and B2 Verbs

Earlier in this chapter, I discuss the change that occurs in Type B verbs in the simple past tense (aorist). Since the aorist and future tenses change the verb stem in a similar way, there isn't much more to tell you here, other than don't forget to add θα.

In Types B1 and B2, the main characteristic is that we add -η- (and less commonly -ε- or -α-) to the end of the verb stem. For example:

>> The verb μιλάω (mee-*la*-o) (*to speak*) becomes θα μιλήσω (tha mee-*lee*-so) (*I will speak*).

>> The verb ρωτάω (ro-*ta*-o) (*to ask*) becomes θα ρωτήσω (tha ro-*tee*-so) (*I will ask*).

Some verbs, instead of having -η- at the end of their stem (like θα μιλήσω), have -α-. For example:

>> The verb γελάω (ye-*la*-o) (*to laugh*) becomes θα γελάσω (tha ye-*la*-so) (*I will laugh*).

>> The verb πεινάω (pee-*na*-o) (*to be hungry*) becomes θα πεινάσω (tha pee-*na*-so) (*I will be hungry*).

Far fewer verbs have -ε- at the end of their stem. For instance:

>> The verb μπορώ (bo-*ro*) (*to be able*) becomes θα μπορέσω (tha bo-*re*-so) (*I will be able*).

>> The verb φορώ (fo-*ro*) (*to wear*) becomes θα φορέσω (tha fo-*re*-so) (*I will wear*).

Determining whether Type B verbs end their stem in -η-, -α-, or -ε- doesn't follow a specific rule. It's a pattern you gradually internalize as you grow your vocabulary and familiarize yourself with different verbs in the aorist tense. To assist with this, I've included Table 4-14, which showcases some fundamental verbs from each category.

TABLE 4-14   **Type B Verbs: Future Simple Conjugation**

Verbs Ending in -ησα	Verbs Ending in -ασα	Verbs Ending in -εσα
μιλάω/ω (mee-*la*-o) (*I speak*)	γελάω/ώ (ye-*la*-o) (*I laugh*)	μπορώ (bo-*ro*) (*I can, I am able to*)
θα μιλήσω (tha mee-*lee*-so) (*I will speak*)	θα γελάσω (tha ye-*la*-so) (*I will laugh*)	θα μπορέσω (tha bo-*re*-so) (*I will be able to*)
θα μιλήσεις (tha mee-*lee*-sees) (*you will speak*, singular)	θα γελάσεις (tha ye-*la*-sees) (*you will laugh*, singular)	θα μπορέσεις (tha bo-*re*-sees) (*you will be able to*, singular)
θα μιλήσει (tha mee-*lee*-see) (*he/she/it will speak*)	θα γελάει (tha ye-*la*-see) (*he/she/it will laugh*)	θα μπορέσει (tha bo-*re*-see) (*he/she/it will be able to*)
θα μιλήσουμε (tha mee-*lee*-soo-me) (*we will speak*)	θα γελάσουμε (tha ye-*la*-soo-me) (*we will laugh*)	θα μπορέσουμε (tha bo-*re*-soo-me) (*we will be able to*)
θα μιλήσετε (tha mee-*lee*-se-te) (*you will speak*, plural)	θα γελάσετε (tha ye-*la*-se-te) (*you will laugh*, plural)	θα μπορέσετε (tha bo-*re*-se-te) (*you will be able to*, plural)
θα μιλήσουν/θα μιλήσουνε (tha mee-*lee*-soon/tha mee-*lee*-soo-ne) (*they will speak*)	θα γελάσουν/θα γελάσουνε (tha ye-*la*-soon/tha ye-*la*-soo-ne) (*they will laugh*)	θα μπορέσουν/θα μπορέσουνε (tha bo-*re*-soon/tha bo-*re*-soo-ne) (*they will able to*)

In the same way you conjugate μιλάω/ω, you conjugate the following:

- >> ρωτάω (ro-*ta*-o) (*to ask*)
- >> απαντάω (a-pa-*da*-o) (*to answer*)
- >> ξυπνάω (ksee-*pna*-o) (*to wake up*)
- >> περπατάω (pe-rpa-*ta*-o) (*to walk*)
- >> σταματάω (sta-ma-*ta*-o) (*to stop*)
- >> αργώ (a-*rgo*) (*to be late*)
- >> τηλεφωνώ (tee-le-fo-*no*) (*to call*)

In the same way you conjugate γελάω/ώ, you conjugate the following:

- >> διψάω (dee-*psa*-o) (*to be thirsty*)
- >> πεινάω (pee-*na*-o) (*to be hungry*)
- >> χαλάω (kha-*la*-o) (*to break*)

In the same way you conjugate μπορώ, you conjugate the following:

➤ φοράω (fo-*ra*-o) (*to wear*)

➤ πονάω (po-*na*-o) (*to be in pain*)

➤ καλώ (ka-*lo*) (*to invite*)

Type Γ1 and Γ2 verbs

Type Γ1 and Γ2 verbs differ from the others because they end in -ομαι and -άμαι. For this reason, the formation of the simple future tense is very different from that of other verb types. I have therefore decided not to include it in this chapter, which presents basic grammar. However, if you would like to learn more grammar, you can join our online school, Greek Learning Hub. You can find out more here: https://greeklearninghub.com/.

Some irregular verbs in the simple future tense

The same verbs that I identified as irregular in the aorist tense are also irregular in the future tense (see Table 4-15). Naturally, I must emphasize that many more verbs form the future and aorist tenses irregularly, but here I focus on the most common verbs of the Greek language.

TABLE 4-15

Some Irregular Verbs in the Simple Future Tense

Verb (Present Tense)	Future Simple (Steegmieos Melodas)
λέω (*le*-o) (*to say*)	θα πω (tha po) (*I will say*)
τρώω (*tro*-o) (*to eat*)	θα φάω (tha *fa*-o) (*I will eat*)
βλέπω (*vle*-po) (*to see*)	θα δω (tha *do*) (*I will see*)
πηγαίνω (pee-ye-no) (*to go*)	θα πάω (tha *pa*-o) (*I will go*)
φέρνω (*fe*-rno) (*to bring*)	θα φέρω (tha *fe*-ro) (*I will bring*)
δίνω (*dee*-no) (*to give*)	θα δώσω (tha *do*-so) (*I will give*)
παίρνω (*pe*-rno) (*to take*)	θα πάρω (tha *pa*-ro) (*I will take*)
μένω (*me*-no) (*to stay*)	θα μείνω (tha *mee*-no) (*I will stay*)

(continued)

TABLE 4-15 *(continued)*

Verb (Present Tense)	Future Simple (Steegmieos Melodas)
έρχομαι (e-rkho-me) (*to come*)	θα έρθω (tha e-rtho) (*I will come*)
πίνω (*pee*-no) (*to drink*)	θα πιω (tha *pyo*) (*I will drink*)
μαθαίνω (ma-*the*-no) (*to learn*)	θα μάθω (tha *ma*-tho) (*I will learn*)
ανεβαίνω (a-ne-*ve*-no) (*to climb, to go up*)	θα ανέβω (tha a-*ne*-vo) (*I will climb, I will go up*)

Using the Subjunctive

In Greek, we use a grammatical mood to express wish, hope, expectation, and intentions, and to make suggestions or negative commands. This is the subjunctive mood. The subjunctive has the following structure: να and verb in the subjunctive mood.

REMEMBER

But how do we use it within a sentence? Very often (but not always), it needs to follow another verb. Specific verbs are followed by να and the subjunctive. In other words, the complete form of the subjunctive is verb + να + verb in the subjunctive.

So, which are these specific verbs that are followed by the subjunctive? There are quite a few, but here I list the most common ones:

>> θέλω να (*the*-lo na) (*I want to*): Example: θέλω να πάω (*the*-lo na *pa*-o) (*I want to go*).

>> πρέπει να (*pre*-pee na) (*I must, it is necessary to*): Example: πρέπει να φάω (*pre*-pee na *fa*-o) (*I must eat*).

>> μπορώ να (bo-*ro* na) (*I can*): Example: μπορώ να βοηθήσω (bo-*ro* na vo-ee-*thee*-so) (*I can help*).

>> εύχομαι να (*ef*-kho-me na) (*I wish that*): Example: εύχομαι να πετύχεις (*ef*-kho-me na pe-*tee*-hees) (*I wish that you succeed*).

>> ελπίζω να (e-*lpee*-zo na) (*I hope*): Example: ελπίζω να έρθει (e-*lpee*-zo na e-rthee) (*I hope he/she comes*).

>> **φοβάμαι να** (fo-*va*-me na) (*I'm afraid that*): Example: **φοβάμαι να μπω** (fo-*va*-me na bo) (*I'm afraid to enter*).

>> **προσπαθώ να** (pro-spa-*tho* na) (*I try to*): Example: **προσπαθώ να μάθω ελληνικά** (pro-spa-*tho* na *ma*-tho e-lee-nee-*ka*) (*I try to learn Greek*).

Additionally, the subjunctive mood is also required after conjunctions such as **για να** (ya na) (*in order to*), **αν και** (an ke) (*even though*), and **μήπως** (mee–pos) (*lest/ maybe*).

As I mention earlier, the subjunctive is formed using **να** and a verb. And how is this verb formed? Well, here's the good news: the verb is formed exactly like the verb in the future tense, but instead of **θα**, you use **να**. Here's an example:

μιλάω (mee-*la*-o) (*I speak*) → **θα μιλήσω** (tha mee-*lee*-so) (*I will speak*) → **να μιλήσω** (na mee-*lee*-so) (*to speak*)

See? The form **μιλήσω** stays the same, and you simply replace **θα** with **να**. Here's another example:

μπορώ (bo-*ro*) (*I am able to*) → **θα μπορέσω** (tha bo-*re*-so) (*I will be able to*) → **να μπορέσω** (na bo-*re*-so) (*to be able to*)

The same applies to all verbs in the subjunctive mood. And the great news is that the verb in the subjunctive is conjugated in the same way as the verb in the future tense. Check it out in Table 4-16.

TABLE 4-16

Conjugating Verbs in the Subjunctive

Future Simple: Παίζω (*pe*-zo) (*I play*)	Subjunctive
θα παίξω (tha *pe*-kso) (*I will play*)	**να παίξω** (na *pe*-kso)
θα παίξεις (tha *pe*-ksees) (*you will play*, singular)	**να παίξεις** (na *pe*-ksees)
θα παίξει (tha *pe*-ksee) (*he/she/it will play*)	**να παίξει** (na *pe*-ksee)
θα παίξουμε (tha *pe*-ksoo-me) (*we will play*)	**να παίξουμε** (na *pe*-ksoo-me)
θα παίξετε (tha *pe*-kse-te) (*you will play*, plural)	**να παίξετε** (na *pe*-kse-te)
θα παίξουν/παίξουνε (tha *pe*-ksoon/*pe*-ksoo-ne) (*they will play*)	**να παίξουν/παίξουνε** (na *pe*-ksoon/*pe*-ksoo-ne)

Talkin' the Talk

PLAY THIS

Athanasios is talking on the phone with his friend Ioanna. (Track 3)

Athanasios: Τι κάνεις, Ιωάννα;
tee *ka*-nees, ee-o-*a*-nna;
How are you, Ioanna?

Ioanna: Καλά! Πρέπει να πάω στο σούπερ μάρκετ σε λίγο.
ka-*la*! *pre*-pee na *pa*-o sto *soo*-per *ma*-rket se *lee*-go.
I'm good! I need to go to the supermarket shortly.

Athanasios: Θέλεις να έρθεις στο σπίτι μου το απόγευμα;
the-lees na e-rthees sto *spee*-tee moo to a-*po*-yev-ma;
Do you want to come to my house this afternoon?

Ioanna: Θέλω αλλά πρέπει να κάνω κάποιες δουλειές στο σπίτι.
the-lo a-*la pre*-pee na *ka*-no *ka*-pyes doo-*lyes* sto *spee*-tee.
I do, but I need to do some chores at home.

Athanasios: Εντάξει. Αν τελειώσεις νωρίς μπορείς να έρθεις.
e-*da*-ksee. an te-*lyo*-sees no-*rees* bo-*rees* na e-rthees.
Alright. If you finish early, you can come.

WORDS TO KNOW

Τι κάνεις;	tee *ka*-nees	How are you?
Πρέπει να πάω.	*pre*-pee na *pa*-o	I need to go.
σε λίγο	se *lee*-go	shortly
Θέλεις να έρθεις;	*the*-lees na e-rthees	Do you want to come?
Πρέπει να κάνω κάποιες δουλειές.	*pre*-pee na *ka*-no *ka*-pyes doo-*lyes*	I need to do some chores.
μπορείς να έρθεις	bo-*rees* na e-rthees	you can come

FUN & GAMES

I'll give you a list of verbs in the present tense. Can you form them into the simple past and simple future tenses as in the example?

Present (Enestotas)	Past Simple (Aoristos)	Future Simple (Steegmieos Melodas)
αγοράζω	αγόρασα	θα αγοράσω
δουλεύω		
μιλάω		
μπορώ		
τρώω		
αγοράζω		
ακούω		
προσπαθώ		
αγαπάω		

IN THIS CHAPTER

» Saying hello to people you
already know

» Introducing yourself and getting
acquainted

» Talking about your country,
profession, and family

» Saying goodbye to people

Chapter **5**

Getting Started with Basic Expressions

The Greeks are a very sociable people. It's easy to strike up a conversation about simple everyday topics while waiting for the bus, ordering your coffee, or waiting for the doctor. They're also very happy when a foreigner tries to speak Greek. As soon as they see your effort, they immediately try to encourage you and make you feel comfortable.

In this chapter, I provide you with the basic expressions that will help you break the ice with any Greek. You find out how to greet people, ask them how they are doing, and exchange information about your nationality, profession, and family. You also find out how to say goodbye to your new Greek friends.

Greeting People You Know

Say γεια!

REMEMBER

The easiest way to start a conversation is to say γεια (ya) (*hello*). And such a small word can start a whole discussion. You can say γεια at all times of the day, from morning until night.

If you meet someone the same age as you or younger, or someone you feel very familiar with when you see them (like family and close friends), then you can say γεια σου (ya soo) (*hello to you*) in the singular. It's a simple and friendly greeting. But if you meet someone older, your boss, or someone you want to show respect to, it's better to say γεια σας (ya sas). Γεια σας is also used when greeting two or more people. So, if you see two girls or a group of students or three friends in a café, you can simply say γεια σας!

TIP

In Greek we use the plural number not only to speak to a group of people but also to speak in a formal way to someone we respect or someone older. For this reason, γεια σας can be used either when talking to a group of people or to a single person when you want to be very polite.

Some greetings in Greek are related to the time of day:

>> In the morning, you can say **καλημέρα** (ka-lee-*me*-ra) (*good morning*).

>> Later, after noon you can say **καλησπέρα** (ka-lee-*spe*-ra) (*good evening*).

>> And in the evening, when you're leaving and saying goodbye to your friends, you can say **καληνύχτα** (ka-lee-*nee*-khta) (*good night*). Find out more about saying goodbye later in this chapter.

Meeting New People

Great, you've said the first greeting. The ice is broken. Now it's time to get to know your conversation partner. In the following sections, you find some phrases that will help you discover more about the Greek person standing in front of you.

Asking for each other's names

Let's start with names. If you want to ask, "What's your name?" in Greek you simply say:

Πώς σε λένε; (pos se *le*-ne)

And again, the rule of the plural that I mentioned earlier applies: If you are talking to a group of people or want to use formal language, then you say:

Πώς σας λένε; (pos sas *le*-ne)

The answer you get 99 percent of the time is Με λένε . . . (me *le*-ne) (*My name is . . .*).

For example, if you're talking to someone named Dimitra, she will tell you: Με λένε Δήμητρα (me *le*-ne *dee*-mee-tra) (*My name is Dimitra*). Dimitra will then ask you: Εσένα; (e-*se*-na) (*And you?*)

This is the moment to say your name: Με λένε . . . (me *le*-ne).

And of course, it is polite to say Χάρηκα (*kha*-ree-ka) (*I'm glad to meet you*) or Χαίρω πολύ (*he*-ro po-*lee*) (*I'm very glad to meet you*).

Talkin' the Talk

Dimitra is meeting some friends for breakfast at a café. Georgia is a new member of the group.

Georgia:	Καλημέρα. ka-lee-*me*-ra. *Good morning.*
Dimitra:	Καλημέρα. ka-lee-*me*-ra. *Good morning.*
Georgia:	Πώς σε λένε; pos se *le*-ne; *What's your name?*
Dimitra:	Με λένε Δήμητρα. Εσένα; me *le*-ne *dee*-mee-tra. e-*se*-na; *My name is Dimitra. And you?*
Georgia:	Με λένε Γεωργία. me *le*-ne ye-o-*ryee*-a. *My name is Georgia.*
Dimitra:	Χαίρω πολύ. *he*-ro po-*lee*. *I'm very glad to meet you.*

WORDS TO KNOW

Καλημέρα.	ka-lee-*me*-ra	*Good morning.*
Πώς σε λένε;	pos se *le*-ne	*What's your name?*
Με λένε . . .	me *le*-ne	*My name is . . .*
Εσένα;	e-*se*-na	*And you?*
Χαίρω πολύ.	*he*-ro po-*lee*	*I'm very glad to meet you.*

Getting acquainted

Great! After you know your conversation partner's name, you may want to know how their day is going. There are many ways to ask:

>> **Τι κάνεις;** (tee *ka*-nees) (*How are you doing? How are you?*)

>> **Πώς είσαι;** (pos *ee*-se) (*How are you?*)

>> **Τι νέα;** (tee *ne*-a) (*What's new?*)

>> **Τι γίνεται;** (tee *yee*-ne-te) (*What's up?*)

If Dimitra is with her friends, or if she wants to politely greet Mrs. Papadopoulou, the neighbor, then she uses the plural form.

>> **Τι κάνετε;** (tee *ka*-ne-te?) (*How are you [plural] doing?*)

>> **Πώς είστε;** (pos *ee*-ste?) (*How are you [plural]?*)

Depending on her mood, Dimitra may answer with one of the following:

>> **Είμαι πολύ καλά.** (*ee*-me po-*lee* ka-*la*) (*I am very well.*)

>> **Είμαι καλά.** (*ee*-me ka-*la*) (*I am well.*)

>> **Δεν είμαι πολύ καλά.** (den *ee*-me po-*lee* ka-*la*) (*I am not very well.*)

>> **Είμαι χάλια.** (*ee*-me *kha*-lya) (*I feel terrible.*)

GRAMMATICALLY SPEAKING

If she tells you είμαι χάλια, then she really needs you! The word χάλια literally means "crap"!

Talkin' the Talk

PLAY THIS

Lukas sees his neighbor, Mrs. Papadopoulou, on a walk. (Track 4)

Lukas:	Γεια σας κυρία Παπαδοπούλου! *ya* sas kee-*ree*-a pa-pa-do-*poo*-loo! *Hello, Mrs. Papadopoulou!*
Mrs. Papadopoulou:	Γεια σου. ya soo. *Hello.*
Lukas:	Πώς είστε; pos *ee*-ste; *How are you?*
Mrs. Papadopoulou:	Δεν είμαι πολύ καλά. Έχω ένα πρόβλημα. den *ee*-me po-*lee* ka-*la*. e-kho e-na *pro*-vlee-ma. *I am not very well. I have a problem.*

WORDS TO KNOW

Γεια σας!	ya sas	*Hello! (formal or plural)*
Γεια σου!	ya sou	*Hello!*
Πώς είστε;	pos *ee*-ste	*How are you? (formal or plural)*
Δεν είμαι πολύ καλά.	den *ee*-me po-*lee* ka-*la*	*I am not very well.*

Talking about Countries, Nationalities, and Languages

Maybe you want to tell your conversation partner where you are from, what language you speak, and your nationality. The following sections explain a few helpful terms in Greek.

Breaking down different places and languages

Since there are many nationalities in the world, I am giving you the 20 nationalities that visit Greece the most each year in Table 5-1. I list the following:

>> χώρα (*kho*-ra) (*country*)

>> εθνικότητα (eth-nee-*ko*-tee-ta) (*nationality*)

>> γλώσσα (*glo*-sa) (*language*)

REMEMBER

Nationalities are divided into masculine and feminine forms. For example, if you talk about a woman from Sweden, you say she is Σουηδέζα (soo-ee-*de*-za) (*Swedish*), while a man would be Σουηδός (soo-ee-*dos*) (*Swedish*).

TABLE 5-1   **Countries, Nationalities, and Languages**

Country	Nationality	Language
Γερμανία (ye-rma-*nee*-a) (*Germany*)	**Γερμανός** (ye-rma-*nos*) (*German;* male) **Γερμανίδα** (ye-rma-*nee*-da) (*German;* female)	γερμανικά (ye-rma-nee-*ka*) (*German*)
Ιταλία (ee-ta-*lee*-a) (*Italy*)	**Ιταλός** (ee-ta-*los*) (*Italian;* male) **Ιταλίδα** (ee-ta-*lee*-da) (*Italian;* female)	ιταλικά (ee-ta-lee-*ka*) (*Italian*)
Γαλλία (ga-*lee*-a) (*France*)	**Γάλλος** (*ga*-los) (*French;* male) **Γαλλίδα** (ga-*lee*-da) (*French;* female)	γαλλικά (ga-lee-*ka*) (*French*)
Ρουμανία (roo-ma-*nee*-a) (*Romania*)	**Ρουμάνος** (roo-*ma*-nos) (*Romanian;* male) **Ρουμάνα** (roo-*ma*-na) (*Romanian;* female)	ρουμάνικα (roo-*ma*-nee-ka) (*Romanian*)
Αμερική/ΗΠΑ (a-me-ree-*kee*/ee-pa) (*America/USA*)	**Αμερικάνος** (a-me-ree-*ka*-nos) *American;* male) **Αμερικάνα** (a-me-ree-*ka*-na) (*American;* female)	αγγλικά (a-nglee-*ka*) (*English*)
Ολλανδία (o-la-*ndee*-a) (*the Netherlands*)	**Ολλανδός** (o-la-ndos) (*Dutch;* male) **Ολλανδέζα** (o-la-*nde*-za) (*Dutch;* female)	ολλανδικά (o-la-ndee-*ka*) (*Dutch*)
Αλβανία (a-lva-*nee*-a) (*Albania*)	**Αλβανός** (a-lva-*nos*) (*Albanian;* male) **Αλβανίδα** (a-lva-*nee*-da) (*Albanian;* female)	αλβανικά (a-lva-nee-*ka*) (*Albanian*)
Αυστρία (af-*stree*-a) (*Austria*)	**Αυστριακός** (af-stree-a-*kos*) (*Austrian;* male) **Αυστριακή** (af-stree-a-*kee*) (*Austrian;* female)	γερμανικά (ye-rma-nee-*ka*) (*German*)

Country	Nationality	Language
Βέλγιο (*ve*-lyee-o) (*Belgium*)	Βέλγος (*ve*-lgos) (*Belgian;* male) Βελγίδα (ve-l*gee*-da) (*Belgian;* female)	γαλλικά (ga-lee-*ka*) (*French*) φλαμανδικά (fla-ma-ndee-*ka*) (*Flemish*)
Κύπρος (*kee*-pros) (*Cyprus*)	Κύπριος (*kee*-pree-os) (*Cypriot;* male) Κύπρια (*kee*-pree-a) (*Cypriot;* female)	ελληνικά (e-lee-nee-*ka*) (*Greek*)
Ελβετία (e-lve-*tee*-a) (*Switzerland*)	Ελβετός (e-lve-*tos*) (*Swiss;* male) Ελβετίδα (e-lve-*tee*-da) (*Swiss;* female)	γερμανικά (ye-rma-nee-*ka*) (*German*) γαλλικά (ga-lee-*ka*) (*French*) ιταλικά (ee-ta-lee-*ka*) (*Italian*)
Τσεχία (tse-*hee*-a) (*Czech Republic*)	Τσέχος (*tse*-khos) (*Czech;* male) Τσέχα (*tse*-kha) (*Czech;* female)	τσεχικά (tse-hee-*ka*) (*Czech*)
Σουηδία (soo-ee-*dee*-a) (Sweden)	Σουηδός (soo-ee-*dos*) (*Swedish;* male) Σουηδέζα (soo-ee-*de*-za) (*Swedish;* female)	σουηδικά (soo-ee-dee-*ka*) (*Swedish*)
Ισπανία (ee-spa-*nee*-a) (*Spain*)	Ισπανός (ee-spa-*nos*) (*Spanish;* male) Ισπανίδα (ee-spa-*nee*-da) (*Spanish;* female)	ισπανικά (ee-spa-nee-*ka*) (*Spanish*)
Καναδάς (ka-na-*das*) (*Canada*)	Καναδέζος (ka-na-*de*-zos) (*Canadian;* male) Καναδέζα (ka-na-*de*-za) (*Canadian;* female)	αγγλικά (a-nglee-*ka*) (*English*) γαλλικά (ga-lee-*ka*) (*French*)
Δανία (da-*nee*-a) (*Denmark*)	Δανός (da-*nos*) (*Danish;* male) Δανή/Δανέζα (da-*nee*/da-*ne*-za) (*Danish;* female)	δανικά/δανέζικα (da-nee-*ka*/da-*ne*-zee-ka) (*Danish*)
Αυστραλία (af-stra-*lee*-a) (*Australia*)	Αυστραλός (af-stra-*los*) (*Australian;* male) Αυστραλή/Αυστραλέζα (af-stra-*lee*/af-stra-*le*-za) (*Australian;* female)	αγγλικά (a-nglee-*ka*) (*English*)
Ρωσία (ro-*see*-a) (*Russia*)	Ρώσος (*ro*-sos) (*Russian;* male) Ρωσίδα (ro-*see*-da) (*Russian;* female)	ρωσικά (ro-see-*ka*) (*Russian*)

TIP

Did you notice that the United States of America also has the acronym ΗΠΑ? These three letters are the initials of the Ηνωμένες Πολιτείες Αμερικής (ee-no-*me*-nes po-lee-*tee*-es a-me-ree-*kees*) the Greek equivalent to USA.

Other nationalities that you may want to know are

>> **Άγγλος** (*a*-nglos) (*English;* male)

>> **Αγγλίδα** (a-*nglee*-da) (*English;* female)

>> **Κινέζος** (kee-*ne*-zos) (*Chinese;* male)

>> **Κινέζα** (kee-*ne*-za) (*Chinese;* female)

>> **Γιαπωνέζος** (ya-po-*ne*-zos) (*Japanese;* male)

>> **Γιαπωνέζα** (ya-po-*ne*-za) (*Japanese;* female)

>> **Ινδός** (ee-*ndos*) (*Indian;* male)

>> **Ινδή** (ee-*ndee*) (*Indian;* female)

Asking people about their nationalities and languages

After you know so many countries, languages, and nationalities, I think it's time to see how you can use them to give or receive information. If you want to know someone's country of origin, you can ask

>> **Από που είσαι;** (a-*po* poo ee-se) (*Where are you from?*)

>> **Από που είστε;** (a-*po* poo ee-ste) (*Where are you from?* [formal/plural])

The answer you'll get is

Είμαι/Είμαστε από . . . (*ee*-me/*ee*-mas-te a-*po*) (*I am/We are from . . .*)

GRAMMATICALLY
SPEAKING

In this answer, the country is always in the accusative case. For example, you say **Είμαι από τη Γερμανία** (*ee*-me a-*po* tee ye-rma-*nee*-a) (*I am from Germany*) or **Είμαι από τον Καναδά** (*ee*-me a-*po* ton ka-na-*da*) (*I am from Canada*). Check out Chapter 3 for more information about the accusative case.

Do you want to ask your friend Dimitra what language she speaks? You should say this:

Τι γλώσσα μιλάς; (tee *glo*-sa mee-*las*) (*What language do you speak?*)

Dimitra will say **Μιλάω . . .** (mee-*la*-o) (*I speak . . .*)

Talkin' the Talk

PLAY THIS

Irini, who's from Greece, meets Johan, who's from Belgium, in a coffee shop in Athens. (Track 5)

Irini: Από που είσαι, Γιόχαν;
a-*po* poo *ee*-se *yo*-khan;
Where are you from, Johan?

Johan: Είμαι από το Βέλγιο. Εσύ;
ee-me a-*po* to *ve*-lyee-o. e-*see*;
I'm from Belgium. And you?

Irini: Εγώ είμαι από την Ελλάδα.
e-*go* *ee*-me a-*po* teen e-*la*-da.
I'm from Greece.

Johan: Τι γλώσσα μιλάς;
tee *glo*-sa mee-*las*;
What language do you speak?

Irini: Μιλάω ελληνικά. Εσύ;
mee-*la*-o e-lee-nee-*ka*. e-*see*;
I speak Greek. And you?

Johan: Εγώ μιλάω γαλλικά και φλαμανδικά και λίγο ελληνικά.
e-*go* mee-*la*-o ga-lee-*ka* ke fla-ma-ndee-*ka* ke *lee*-go
e-lee-nee-*ka*.
I speak French and Flemish and a little Greek.

WORDS TO KNOW

Από πού είσαι;	a-*po* poo *ee*-se	*Where are you from?*
Είμαι από τον/ τη(ν)/το . . .	*ee*-me a-*po* ton/teen/to	*I'm from . . .*
Τι γλώσσα μιλάς;	tee *glo*-sa mee-*las*	*What language do you speak?*
Μιλάω . . .	mee-*la*-o	*I speak . . .*
εγώ	e-*go*	*I*

Speaking About Your Profession

What do you do for a living?

This is one of the first questions we ask when we meet someone. If you want to ask this question in Greek, you say:

Τι δουλειά κάνεις; (tee doo-*lya* ka-nees) (*What do you do?*)

Hundreds of professions exist, and it would be difficult to translate them all in this chapter. However, in the following sections I tell you about the 20 most common professions in Greece and how to ask and answer questions about them.

Noting common professions

GRAMMATICALLY SPEAKING

Before I begin, I must emphasize that in the Greek language, some professions have different words for the masculine and feminine forms. For example: ο μάγειρας (o ma-yee-ras) (*the cook;* male) and η μαγείρισσα (ee ma-*yee*-ree-sa) (*the cook;* female). However, some professions have only one form for both masculine and feminine — for example, the word δικηγόρος (dee-kee-*go*-ros) (*lawyer*). To understand the gender of the professional, we observe the article. If the lawyer is a man, we say ο δικηγόρος (o dee-kee-*go*-ros). If the lawyer is a woman, we say η δικηγόρος (ee dee-kee-*go*-ros).

Table 5-2 lists professions with both masculine and feminine forms.

TABLE 5-2

Professions with Masculine and Feminine Forms

Masculine	Feminine	Translation
νοσοκόμος (no-so-*ko*-mos)	**νοσοκόμα** (no-so-*ko*-ma)	Nurse
μάγειρας (*ma*-yee-ras)	**μαγείρισσα** (ma-yee-ree-sa)	Cook
εργάτης (e-*rga*-tees)	**εργάτρια** (e-*rga*-tree-a)	Worker
προγραμματιστής (pro-gra-ma-tee-*stees*)	**προγραμματίστρια** (pro-gra-ma-*tee*-stree-a)	Developer
πωλητής (po-lee-*tees*)	**πωλήτρια** (po-*lee*-tree-a)	Retail sales associate
λογιστής (lo-yee-*stees*)	**λογίστρια** (lo-*yee*-stree-a)	Accountant
δάσκαλος (*da*-ska-los)	**δασκάλα** (da-*ska*-la)	Teacher

Masculine	Feminine	Translation
διαφημιστής (dee-a-fee-mee-*stees*)	**διαφημίστρια** (dee-a-fee-*mee*-stree-a)	Marketer
σερβιτόρος (se-rvee-*to*-ros)	**σερβιτόρα** (se-rvee-*to*-ra)	Waiter/waitress
αγρότης (a-*gro*-tees)	**αγρότισσα** (a-*gro*-ti-sa)	Farmer

Table 5-3 lists professions that have only one form for both masculine and feminine.

TABLE 5-3

Professions with Only One Form

Masculine & Feminine	Translation
γιατρός (ya-*tros*)	Doctor
ταμίας (ta-*mee*-as)	Cashier
μηχανικός (mee-kha-nee-*kos*)	Engineer
τεχνικός (te-chnee-*kos*)	Technician
δικηγόρος (dee-kee-*go*-ros)	Lawyer
ψυχολόγος (psee-kho-*lo*-gos)	Psychologist
γραμματέας (gra-ma-*te*-as)	Secretary
οδηγός (o-dee-*gos*)	Driver
ηπάλληλος γραφείου (ee-*pa*-lee-los gra-*fee*-oo)	Administrative officer
αστυνόμος (a-stee-*no*-mos)	Police officer

Asking and answering questions

So, suppose your Greek neighbor asks you: **Τι δουλειά κάνεις;** (tee doo-*lya ka*-nees) *(What do you do for a living?)* You can say: **Είμαι** (*ee*-me) *(I am)* and your profession.

Now, if you want to talk about someone else, the questions and answers go like this:

> **Τι δουλειά κάνει η Μαρία;** (tee doo-*lya ka*-nee ee ma-*ree*-a) *(What does Maria do for a living?)*

Η Μαρία είναι δικηγόρος. (ee ma-*ree*-a *ee*-ne dee-kee-*go*-ros) (*Maria is a lawyer.*)

Τι δουλειά κάνει ο Παντελής; (tee doo-*lya* ka-nee o pa-nde-*lees*) (*What does Pantelis do for a living?*)

Ο Παντελής είναι αγρότης. (o pa-nde-*lees ee*-ne a-*gro*-tees) (*Pantelis is a farmer.*)

Chatting About Your Family

Family makes a house a home.

This is a phrase we often find written on a magnet on Mom's fridge. This phrase shows how important family is, and for this reason, the topic of family couldn't be missing from this chapter with basic expressions.

The word family in Greek is οικογένεια (ee-ko-*ye*-nee-a). Let's look at the family members in Greek (with their appropriate articles).

>> η οικογένειά μου (ee ee-ko-ye-nee-*a* moo) (*my family*)

>> ο πατέρας or ο μπαμπάς (o pa-*te*-ras) or (o ba-*bas*) (*father, Dad*)

>> η μητέρα or η μαμά (ee mee-*te*-ra) or (ee ma-*ma*) (*mother, Mom/Mum*)

TIP

Μπαμπάς and μαμά are more tender words; children use these names when talking to their parents.

>> ο παππούς (o pa-*poos*) (*grandfather*)

>> η γιαγιά (ee ya-*ya*) (*grandmother*)

TIP

When you talk about both together, you can say οι παππούδες (ee pa-*poo*-des).

>> ο θείος (o *thee*-os) (*uncle*)

>> η θεία (ee *thee*-a) (*aunt*)

TIP

If you want to talk about all your uncles and aunts together, you can say οι θείοι (ee *thee*-ee).

>> ο ξάδελφος (o *ksa*-de-lfos) (*cousin,* male)

>> η ξαδέλφη (ee ksa-*de*-lfee) (*cousin,* female)

TIP

If you have many male and female cousins, you can call them τα ξαδέλφια (ta ksa-*de*-lfya).

>> **ο γιός** (o yos) (*son*)

>> **η κόρη** (ee *ko*-ree) (*daughter*)

>> **τα παιδιά** (ta pe-*dya*) (*children*)

>> **ο αδελφός** (o a-de-*lfos*) (*brother*)

>> **η αδελφή** (ee a-de-*lfee*) (*sister*)

>> **τα αδέλφια** (ta a-*del*-fya) (*siblings*)

You can use the following vocabulary to talk about your relationship status:

>> When someone is married, we say that person is **παντρεμένος** (pa-dre-*me*-nos) (male) or **παντρεμένη** (pa-dre-*me*-nee) (female).

>> When someone is single, you say that person is **ελεύθερος** (e-*lef*-the-ros) (male) or **ελεύθερη** (e-*lef*-the-ree) (female).

>> When someone is in a relationship, that person can say **είμαι σε σχέση** (*ee*-me se *skhe*-see) or **έχω σχέση** (*e*-kho *skhe*-see).

Suppose you're learning about your new friend Dimitra's family. You may hear statements like the following:

Ο μπαμπάς της είναι ο Νίκος και η μαμά της η Ελένη. (o ba-*bas* tees *ee*-ne o *nee*-kos ke ee ma-*ma* tees ee e-*le*-nee) (*Her dad is Nikos, and her mom is Eleni.*)

Έχει τρία αδέλφια, τον Κώστα, τη Βασιλική, και τον Φίλιππο. (e-hee *tree*-a a-de-lfya ton *Ko*-sta tee va-see-lee-*kee* ke ton *fee*-lee-po) (*She has three siblings, Kostas, Vasiliki, and Filippos.*)

Η Βασιλική είναι παντρεμένη με τον Πάνο. (ee va-see-lee-*kee* *ee*-ne pa-dre-*me*-nee me ton *pa*-no) (*Vasiliki is married to Panos.*)

Ο Κώστας και ο Φίλιππος είναι ελεύθεροι. (o *ko*-stas ke o *fee*-lee-pos *ee*-ne e-*lef*-the-ree) (*Kostas and Filippos are single.*)

Η Δήμητρα έχει και οκτώ ξαδέλφια, πέντε κορίτσια και τρία αγόρια. (ee *dee*-mee-tra *e*-hee ke o-*kto* ksa-de-lfya, *pe*-nde ko-*ree*-tsya ke *tree*-a a-*go*-rya) (*Dimitra also has eight cousins, five girls and three boys.*)

Talkin' the Talk

Dimitra meets her new friend Georgia at the café. They talk about their families.

Georgia: Έχεις αδέλφια;
          e-hees a-*de*-lfya;
          Do you have any siblings?

Dimitra: Ναι, έχω τρία αδέλφια, δύο αδελφούς και μια αδελφή. Εσύ;
          ne, *e*-kho *tree*-a a-*de*-lfya, *dee*-o a-de-*lfoos* ke mya a-de-*lfes*. e-*see*;
          Yes, I have three siblings, two brothers and one sister. And you?

Georgia: Εγώ έχω μια αδελφή, την Μαρίνα.
          e-*go* e-kho mya a-de-*lfee,* teen ma-*ree*-na.
          I have one sister, Marina.

Dimitra: Είσαι παντρεμένη;
          ee-se pa-dre-*me*-nee;
          Are you married?

Georgia: Όχι, είμαι ελεύθερη. Εσύ;
          o-hee, *ee*-me e-*lef*-the-ree. e-*see*;
          No, I am single. And you?

Dimitra: Δεν είμαι παντρεμένη αλλά είμαι σε σχέση.
          Den *ee*-me pa-dre-*me*-nee a-*la* *ee*-me se *skhe*-see.
          I'm not married, but I'm in a relationship.

WORDS TO KNOW		
Έχεις αδέλφια;	*e*-hees a-*de*-lfya	*Do you have any siblings?*
αδελφή	a-de-*lfee*	*sister*
Είσαι παντρεμένος/ παντρεμένη;	*ee*-se pa-dre-*me*-nos/ pa-dre-*me*-nee	*Are you married? (male, female)*
ελεύθερος, ελεύθερη	e-*lef*-the-ros, e-*lef*-the-ree	*single (male, female)*
Είμαι σε σχέση.	*ee*-me se *skhe*-see	*I am in a relationship.*

Saying Goodbye

TIP

All right, it's time to leave and say goodbye to your new Greek friends. What can you say? Of course, a simple γεια (ya) is enough, but if you want variety, you can say αντίο (a-*dee*-o) (*goodbye*) or γεια χαρά (ya kha-*ra*) (*bye*). And of course, if you want to see them again (I hope you do), you can say τα λέμε (ta *le*-me) (*see you later*).

FUN & GAMES

Can you match the questions with their answers?

Πώς σε λένε;	Ναι, έχω δύο αδέλφια.
Τι δουλειά κάνεις;	Είμαι από την Ελλάδα.
Είσαι παντρεμένη;	Με λένε Ελένη.
Πώς είστε κύριε Γιώργο;	Όχι, είμαι ελεύθερη.
Έχεις αδέλφια;	Μιλάω ελληνικά και αγγλικά.
Τι γλώσσες μιλάς;	Είμαι καλά.
Από πού είσαι;	Είμαι δικηγόρος.

Chapter **6**

Figuring Out Numbers, Dates, and Times

Greece has a long history with mathematics, as it was one of the first countries in the world to develop the science of mathematics. In this chapter, you find out how to count numbers in Greek as well as how to talk about years, months, days of the week, and the time. Are you ready?

Counting Numbers 1 to 1,000

If you can't sleep, then it will help you to start counting sheep. But if you want to fall asleep very quickly, then try counting sheep in Greek. I promise you that you'll fall asleep in a few minutes. But how do you count in Greek? Just read this section, and you'll be ready to snooze in no time!

TIP

In Greek, you have two options for the word "number":

» αριθμός (a-ree-*thmos*)

» νούμερο (*noo*-me-ro)

From 0 to 10

Let's start with the numbers from 0 to 10. Look at Table 6-1.

TABLE 6-1

Numbers 0–10

Number	Greek
0	μηδέν (mee-*den*)
1	ένα (*e*-na)
2	δύο (*dee*-o)
3	τρία (*tree*-a)
4	τέσσερα (*te*-se-ra)
5	πέντε (*pe*-nde)
6	έξι (*e*-ksee)
7	εφτά (e-*fta*) or επτά (e-*pta*)
8	οκτώ (o-*kto*) or οχτώ (o-*khto*)
9	εννιά (e-*nya*) or εννέα (e-*ne*-a)
10	δέκα (*de*-ka)

From 11 to 19

After you know the first ten numbers, it's time to move on. Table 6-2 has numbers 11 to 19.

TABLE 6-2

Numbers 11–19

Number	Greek
11	έντεκα (e-de-ka)
12	δώδεκα (*do*-de-ka)
13	δεκατρία (de-ka-*tree*-a)
14	δεκατέσσερα (de-ka-*te*-se-ra)
15	δεκαπέντε (de-ka-*pe*-nde)

Number	Greek
16	δεκαέξι (de-ka-*e*-ksee)
17	δεκαεπτά (de-ka-e-*pta*) or δεκαεφτά (de-ka-e-*fta*)
18	δεκαοκτώ (de-ka-o-*kto*) or δεκαοχτώ (de-ka-o-*khto*)
19	δεκαεννιά (de-ka-e-*nya*) or δεκαεννέα (de-ka-e-*ne*-a)

From 20 to 99

TIP

Do you see anything interesting about the numbers 13 to 19 in Table 6-2? How do we say them? First, we say the tens (ten) and then the units (three, four, five, and so on). We count all the numbers from 13 and above in the same way.

So how do we read 21? You combine the words for 20 and 1. It's είκοσι ένα (*ee*-ko-see *e*-na).

What about 37? You combine the words for 30 and 7. It's τριάντα επτά (tree-*a*-nda e-*pta*).

And 44? You get the idea: Combine the words for 40 and 4. It's σαράντα τέσσερα (sa-*ra*-nda *te*-se-ra).

And now that I've explained this to you, let's look at the tens up to 90 in Table 6-3.

TABLE 6-3

Numbers 20–90 by Tens

Number	Greek
20	είκοσι (*ee*-ko-see)
30	τριάντα (tree-*a*-nda)
40	σαράντα (sa-*ra*-nda)
50	πενήντα (pe-*nee*-nda)
60	εξήντα (e-*ksee*-nda)
70	εβδομήντα (e-vdo-*mee*-nda)
80	ογδόντα (o-*gdo*-nda)
90	ενενήντα (e-ne-*nee*-nda)

From 100 to 999

You're doing very well. But if counting 100 sheep in Greek hasn't put you to sleep, maybe it would help to learn to count to 1,000. Check out Table 6-4.

TABLE 6-4

Numbers 100–1,000

Number	Greek
100	εκατό (e-ka-*to*)
200	διακόσια (dya-*ko*-sya)
300	τριακόσια (tree-a-*ko*-sya)
400	τετρακόσια (te-tra-*ko*-sya)
500	πεντακόσια (pe-nda-*ko*-sya)
600	εξακόσια (e-ksa-*ko*-sya)
700	επτακόσια (e-pta-*ko*-sya) or εφτακόσια (e-fta-*ko*-sya)
800	οκτακόσια (o-kta-*ko*-sya) or οχτακόσια (o-khta-*ko*-sya)
900	εννιακόσια (e-nya-*ko*-sya)
1,000	χίλια (*hee*-lya)

GRAMMATICALLY SPEAKING

Pay attention! The number 100 is εκατό (e-ka-*to*) but in other numbers like 101, 102, 110, and 135, we add a final –ν (n) to the word. Let's look at some examples:

>> For 101, you say εκατόν ένα (e-ka-*ton* e-na).

>> For 135, you say εκατόν τριάντα πέντε (e-ka-*ton* tree-*a*-nda pe-nde).

>> For 179, you say εκατόν εβδομήντα εννιά (e-ka-*ton* e-vdo-*mee*-nda e-*nya*).

This rule doesn't apply to the other hundreds, though. For example:

>> For 299, you say διακόσια ενενήντα εννιά (dya-*ko*-sya e-ne-*nee*-nda e-*nya*).

>> For 341, you say τριακόσια σαράντα ένα (tree-a-*ko*-sya sa-*ra*-nda e-na).

>> For 564, you say πεντακόσια εξήντα τέσσερα (pe-nda-*ko*-sya e-*ksee*-nda *te*-se-ra).

>> For 805, you say οκτακόσια πέντε (o-kta-*ko*-sya *pe*-nde).

Age is just a number

In Greece, it isn't considered very polite to ask someone's age, especially a woman's age. Nevertheless, we couldn't go through this chapter without mentioning this topic — the chapter is about numbers, after all. The word for age is ηλικία (ee-lee-*kee*-a).

The question is

> **Πόσο χρονών είσαι?** (*po*-so khro-*non* ee-se) (*How old are you?*)

And the usual answer is

> **Είμαι . . . χρονών** (*ee*-me . . . khro-*non*) (*I am . . . years old.*)

Just add the correct number to your answer.

Nevertheless, you may hear a woman jokingly say Είμαι όσο φαίνομαι (*ee*-me *o*-so *fe*-no-me) (*I am as old as I look*).

Talkin' the Talk

Stella and Panos have just met on a sightseeing tour. As they get to know each other, they ask each other about their age. (Track 6)

Stella: Πάνο, πόσο χρονών είσαι;
pa-no po-so khro-*non* ee-se;
Panos, how old are you?

Panos: Είμαι τριάντα πέντε χρονών. Εσύ;
ee-me tree-*a*-nda *pe*-nde khro-*non*. e-*see*;
I am 35 years old. And you?

Stella: Εγώ είμαι σαράντα εννιά χρονών.
e-*go* ee-me sa-*ra*-nda e-*nya* khro-*non*.
I am 49 years old.

WORDS TO KNOW

ηλικία	ee-lee-*kee*-a	*age*
Πόσο χρονών είσαι;	*po*-so khro-*non ee*-se	*How old are you?*
Είμαι . . . χρονών.	*ee*-me . . . khro-*non*	*I am . . . years old.*

Naming the Days of the Week

After you have a handle on numbers in Greek, it's a good time to tell you the days of the week so you can eventually talk about specific dates on the calendar (see the next section). Let's start with some basic words:

>> **η ημέρα** (ee ee-*me*-ra) (*the day*)

>> **η εβδομάδα** (ee e-vdo-*ma*-da) (*the week*)

>> **οι ημέρες της εβδομάδας** (ee ee-*me*-res tees e-vdo-*ma*-das) (*the days of the week*)

>> **η καθημερινή** (ee ka-thee-me-ree-*nee*) (*the weekday*)

>> **το Σαββατοκύριακο** (to sa-va-to-*kee*-rya-ko) (*the weekend*)

REMEMBER

All right, now let's look at the seven days:

>> **Δευτέρα** (de-*fte*-ra) (*Monday*)

>> **Τρίτη** (*tree*-tee) (*Tuesday*)

>> **Τετάρτη** (te-*ta*-rtee) (*Wednesday*)

>> **Πέμπτη** (*pe*-mptee) (*Thursday*)

>> **Παρασκευή** (pa-ra-skev-*ee*) (*Friday*)

>> **Σάββατο** (*sa*-va-to) (*Saturday*)

>> **Κυριακή** (kee-rya-*kee*) (*Sunday*)

So, if you want to ask about the day, you can say:

Τι μέρα είναι σήμερα; (tee *me*-ra *ee*-ne *see*-me-ra) (*What day is it today?*)

Είναι Παρασκευή. (*ee*-ne pa-ra-skev-*ee*) (*It is Friday.*)

Τι μέρα είναι αύριο; (tee *me*-ra *ee*-ne *av*-ree-o) (*What day is it tomorrow?*)

Είναι Σάββατο. (*ee*-ne *sa*-va-to) (*It is Saturday.*)

Listing Months and Years

After you know the days of the week, it's time to look at the months. In Greek, the word for "month" is μήνας (*mee*-nas).

>> **Ιανουάριος** (ee-a-noo-*a*-ree-os) (*January*)

>> **Φεβρουάριος** (fe-vroo-*a*-ree-os) (*February*)

>> **Μάρτιος** (*ma*-rtee-os) (*March*)

>> **Απρίλιος** (a-*pree*-lee-os) (*April*)

>> **Μάιος** (*ma*-ee-os) (*May*)

>> **Ιούνιος** (ee-*oo*-nee-os) (*June*)

>> **Ιούλιος** (ee-*oo*-lee-os) (*July*)

>> **Αύγουστος** (*av*-goo-stos) (*August*)

>> **Σεπτέμβριος** (se-*pte*-mvree-os) (*September*)

>> **Οκτώβριος** (o-*kto*-vree-os) (*October*)

>> **Νοέμβριος** (no-*em*-vree-os) (*November*)

>> **Δεκέμβριος** (de-*kem*-vree-os) (*December*)

In Greek the word for "year" is η χρονιά (ee khro-*nya*) or το έτος (to *e*-tos). If you know how to count in Greek (as you find out earlier in this chapter), you can easily say the year. So let's look at some examples:

>> For 1981, you say **χίλια εννιακόσια ογδόντα ένα** (*hee*-lya e-nya-*ko*-sya o-*gdo*-nda *e*-na).

>> For 1992, you say **χίλια εννιακόσια ενενήντα δύο** (*hee*-lya e-nya-*ko*-sya e-ne-*nee*-nda *dee*-o).

>> For 2004, you say **δύο χιλιάδες τέσσερα** (*dee*-o hee-*lya*-des *te*-se-ra).

Telling Time

Suppose you want to arrange a coffee meeting with your friend Panagiota. How do you go about it? You need to arrange the day, the time, and the place. In this section, I talk about telling time, as you would see it on an analog clock.

The basics

The time in Greek is η ώρα (ee *o*-ra). If you want to ask what time it is, you say

Τι ώρα είναι; (tee *o*-ra *ee*-ne) (*What time is it?*)

And the usual answer is

Είναι . . . (*ee*-ne) (*It is . . .*)

On an analog clock, the following rules apply (see the times described in Figure 6-1):

>> When the time is on the hour, you say **ακριβώς** (a-kree-*vos*). So, for example, you say **Η ώρα είναι πέντε ακριβώς** (ee *o*-ra *ee*-ne *pe*-nde a-kree-*vos*) (*It is five o'clock*).

>> Half past the hour in Greek is **και μισή** (ke mee-*see*). So here, you read seven-thirty as **εφτά και μισή** (e-*fta* ke mee-*see*) or **εφτάμιση** (e-*fta*-mee-see).

>> When the minute hand is on the right side of the clock, you say **και** (ke). For example, **Η ώρα είναι πέντε και δέκα.** (ee *o*-ra *ee*-ne *pe*-nde ke *de*-ka) (*The time is five-ten; the time is ten minutes past five.*)

>> When the minute hand is on the left side of the clock, you say **παρά** (pa-*ra*) and the hour that is coming. So, if it's 7:50, you read **οκτώ παρά δέκα** (o-*kto* pa-*ra de*-ka) (*ten to eight*).

>> When the time is a quarter past the hour, you say **και τέταρτο** (ke *te*-ta-rto). For example, for 5:15, you say **πέντε και τέταρτο** (*pe*-nde ke *te*-ta-rto) (*quarter past five*).

>> If the time is a quarter to the hour, you say **παρά τέταρτο** (pa-*ra te*-ta-rto) and the hour that is coming. For 7:45, you say **οκτώ παρά τέταρτο** (o-*kto* pa-*ra te*-ta-rto) (*quarter to eight*).

Other helpful guidelines

If the time is one o'clock, you say η ώρα είναι μία (ee *o*-ra *ee*-ne *mee*-a) and not ένα (*e*-na). Look at these cases:

>> For 1:15, you say **Η ώρα είναι μία και τέταρτο.** (ee *o*-ra *ee*-ne *mee*-a ke *te*-ta-rto) (*The time is a quarter past one.*)

>> For 1:30, you say **Η ώρα είναι μία και μισή.** (ee *o*-ra *ee*-ne *mee*-a ke mee-*see*) (*The time is half past one.*)

FIGURE 6-1:
Telling time.

© John Wiley & Sons, Inc.

GRAMMATICALLY
SPEAKING

You also need to be careful with the numbers 3 and 4, which change when used to tell the time. For 3, we say τρεις (trees) and for 4, we say τέσσερις (*te*-se-rees). Let's read the following:

» For 3:05, you say **Η ώρα είναι τρεις και πέντε.** (ee *o*-ra *ee*-ne trees ke *pe*-nde) (*The time is five past three.*)

» For 3:55, you say **Η ώρα είναι τέσσερις παρά πέντε.** (ee *o*-ra *ee*-ne *te*-se-rees pa-*ra pe*-nde) (*The time is five to four.*)

» For 4:25, you say **Η ώρα είναι τέσσερις και είκοσι πέντε.** (ee *o*-ra *ee*-ne *te*-se-rees ke *ee*-ko-see *pe*-nde) (*The time is twenty-five past four.*)

» For 4:45, you say **Η ώρα είναι πέντε παρά τέταρτο.** (ee *o*-ra *ee*-ne *pe*-nde pa-*ra te*-ta-rto) (*The time is a quarter to five.*)

Since I've told you the basics, let's see how you can have a conversation and schedule a meeting with someone or arrange your schedule:

» **Τι ώρα είναι η συνάντηση;** (tee *o*-ra *ee*-ne ee see-*na*-dee-see) (*What time is the meeting?*)

» **Τι ώρα έχεις ραντεβού με τον γιατρό;** (tee *o*-ra *e*-hees ra-de-*voo* me ton ya-*tro*) (*What time is your appointment with the doctor?*)

» **Το ραντεβού είναι στις . . .** (to ra-de-*voo ee*-ne stees) (*The appointment is at . . .*)

» **Έχετε ώρα;** (*e*-he-te *o*-ra) (*Do you have time?*)

Talkin' the Talk

Marina and Niki are arranging a meeting on Saturday evening.

Marina: Γεια σου, Νίκη. Θέλεις να πάμε για ποτό το Σάββατο;
ya soo *nee*-kee. *the*-lees na *pa*-me ya po-*to* to *sa*-va-to;
Hi Niki. Do you want to go out for a drink on Saturday?

Niki: Θέλω! Τι ώρα;
the-lo! tee *o*-ra;
I want to! What time?

Marina: Μπορείς στις επτά;
bo-*rees* stees e-*pta*;
Are you available at seven?

Niki: Προτιμώ να βρεθούμε στις οκτώ ακριβώς.
pro-tee-*mo* na vre-*thoo*-me stees o-*kto* a-kree-*vos*.
I prefer to meet at eight exactly.

Marina: Δεν υπάρχει πρόβλημα! Τα λέμε το Σάββατο!
den ee-*pa*-rhee *pro*-vlee-ma! ta *le*-me to *sa*-va-to!
No problem! See you on Saturday!

WORDS TO KNOW

Θέλεις να πάμε . . .	*the*-lees na *pa*-me	*Do you want to go . . .*
Τι ώρα;	tee *o*-ra	*What time?*
Μπορείς στις επτά;	bo-*rees* stees e-*pta*	*Are you available at seven?*
οκτώ ακριβώς	o-*kto* a-kree-*vos*	*eight o'clock exactly*
Δεν υπάρχει πρόβλημα!	den ee-*pa*-rhee *pro*-vlee-ma	*No problem!*

Talking About Yesterday, Today, and Tomorrow

Some words help us talk about the present, the past, and the future. Earlier in this chapter, I discuss the months, the days, and the time; let's take a moment to look at words that will help us put the events of our lives in chronological order. (See Chapter 4 for more about present, past, and future verb tenses.)

The present

Words and phrases related to the present, or **to παρόν** (to pa-*ron*), include the following:

>> **τώρα** (*to*-ra) (*now*)

>> **αυτή τη στιγμή** (af-*tee* tee stee-*gmee*) (*at this moment*)

>> **σήμερα** (*see*-me-ra) (*today*)

>> **αυτή την ώρα** (af-*tee* teen o-ra) (*at this time*)

>> **μόλις** (*mo*-lees) (*just now*)

The past

Many words help us talk about the past, or **to παρελθόν** (to pa–rel-*thon*). However, here are the most basic ones:

>> **εχθές** (e-*khthes*) (*yesterday*)

>> **προχθές** (pro-*khthes*) (*the day before yesterday*)

>> **τον προηγούμενο μήνα** (ton pro-ee-*goo*-me-no *mee*-na) (*last month*)

>> **την προηγούμενη εβδομάδα** (teen pro-ee-*goo*-me-nee e-vdo-*ma*-da) (*last week*)

>> **πριν από ένα μήνα, ένα χρόνο** (preen a-*po* e-na *mee*-na, e-na *khro*-no) (*one month ago, one year ago*)

>> **πριν** (preen) (*before*)

The future

To talk about situations or plans that will happen in the future, or το μέλλον (to *me*-lon), you can use some of these words:

» μετά (me-*ta*) (*after*)

» αύριο (*av*-ree-o) (*tomorrow*)

» αργότερα (a-*rgo*-te-ra) (*later*)

» στη συνέχεια (stee see-*ne*-hee-a) (*subsequently, next*)

FUN & GAMES

What is the time in Greek? Match the times to the correct Greek phrases.

6:10	Η ώρα είναι έξι και μισή.
6:45	Η ώρα είναι έξι ακριβώς.
6:00	Η ώρα είναι επτά παρά είκοσι πέντε.
6:15	Η ώρα είναι έξι και δέκα.
6:35	Η ώρα είναι επτά παρά τέταρτο.
6:30	Η ώρα είναι έξι και τέταρτο.

Chapter 7

Speaking Greek at Home

One easy way to kickstart your Greek language journey is to identify and name everyday items around you at home. Enhance your skills by discussing furniture and rooms and detailing the daily tasks you perform in Greek. This chapter guides you through these practices and more.

Talking About Your Daily Routines

Happiness, they say, lies in the small things: a warm coffee in the morning, a walk in the park with the dog, an evening of board games with the children, a nice meal with friends. That is, the simple daily routine — or in Greek η ρουτίνα (ee roo-*tee*-na) that we all love. So in this section, I look at the vocabulary that will help us talk about our daily habits, and by the way that is η καθημερινή συνήθεια (ee ka-thee-me-ree-*nee* see-*nee*-thee-a) (*the daily habit*).

GRAMMATICALLY
SPEAKING

When you talk about your daily routine, meaning things that happen repeatedly every day, then the verbs are in ενεστώτας (e-ne-*sto*-tas) (*present tense*). See Chapter 4 for details on verbs and their tenses.

The morning

Πρωί (pro-*ee*) (*morning*) is when the following words and phrases will come in handy:

>> **Ξυπνάω.** (ksee-*pna*-o) (*I wake up.*)

>> **Σηκώνομαι από το κρεβάτι.** (see-*ko*-no-me a-*po* to kre-*va*-tee) (*I get out of bed.*)

>> **Φοράω τα ρούχα μου.** (fo-*ra*-o ta *roo*-kha moo) (*I put on my clothes.*)

>> **Πλένω τα δόντια μου.** (*ple*-no ta *do*-ntya moo) (*I brush my teeth.*)

>> **Χτενίζω τα μαλλιά μου.** (hte-*nee*-zo ta ma-*lya* moo) (*I comb my hair.*)

>> **Πίνω καφέ.** (*pee*-no ka-*fe*) (*I drink coffee.*)

>> **Τρώω πρωινό.** (*tro*-o pro-ee-*no*) (*I eat breakfast.*)

>> **Φεύγω για τη δουλειά.** (*fev*-go ya tee doo-*lya*) (*I leave for work.*)

>> **Πάω τα παιδιά σχολείο.** (*pa*-o ta pe-*dya* skho-*lee*-o) (*I take the children to school.*)

The afternoon

CULTURAL WISDOM

In Greece, the hours between 13:00 (1 p.m.) and 16:00 (4 p.m.) are called μεσημέρι (me-see-*me*-ree) (*midday*). It's the time when you have your lunch and your children finish school. During those hours, the following usually take place:

>> **Τρώω μεσημεριανό.** (*tro*-o me-see-me-rya-*no*) (*I eat lunch.*)

>> **Κάνω διάλειμμα.** (*ka*-no dee-*a*-lee-ma) (*I take a break.*)

>> **Παίρνω τα παιδιά από το σχολείο.** (*pe*-rno ta pe-*dya* a-*po* to skho-*lee*-o) (*I pick up the children from school.*)

>> **Ξεκουράζομαι.** (kse-koo-*ra*-zo-me) (*I rest.*)

CULTURAL WISDOM

The Greeks love a midday nap, especially in the summer when it's very hot. In small villages and towns, many shops close for two hours at noon so the shopkeepers can rest. Nevertheless, this doesn't apply to cities where people have the typical 9–5 job and, of course, the midday rest is impossible.

From 16:00 (4 p.m.) until around 19:00 (7 p.m.), it is called απόγευμα (a-*po*-yev-ma) (*afternoon*). What happens during those hours?

>> **Σχολάω από τη δουλειά, από το σχολείο.** (skho-*la*-o a-*po* tee doo-*lya*, a-po to skho-*lee*-o) (*I finish work, school.*)

Σχολάω is a verb that can be used when we talk about finishing work *or* school at the end of the day. It means "I finish work" or "I finish school."

The regular school schedule in Greece ends around 1:30 or 2 p.m., but many children stay at school for more hours, approximately until 4 p.m., if their parents are working.

» **Πηγαίνω στο γυμναστήριο.** (pee-*ye*-no sto yee-mna-*stee*-ree-o) (*I go to the gym.*)

» **Διαβάζω τα μαθήματά μου.** (dya-*va*-zo ta ma-*thee*-ma-*ta* moo) (*I do my homework.*)

» **Βγάζω τον σκύλο βόλτα.** (*vga*-zo ton *skee*-lo vo-lta) (*I walk the dog.*)

» **Κάνω ένα χόμπι.** (*ka*-no *e*-na *kho*-bee) (*I do a hobby.*)

The evening

The evening, which in Greek is called βράδυ (*vra*-dee), is the time when people settle down and prepare to sleep. Here are some helpful phrases to know:

» **Βλέπω τηλεόραση.** (*vle*-po tee-le-o-ra-see) (*I watch television.*)

» **Διαβάζω ένα βιβλίο.** (dya-*va*-zo *e*-na vee-*vlee*-o) (*I read a book.*)

» **Τρώω βραδινό.** (*tro*-o vra-dee-*no*) (*I eat dinner.*)

» **Φοράω τις πιτζάμες μου.** (fo-*ra*-o tees pee-*tza*-mes moo) (*I put on my pajamas.*)

» **Ξαπλώνω στο κρεβάτι.** (ksa-*plo*-no sto kre-*va*-tee) (*I lie down in bed.*)

» **Κοιμάμαι.** (kee-*ma*-me) (*I sleep.*)

Many foreigners observe that Greeks eat their last meal of the day very late. It's true that you may see families having dinner at 21:00 (9 p.m.) or 22:00 (10 p.m.) in the evening, especially on weekends or when they are on vacation.

Naming the Rooms of a House

Home sweet home, or as we say in Greek, σπίτι μου, σπιτάκι μου (*spee*-tee moo, spee-*ta*-kee moo). Here we talk about the rooms of the house, which in Greek we call σπίτι (*spee*-tee).

REMEMBER

In Greek, the word σπίτι is more general than the English word "house." It describes any dwelling where people live, regardless of whether it is a single-family home, an apartment, a mansion, and so on. Additionally, the same word is translated as "home" and indicates a place where we feel warmth, love, and security.

CULTURAL WISDOM

But where do Greeks live? The majority of the population in Greece lives in cities where the typical type of housing is apartment buildings, or η πολυκατοικία (ee po-lee-ka-tee-*kee*-a). An apartment, or το διαμέρισμα (to dya-*me*-ree-sma), in Greece usually has one to two bedrooms, a living room, a kitchen, and almost always a balcony.

Every room in a house has a πόρτα (*po*-rta) (*door*), a παράθυρο (pa-*ra*-thee-ro) (*window*), a δάπεδο (*da*-pe-do) (*floor*), a ταβάνι (ta-*va*-nee) (*ceiling*), and τοίχους (*tee*-khoos) (*walls*).

So, let's see the basic rooms and fixtures (shown in Figure 7-1).

>> το δωμάτιο (to do-*ma*-tee-o) (*the room*)

>> το σαλόνι (to sa-*lo*-nee) (*the living room*)

>> η κουζίνα (ee koo-*zee*-na) (*the kitchen*)

>> το υπνοδωμάτιο (to ee-pno-do-*ma*-tee-o) (*the bedroom*)

>> ο διάδρομος (o dee-*a*-dro-mos) (*the hallway*)

>> το μπάνιο (to *ba*-nyo) (*the bathroom*)

>> η τουαλέτα (ee too-a-*le*-ta) (*the toilet*)

>> η αποθήκη (ee a-po-*thee*-kee) (*the storage room*)

>> ο κήπος (o *kee*-pos) (*the garden*)

>> το μπαλκόνι (to ba-*lko*-nee) (*the balcony*)

Apartments in Greece have balconies. The balcony is a space where we can place our γλάστρες (*gla*-stres) (*flowerpots*), τραπέζι (tra-*pe*-zee) (*table*), and καρέκλες (ka-*re*-kles) (*chairs*), and of course, hang our clothes to dry on the απλώστρα (a-*plo*-stra) (*clothesline*). Because the weather in Greece is good most of the time, we don't usually have a στεγνωτήριο (ste-gno-*tee*-ree-o) (*dryer*) in our homes. We hang the washed clothes to dry outside on the balcony or in the yard.

CULTURAL WISDOM

Were you invited to a Greek home? I have some tips to make a good impression. First, it's good to go to the house with a treat, a box of sweets, a cake, or flowers. It's also very important to accept any treat offered by the hosts. It isn't polite to be offered something and not eat or drink it.

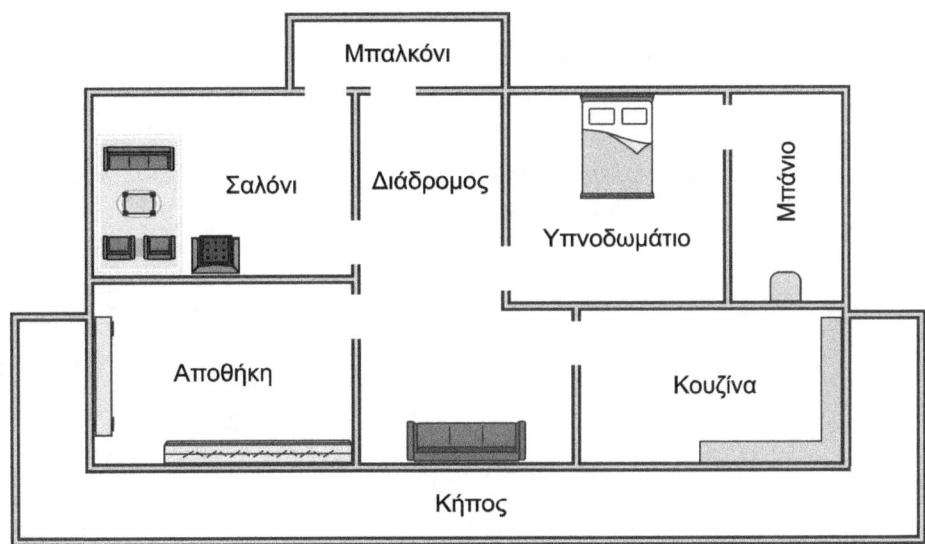

FIGURE 7-1:
Rooms of a
home in Greek.

© John Wiley & Sons, Inc.

Chatting About Furniture and Fixtures

Earlier in this chapter I tell you about the rooms; now it's time to tell you about the furniture in each room. Furniture in Greek is έπιπλο (*e*-pee-plo).

TIP

In the following sections, you discover a lot of vocabulary related to the house. Do you want to remember all these words? A smart way is to put sticky notes on the objects in your house that have the Greek name written on them. So every time you approach or use a specific object, you'll read the Greek word. Good idea, right?

The bedroom

Το υπνοδωμάτιο (to ee-pno-do-*ma*-tee-o) (*the bedroom*) has the following items:

» το κρεβάτι (to kre-*va*-tee) (*the bed*)

» το μαξιλάρι (to ma-ksee-*la*-ree) (*the pillow*)

» το σεντόνι (to se-*do*-nee) (*the bed sheet*)

» η κουβέρτα (ee koo-*ve*-rta) (*the blanket*)

» το πάπλωμα (to *pa*-plo-ma) (*the duvet/comforter*)

» το κομοδίνο (to ko-mo-*dee*-no) (*the nightstand*)

>> η ντουλάπα (ee doo-*la*-pa) (*the wardrobe/closet*)

>> το στρώμα (to *stro*-ma) (*the mattress*)

Figure 7-2 shows a bedroom with a bed, a nightstand, and a large closet. Note the Greek words in the figure.

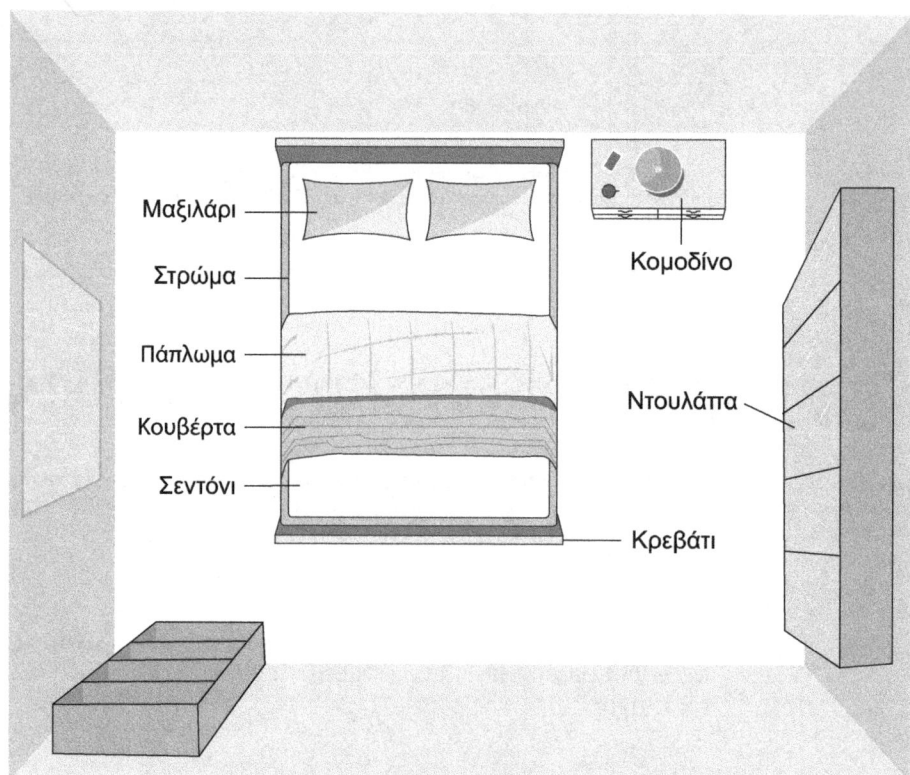

Labels in figure: Μαξιλάρι, Στρώμα, Πάπλωμα, Κουβέρτα, Σεντόνι, Κομοδίνο, Ντουλάπα, Κρεβάτι

FIGURE 7-2: Items in a bedroom.

The living room

Το σαλόνι (to sa-*lo*-nee) (*the living room*) includes the following:

>> ο καναπές (o ka-na-*pes*) (*the sofa*)

>> η πολυθρόνα (ee po-lee-*thro*-na) (*the armchair*)

>> το τραπεζάκι (to tra-pe-*za*-kee) (*the coffee table*)

>> η τηλεόραση (ee tee-le-*o*-ra-see) (*the television*)

>> **η βιβλιοθήκη** (ee vee-vlee-o-*thee*-kee) (*the bookshelf*)

>> **το χαλί** (to kha-*lee*) (*the carpet/rug*)

>> **το φωτιστικό** (to fo-tee-stee-*ko*) (*the lamp*)

>> **η κουρτίνα** (ee koo-*rtee*-na) (*the curtain*)

>> **το παράθυρο** (to pa-*ra*-thee-ro) (*the window*)

>> **το τζάκι** (to *tza*-kee) (*the fireplace*)

>> **ο πίνακας** (o *pee*-na-kas) (*the painting/artwork*)

Figure 7-3 shows a living room with a sofa, an armchair, a coffee table, a book-shelf, and a lamp. Note the Greek words in the figure.

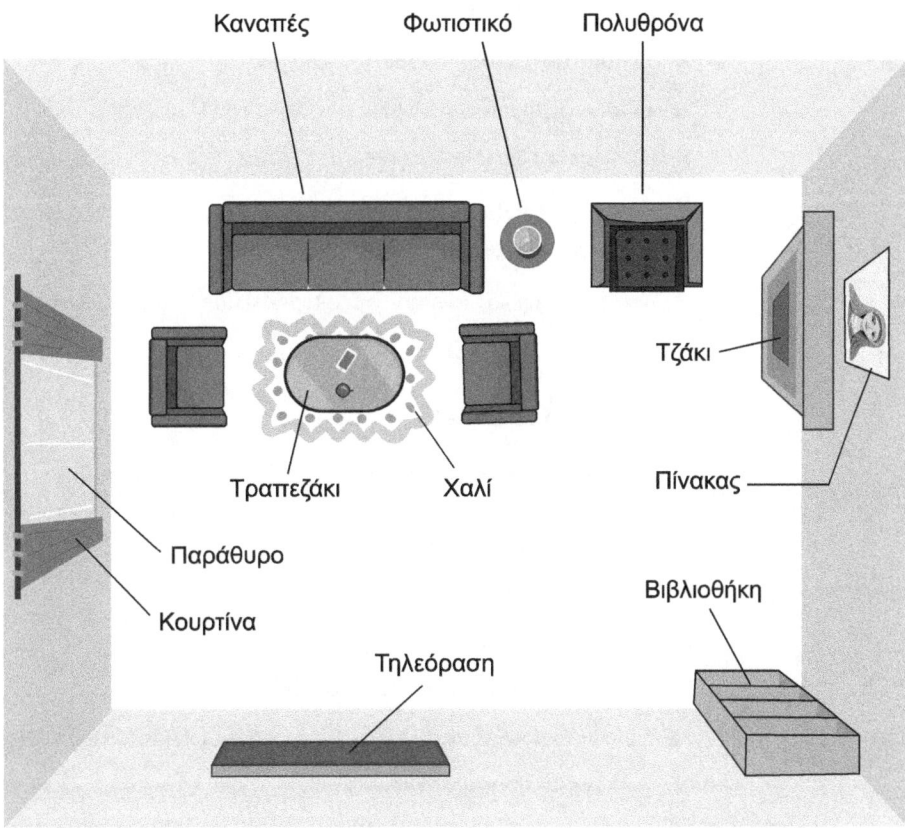

FIGURE 7-3: Items in a living room.

© *John Wiley & Sons, Inc.*

The kitchen

CULTURAL WISDOM

Η Κουζίνα (ee koo-*zee*-na) (*the kitchen*) in Greek households often serves as the heart of the home. It's not just a place for cooking; it's where traditions are passed down, culinary skills are honed, and family recipes are cherished and shared from generation to generation. The kitchen also holds a social significance. It's where family members come together to prepare meals, engage in lively conversations, and share their daily experiences. In many Greek homes, meals are a communal affair, and the kitchen is where the day begins and ends with shared moments over breakfast, lunch, or dinner.

Here are some useful words and phrases for the kitchen:

>> το ψυγείο (to psee-*yee*-o) (*the refrigerator*)

>> ο φούρνος (o *foo*-rnos) (*the oven*)

>> το ντουλάπι (to doo-*la*-pee) (*the cabinet*)

>> το πλυντήριο πιάτων (to plee-*dee*-ree-o *pya*-ton) (*the dishwasher*)

>> ο νεροχύτης (o ne-ro-*hee*-tees) (*the sink*)

>> το τραπέζι (to tra-*pe*-zee) (*the table*)

>> η καρέκλα (ee ka-*re*-kla) (*the chair*)

>> ο απορροφητήρας (o a-po-ro-fee-*tee*-ras) (*the range hood*)

The bathroom

Το μπάνιο (to *ba*-nyo) (*the bathroom*) includes the following:

>> ο νιπτήρας (o nee-*ptee*-ras) (*the sink*)

>> η βρύση (ee *vree*-see) (*the faucet/tap*)

>> ο καθρέφτης (o ka-*thre*-ftees) (*the mirror*)

>> η λεκάνη (ee le-*ka*-nee) (*the toilet bowl*)

>> η βούρτσα τουαλέτας (ee *voo*-rtsa too-a-*le*-tas) (*the toilet brush*)

>> το ντους (to doos) (*the shower*)

>> η ντουζιέρα (ee doo-*zye*-ra) (*the showerhead*)

>> η μπανιέρα (ee ba-*nye*-ra) (*the bathtub*)

>> η κρεμάστρα πετσετών (ee kre-*ma*-stra pe-tse-*ton*) (*the towel rack*)

CULTURAL
WISDOM

Fun fact: When you use the toilet in Greece, you shouldn't throw toilet paper into the bowl. A small basket is next to the toilet bowl for the paper. This practice is in place because the plumbing systems in many areas of Greece, particularly in older buildings, aren't designed to handle toilet paper.

Cleaning Your House

CULTURAL
WISDOM

So, you have a nice home with all the amenities. However, it's very important to be able to keep your house clean. Having a clean house is so important that we even have a saying for it:

Η καθαριότητα είναι η μισή αρχοντιά. (ee ka-tha-ree-*o*-tee-ta *ee*-ne ee mee-*see* ar-kho-*dya*) (*Cleanliness is half of nobility.*)

This saying emphasizes the importance of cleanliness and hygiene. It implies that maintaining a clean and tidy environment is a significant aspect of one's dignity, respectability, and overall well-being.

Here are some verbs that help you talk about house cleaning:

>> **Σκουπίζω.** (skoo-*pee*-zo) (*I sweep.*)

>> **Σφουγγαρίζω.** (sfoo-ga-*ree*-zo) (*I mop.*)

>> **Καθαρίζω.** (ka-tha-*ree*-zo) (*I clean.*)

>> **Συγυρίζω.** (see-yee-*ree*-zo) (*I tidy up.*)

>> **Ξεσκονίζω.** (kse-sko-*nee*-zo) (*I dust.*)

>> **Πλένω.** (*ple*-no) (*I wash.*)

>> **Βάζω πλυντήριο.** (*va*-zo plee-*dee*-ree-o) (*I do the laundry.*)

And to do all these things, you naturally need, apart from a lot of patience, some items:

>> **σκούπα** (*skoo*-pa) (*broom*)

>> **φαράσι** (fa-*ra*-see) (*dustpan*)

>> **σφουγγαρίστρα** (sfoo-ga-*ree*-stra) (*mop*)

>> **κουβάς** (koo-*vas*) (*bucket*)

>> **σακούλα σκουπιδιών** (sa-*koo*-la skoo-pee-*dyon*) (*trash bag*)

>> κάδος απορριμμάτων (*ka*-dos a-po-ree-*ma*-ton) (*trash can*)

>> υγρό πιάτων (ee-*gro pya*-ton) (*dish soap*)

>> απορρυπαντικό (a-po-ree-pa-dee-*ko*) (*detergent*)

Talkin' the Talk

PLAY THIS

Mihalis and Panagiota discuss how to divide the household chores. (Track 7)

Mihalis: Εγώ θα ξεκινήσω από την κουζίνα.
e-*go* tha kse-kee-*nee*-so a-*po* teen koo-*zee*-na.
I will start with the kitchen.

Panagiota: Τι θα κάνεις στην κουζίνα;
tee tha *ka*-nees steen koo-*zee*-na;
What will you do in the kitchen?

Mihalis: Θα πλύνω τα πιάτα, θα καθαρίσω τον φούρνο, θα σκουπίσω, και θα σφουγγαρίσω το πάτωμα. Εσύ τι θα κάνεις;
tha *plee*-no ta *pya*-ta, tha ka-tha-*ree*-so ton *foo*-rno, tha skoo-*pee*-so, ke tha sfoo-ga-*ree*-so to *pa*-to-ma. e-*see* tee tha *ka*-nees;
I will wash the dishes, clean the oven, sweep, and mop the floor. What will you do?

Panagiota: Εγώ θα καθαρίσω το σαλόνι. Θα σκουπίσω το χαλί, θα ξεσκονίσω, και θα σφουγγαρίσω.
e-*go* tha ka-tha-*ree*-so to sa-*lo*-nee. tha skoo-*pee*-so to kha-*lee*, tha kse-sko-*nee*-so, ke tha sfoo-ga-*ree*-so.
I will clean the living room. I will vacuum the carpet, dust, and mop.

Mihalis: Που είναι ο κουβάς και η σφουγγαρίστρα;
poo *ee*-ne o koo-*vas* ke ee sfoo-ga-*ree*-stra;
Where are the bucket and mop?

Panagiota: Στην αποθήκη.
steen a-po-*thee*-kee.
In the storage room.

Mihalis: Και οι μεγάλες σακούλες σκουπιδιών;
ke ee me-*ga*-les sa-*koo*-les skoo-pee-*dyon*;
And the large garbage bags?

Panagiota: Στην κουζίνα, μέσα στο τρίτο συρτάρι.
steen koo-*zee*-na, *me*-sa sto *tree*-to see-*rta*-ree.
In the kitchen, in the third drawer.

Mihalis: Ωραία λοιπόν, ας ξεκινήσουμε.
o-*re*-a lee-*pon*, as kse-kee-*nee*-soo-me.
All right then, let's get started.

WORDS TO KNOW

Εγώ θα ξεκινήσω.	e-*go* tha kse-kee-*nee*-so	*I will start.*
Θα πλύνω τα πιάτα.	tha *plee*-no ta *pya*-ta	*I will wash the dishes.*
Θα καθαρίσω.	tha ka-tha-*ree*-so	*I will clean.*
Θα σκουπίσω.	tha skoo-*pee*-so	*I will sweep.*
Θα σφουγγαρίσω το πάτωμα.	tha sfoo-ga-*ree*-so to *pa*-to-ma	*I will mop the floor.*
Θα σκουπίσω το χαλί.	tha skoo-*pee*-so to kha-*lee*	*I will vacuum the carpet.*
Θα ξεσκονίσω.	tha kse-sko-*nee*-so	*I will dust.*
κουβάς	koo-*vas*	*bucket*
σφουγγαρίστρα	sfoo-ga-*ree*-stra	*mop*
σακούλες σκουπιδιών	sa-*koo*-les skoo-pee-*dyon*	*garbage bags*
συρτάρι	see-*rta*-ree	*drawer*

FUN & GAMES

Can you name the furniture in this house?

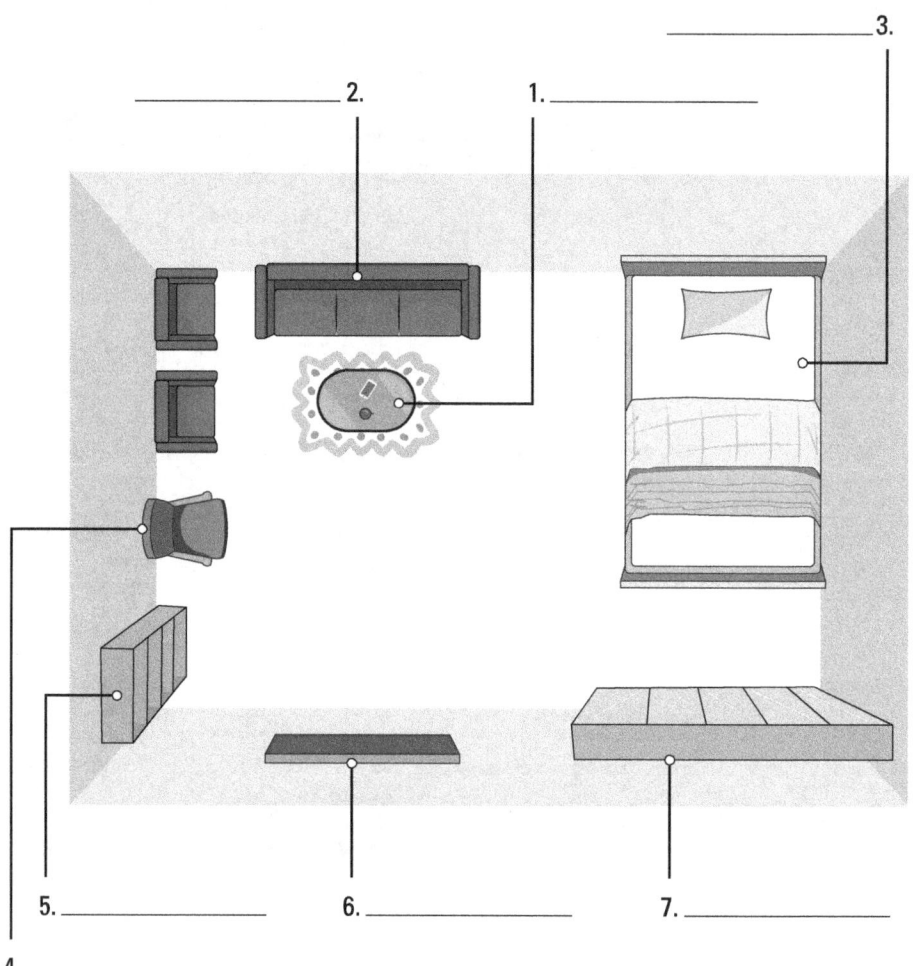

1. _____

2. _____

3. _____

4. _____

5. _____

6. _____

7. _____

2

Greek in Action

Get places easily by speaking Greek.

Discover what to say when you go shopping in Greece.

Explore Greek entertainment and nightlife.

Care for your health and body while using Greek vocabulary.

Take care of business matters in Greek.

Chapter **8**

Moving Around

I f you're someone who loves to wander and explore, this chapter will be especially useful. I dive into essential words and phrases that can help you ask for directions, share your travel plans, and choose the right mode of transportation to reach your destination. Whether you're checking schedules, asking about ticket prices, or figuring out the fastest way to get somewhere, having the right vocabulary at your fingertips can make your journey smoother and more enjoyable.

Asking for Directions

Imagine this: You're traveling to Thessaloniki for the first time and you want to find the White Tower, the most famous landmark in the city. But you've gotten lost and don't know which way to go. Wouldn't it be good to ask someone for directions? Definitely! But how will you do that? With the help of the words and phrases I share with you in the following sections.

CULTURAL WISDOM

You should know that Greeks are very open to helping someone find their way (especially if you try to speak Greek!). Directions in Greek are οδηγίες (o-dee-*yee*-es). When you ask for directions, you say Ζητάω οδηγίες (zee-*ta*-o o-dee-*yee*-es) (*I'm asking for directions*). When you want to ask someone for help, it's polite to say Μπορείτε να με βοηθήσετε; (bo-*ree*-te na me vo-ee-*thee*-se-te) (*Can you help me?*).

Wondering where something is

REMEMBER

Now, let's look at the most basic phrase you need to ask for directions: Πού είναι . . .; (poo *ee*-ne) (*Where is . . .?*) After this phrase, you add the place you want to go with its article. For example:

> **Πού είναι ο Λευκός Πύργος;** (poo *ee*-ne o lef-*kos* pee-rgos) (*Where is the White Tower?*)

> **Πού είναι η Ακρόπολη;** (poo *ee*-ne ee a-*kro*-po-lee) (*Where is the Acropolis?*)

> **Πού είναι ο σταθμός του τρένου;** (poo *ee*-ne o sta-*thmos* too *tre*-noo) (*Where is the train station?*)

> **Πού είναι το αρχαιολογικό μουσείο;** (poo *ee*-ne to a-rhe-o-lo-yee-*ko* moo-*see*-o) (*Where is the archaeological museum?*)

The same structure applies to the phrase Πόσο μακριά είναι . . .; (*po*-so ma-kree-*a* *ee*-ne) (*How far is . . .?*) It's followed by the place you want to go with its article. For example:

> **Πόσο μακριά είναι το δημαρχείο;** (*po*-so ma-kree-*a* *ee*-ne to dee-ma-*rhee*-o) (*How far is the town hall?*)

See Chapter 3 for an introduction to articles in Greek.

Understanding directions you hear

After you've asked how to get somewhere, here are possible directions that might be given to you:

> **Στρίψε αριστερά.** (*stree*-pse a-ree-ste-*ra*) (*Turn left.*)

> **Στρίψε δεξιά.** (*stree*-pse de-ksee-*a*) (*Turn right.*)

Αριστερά means *left* and δεξιά means *right*. Στρίψε means *turn*. In more everyday language, someone may say:

» στο αριστερό σου χέρι (sto a-ree-ste-*ro* soo *he*-ree) (*on your left-hand side*)

» στο δεξί σου χέρι (sto de-*ksee* soo *he*-ree) (*on your right-hand side*)

For example:

> **Το σούπερ μάρκετ είναι στο δεξί σου χέρι.** (to *soo*-per *ma*-rket *ee*-ne sto de-*ksee* soo *he*-ree) (*The supermarket is on your right-hand side.*)

Also, if you need to turn a few blocks down, they may say:

> **Στρίψε στο . . . (πρώτο, δεύτερο, τρίτο) στενό.** (*stree*-pse sto [*pro*-to, *def*-te-ro, *tree*-to] ste-*no*) (*Turn to the [first, second, third] street.*)

Στενό means *street* and before it, they will use an ordinal number that will show you how many blocks you have to pass before you turn.

Ευθεία (ef-*thee*-a) means *straight.* When someone wants to tell you to go straight, they say:

> **Προχώρα ευθεία** (pro-*kho*-ra ef-*thee*-a) or **Πήγαινε ευθεία** (*pee*-ye-ne ef-*thee*-a).

If you need to cross a street on your way, you may hear:

> **Διάσχισε τον δρόμο.** (dee-*a*-skhee-se ton *dro*-mo) (*Cross the road.*)
>
> **Πέρνα απέναντι.** (*pe*-rna a-*pe*-na-dee) (*Cross over.*)

Knowing other helpful words

Beyond the phrases in the previous sections, here are some additional words you need to know and may hear from someone giving directions:

» **διασταύρωση** (dee-a-*stav*-ro-see) (*intersection*)

» **φανάρι** (fa-*na*-ree) (*traffic light*)

» **διάβαση πεζών** (dee-*a*-va-see pe-*zon*) (*pedestrian crossing*)

When something is close, you say **κοντά** (ko-*da*), and when something is far, you say **μακριά** (ma-kree-*a*).

TIP

Η οδός (ee o-*dos*) versus **ο δρόμος** (o *dro*-mos): In Greek, both these words mean *the road,* but they have somewhat different usages.

» The word **οδός** is more formal and is usually used when referring to street names — for example, **οδός Ίδης** (o-*dos* ee-dees) (*Idis Street*) and **οδός Αθηνάς** (o-*dos* a-thee-*nas*) (*Athenas Street*).

» The word **δρόμος** is more informal and is used in daily conversations. For example: **Περπατάω στον δρόμο** (pe-rpa-*ta*-o ston *dro*-mo) (*I walk on the road*).

There are also the words **σοκάκι** (so-*ka*-kee) (*alley*) and **λεωφόρος** (le-o-*fo*-ros) (*avenue*).

CULTURAL WISDOM

You'll notice that Greeks, when giving directions, use body language, especially their hands, making gestures toward the direction you need to go. This makes the directions very vivid and sometimes funny.

Talkin' the Talk

PLAY THIS

Simon, who is from England, asks Irini for directions to the White Tower in Thessaloniki. (Track 8)

Simon: Συγγνώμη, μπορείτε να με βοηθήσετε;
see-*gno*-mee, bo-*ree*-te na me vo-ee-*thee*-se-te;
Excuse me, can you help me?

Irini: Ναι, βεβαίως. Τι χρειάζεστε;
ne, ve-*ve*-os. tee hree-*a*-ze-ste;
Yes, of course. What do you need?

Simon: Πού είναι ο Λευκός Πύργος;
poo *ee*-nee o lef-*kos pee*-rgos;
Where is the White Tower?

Irini: Ο Λευκός Πύργος είναι κοντά. Πηγαίνετε ευθεία και στρίψτε δεξιά στη γωνία.
o lef-*kos pee*-rgos *ee*-nee ko-*da*. pee-*ye*-ne-te ef-*thee*-a ke *stree*-pste de-ksee-*a* stee go-*nee*-a.
The White Tower is close. Go straight and turn right at the corner.

Simon: Και μετά;
ke me-*ta*;
And then?

Irini: Συνεχίστε μέχρι την επόμενη διασταύρωση. Εκεί, στρίψτε αριστερά και θα δείτε τον Λευκό Πύργο ακριβώς μπροστά σας.
see-ne-*hee*-ste *me*-hree teen e-*po*-me-nee dee-a-*stav*-ro-see. e-*kee*, *stree*-pste a-ree-ste-*ra* ke tha *dee*-te ton lef-*ko pee*-rgo a-kree-*vos* bro-*sta* sas.
Continue to the next intersection. There, turn left, and you'll see the White Tower right in front of you.

Simon: Είναι μακριά;
ee-ne ma-kree-*a*;
Is it far?

Irini:	**Όχι, είναι κοντά. Μόνο δέκα λεπτά με τα πόδια.**
	o-hee, *ee*-ne ko-*da*. *mo*-no *de*-ka le-*pta* me ta *po*-dya.
	No, it's close. Only ten minutes on foot.
Simon:	**Ευχαριστώ πολύ!**
	ef-kha-ree-*sto* po-*lee*!
	Thank you very much!
Irini:	**Παρακαλώ!**
	pa-ra-ka-*lo*!
	You're welcome!

WORDS TO KNOW

Μπορείτε να με βοηθήσετε;	bo-*ree*-te na me vo-ee-*thee*-se-te?	*Can you help me?*
Πού είναι . . .;	poo *ee*-ne	*Where is . . .?*
κοντά	ko-*da*	*near*
Πηγαίνετε ευθεία.	pee-*ye*-ne-te ef-*thee*-a	*Go straight.*
Στρίψτε δεξιά.	*stree*-pste de-ksee-*a*	*Turn right.*
διασταύρωση	dee-a-*stav*-ro-see	*intersection*
Στρίψτε αριστερά.	*stree*-pste a-ree-ste-*ra*	*Turn left.*
μακριά	ma-kree-*a*	*far*
με τα πόδια	me ta *po*-dya	*on foot*

Talking About Means of Transportation

Let's say you want to go somewhere farther away and need some μέσο μεταφοράς (*me*-so me-ta-fo-*ras*) (*means of transportation*). How can you talk about it? And what means of transportation do Greeks use the most? You find out in the following sections.

Common means of transportation

CULTURAL WISDOM

In the cities, Greeks use cars and motorcycles the most. Motorcycles are extremely popular because the good weather in Greece and the heavy traffic on the streets make them a very convenient mean of transportation. So, we have

» το αυτοκίνητο (to af-to-*kee*-nee-to) (*the car*)

» το παπάκι (to pa-*pa*-ki) (*the minibike*)

» το μηχανάκι (to mee-kha-*na*-kee) (*the motobike*)

» η μοτοσικλέτα (ee mo-to-see-*kle*-ta) (*the motorcycle*)

CULTURAL WISDOM

In Greece, bicycles aren't very popular in big cities because the terrain isn't flat, making cycling very difficult on the hills and slopes. Also, the cities don't have dedicated bike lanes, making cycling dangerous. However, some cities, because they are located in a valley, are suitable for bicycle use, such as Larissa, Trikala, Messolonghi, and a few more. A bicycle in Greek is το ποδήλατο (to po-*dee*-la-to), and Κάνω ποδήλατο (*ka*-no po-*dee*-la-to) is "I cycle."

Beyond these, on the streets of Greece, you'll also see some other vehicles:

» το λεωφορείο (to le-o-fo-*ree*-o) (*the bus*)

» το πούλμαν (to *poo*-lman) (*the coach*)

» το φορτηγό (to fo-rtee-*go*) (*the lorry, the truck*)

If you want to go somewhere quickly and you don't have your own car, you can take a taxi. Το ταξί (to ta-*ksee*) in Greece is yellow, and you can stop it just by raising your hand as it passes.

TIP

Taxi drivers are usually friendly and like to talk with their passengers, so a taxi ride can be a perfect opportunity to practice your Greek.

In Greece, railways are also inside and outside the city. What are they?

» το μετρό (to me-*tro*) (*the subway*)

» το τραμ (to tram) (*the tram*)

» το τρένο (to *tre*-no) (*the train*)

WARNING

The railway network for trains in Greece isn't very developed. A few lines run limited routes.

Το λεωφορείο, το τραμ, το μετρό, and το τρένο are μέσα μαζικής μεταφοράς (*me*-sa ma-zee-*kees* me-ta-fo-*ras*) (*means of mass transportation*). When someone wants to take one of these, they have to wait at the stop:

>> η στάση του λεωφορείου (ee *sta*-see too le-o-fo-*ree*-oo) (*the bus stop*)

>> η στάση του τραμ (ee *sta*-see too tram) (*the tram stop*)

>> η στάση του μετρό (ee *sta*-see too me-*tro*) (*the metro station*)

>> ο σταθμός του τρένου (o sta-*thmos* too *tre*-noo) (*the railway station*)

You also need to get a ticket for these means of transportation. How can you buy it? Just say Ένα εισιτήριο, παρακαλώ (*e*-na ee-see-*tee*-ree-o pa-ra-ka-*lo*) (*One ticket, please*). The ticket seller will give you the appropriate one.

Other useful questions are as follows:

Πού είναι η στάση (του μετρό, του λεωφορείου, του τραμ); (poo *ee*-ne ee *sta*-see [too me-*tro*/too le-o-fo-*ree*-oo/too tram]) (*Where is the metro/bus/tram station?*)

Τι ώρα περνάει (το μετρό, το λεωφορείο, το τραμ); (tee o-ra pe-*rna*-ee [to me-*tro*/to le-o-fo-*ree*-o/to tram]) (*What time does the metro/bus/tram leave?*)

Τι ώρα φεύγει το τρένο; (tee o-ra *fev*-yee to *tre*-no) (*What time does the train leave?*)

CULTURAL WISDOM

Greeks also use ships a lot because Greece has many islands that they like to visit. So, passenger ships leave daily from the country's major ports to all the Greek islands. A ship is called το καράβι (to ka-*ra*-vee) or το πλοίο (to *plee*-o). The place where ships are located is το λιμάνι (to lee-*ma*-nee).

When you want to take an even longer trip, you use το αεροπλάνο (to a-e-ro-*pla*-no) (*the airplane*). You can take an airplane from το αεροδρόμιο (to a-e-ro-*dro*-mee-o) (*the airport*).

Special means of transportation

Of course, other means of transportation may not be available to the general public but are used for special purposes. Let's see some of them:

>> το ασθενοφόρο (to a-sthe-no-*fo*-ro) (*the ambulance*)

>> το πυροσβεστικό όχημα (to pee-ro-sve-stee-*ko* o-hee-ma) (*the fire truck*)

>> το τρακτέρ (to tra-*kter*) (*the tractor*)

>> το περιπολικό (to pe-ree-po-lee-*ko*) (*the police car*)

>> το ελικόπτερο (to e-lee-*ko*-pte-ro) (*the helicopter*)

Talkin' the Talk

PLAY THIS

Alexandra is on a street in Athens. She talks to a passerby, Panagiotis, about her options for transportation. (Track 9)

Alexandra: Συγγνώμη, μπορείτε να μου πείτε ποια μέσα μεταφοράς υπάρχουν εδώ κοντά;
see-*gno*-mee, bo-*ree*-te na moo *pee*-te py*a* *me*-sa me-ta-fo-*ras* ee-*pa*-rkhoon e-*do* ko-*da*;
Excuse me, can you tell me what means of transportation are available nearby?

Panagiotis: Ναι, βεβαίως. Μπορείτε να χρησιμοποιήσετε το λεωφορείο, το μετρό, το ταξί, ή το ποδήλατο.
ne, ve-*ve*-os. bo-*ree*-te na hree-see-mo-pee-*ee*-se-te to le-o-fo-*ree*-o, to me-*tro*, to ta-*ksee,* ee to po-*dee*-la-to.
Yes, of course. You can use the bus, the metro, a taxi, or a bicycle.

Alexandra: Πόσο κοστίζει το εισιτήριο για το λεωφορείο;
po-so ko-*stee*-zee to ee-see-*tee*-ree-o ya to le-o-fo-*ree*-o;
How much does the bus ticket cost?

Panagiotis: Το εισιτήριο για το λεωφορείο κοστίζει **1.60** ευρώ.
to ee-see-*tee*-ree-o ya to le-o-fo-*ree*-o ko-*stee*-zee 1.60 ev-*ro.*
The bus ticket costs 1.60 euros.

Alexandra: Πού είναι η στάση του λεωφορείου;
poo *ee*-ne ee *sta*-see too le-o-fo-*ree*-oo;
Where is the bus stop?

Panagiotis: Η στάση είναι δίπλα στο πάρκο, στη γωνία.
ee *sta*-see *ee*-ne *dee*-pla sto *pa*-rko, stee go-*nee*-a.
The stop is next to the park, on the corner.

Alexandra: Ευχαριστώ πολύ. Μπορώ να βρω ταξί εδώ;
ef-kha-ree-*sto* po-*lee.* bo-*ro* na vro ta-*ksee* e-*do*;
Thank you very much. Can I find a taxi here?

Panagiotis: Ναι, υπάρχουν πολλά ταξί στην πλατεία.
ne, ee-*pa*-rkhoon po-*la* ta-*ksee* steen pla-*tee*-a.
Yes, there are many taxis in the square.

Alexandra: Ευχαριστώ!
ef-kha-ree-*sto!*
Thanks!

WORDS TO KNOW

μέσα μεταφοράς	*me*-sa me-ta-fo-*ras*	*means of transportation*
λεωφορείο	le-o-fo-*ree*-o	*bus*
μετρό	me-*tro*	*metro, subway*
ταξί	ta-*ksee*	*taxi*
ποδήλατο	po-*dee*-la-to	*bicycle*
Πόσο κοστίζει το εισιτήριο . . . ;	*po*-so ko-*stee*-zee to ee-see-*tee*-ree-o	*How much does the ticket cost?*
Το εισιτήριο για το λεωφορείο κοστίζει . . .	to ee-see-*tee*-ree-o ya to le-o-fo-*ree*-o ko-*stee*-zee	*The bus ticket costs . . .*
στάση του λεωφορείου	*sta*-see too le-o-fo-*ree*-oo	*bus stop*
δίπλα	*dee*-pla	*next to*
γωνία	go-*nee*-a	*corner*

Asking People Where They're Going

Πού πηγαίνεις; (poo pee–*ye*-nees) (*Where are you going?*)

This could be your mom's voice when she sees you leaving the house. And of course, if your mom is Greek, it's common for her to continue with this phrase: Ζακέτα να πάρεις! (za–*ke*-ta na *pa*-rees) (*Take your jacket!*). I don't know why, but Greek moms always fear that you'll catch a cold, so it's very important to dress warmly.

REMEMBER

When you want to say where you're going, you can say Πηγαίνω στον/στη(ν)/στο (pee–*ye*-no ston/stee[n]/sto) and then the place you're going to.

If the place you're going to is masculine in form, you say πηγαίνω στον . . . (pee–*ye*-no ston):

Πηγαίνω στον γιατρό. (pee-*ye*-no ston ya-*tro*) (*I'm going to the doctor.*)

Πηγαίνω στον σταθμό του τρένου. (pee-*ye*-no ston sta-*thmo* too *tre*-noo) (*I am going to the train station.*)

If it's feminine, you say πηγαίνω στην . . . (pee-*ye*-no steen):

> **Πηγαίνω στην πλατεία.** (pee-*ye*-no steen pla-*tee*-a) (*I'm going to the square.*)

> **Πηγαίνω στην καφετέρια.** (pee-*ye*-no steen ka-fe-*te*-ree-a) (*I'm going to the café.*)

If it's neuter, you say πηγαίνω στο . . . (pee-*ye*-no sto):

> **Πηγαίνω στο κέντρο.** (pee-*ye*-no sto *ken*-dro) (*I'm going to the center.*)

> **Πηγαίνω στο χωριό μου.** (pee-*ye*-no sto kho-*ryo* mou) (*I'm going to my village.*)

See Chapter 3 for an introduction to the gender of Greek words.

You may also want to say what means of transportation you use. Then you say Πηγαίνω με τον/τη(ν)/το (pee-*ye*-no me ton/tee[n]/to) (*I go by . . .*). Again, the article depends on the gender of the transportation means you use:

> **Πηγαίνω με το αυτοκίνητο.** (pee-*ye*-no me to af-to-*kee*-nee-to) (*I'm going by car.*)

> **Πηγαίνω με τη μοτοσικλέτα.** (pee-*ye*-no me tee mo-to-see-*kle*-ta) (*I'm going by motorcycle.*)

> **Πηγαίνω με το τρένο.** (pee-*ye*-no me to *tre*-no) (*I'm going by train.*)

If you don't want to take a vehicle and prefer to walk, you say με τα πόδια (me ta po-dya) (*on foot*).

> **Πηγαίνω στο κέντρο με τα πόδια.** (pee-*ye*-no sto *ke*-ndro me ta *po*-dya) (*I'm going to the center on foot.*)

So, if your mom asks you Πού πηγαίνεις, you can answer her: Πηγαίνω στο σινεμά με το λεωφορείο. (pee-*ye*-no sto see-ne-*ma* me to le-o-fo-*ree*-o) (*I'm going to the cinema by bus.*) And don't forget to take your jacket!

FUN & GAMES

Help Vasiliki get to her destination. Look at the map and put the instructions in the right order.

Στρίψε αριστερά (2)

Το σούπερ μάρκετ είναι στο αριστερό σου χέρι

Από το σπίτι προχώρα ευθεία

Στρίψε δεξιά (2)

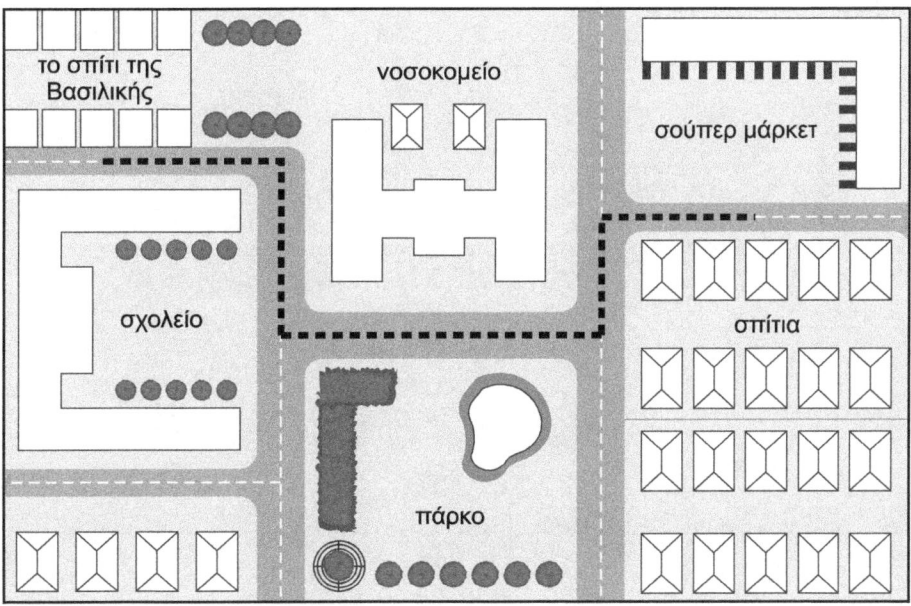

1. _____
2. _____
3. _____
4. _____
5. _____
6. _____

Chapter **9**

Shopping Made Easy

et's say you're in the center of Thessaloniki and want to go shopping. Around you, there's a variety of stores with clothes, household items, groceries, souvenirs, and the like. You're ready to enter the first store when anxiety strikes. You think, "How will I communicate? Do they speak English? Darn it! If only I knew a few words related to shopping, it might be easier . . ."

This, of course, is a hypothetical scenario because you're about to read this chapter, which contains vocabulary related to stores, products, and shopping. Happy studying — and happy shopping!

Retail Therapy: Shopping for Clothes

REMEMBER

Jokingly, we often say that shopping has therapeutic properties, and if you go shopping on a day you're feeling down, you'll feel better. I'm not sure about that. But what I am sure of is that the word "shopping" in Greek is τα ψώνια (ta *pso*-nya). Additionally, the word "to buy" in Greek has two versions: αγοράζω (a-go-*ra*-zo) and ψωνίζω (pso-*nee*-zo).

Talking with the shop staff

The word "store" in Greek can be either το μαγαζί (to ma-ga-zee) or το κατάστημα (to ka-ta-stee-ma). When entering a store the υπάλληλος (ee-pa-lee-los) (employee) will approach you, the customer, or ο πελάτης (o pe-la-tees).

GRAMMATICALLY SPEAKING

The word υπάλληλος is the same for both men and women. The only thing that changes to specify the gender of the employee is the article. For example: ο υπάλληλος (masculine) and η υπάλληλος (feminine).

The employee will probably say one of the following:

> Πώς μπορώ να σας βοηθήσω; (pos bo-ro na sas vo-ee-thee-so) (How can I help you?)

> Ψάχνετε κάτι συγκεκριμένο; (psa-khne-te ka-tee see-ge-kree-me-no) (Are you looking for something specific?)

Then you can say what you want. If you're just browsing products without necessarily intending to shop, you can say:

> Ρίχνω μια ματιά. (ree-khno mya ma-tya) (I'm just looking.)

Finding the right size

In a clothing or shoe store, you'll naturally be looking for the size that fits you, so you can ask the shop assistant: Το έχετε σε . . . ; (to e-he-te se) (Do you have this in [size]?)

TIP

For shoe sizes, Greeks use the term νούμερο (noo-me-ro). For clothing sizes, we use the word μέγεθος (me-ye-thos). For clothing sizes, Greeks also use English terminology, even in writing: small, medium, and large.

CULTURAL WISDOM

In Greece, shoe sizes are in the European (EU) system, which is common across most continental European countries. It starts from 15 (the infant size) and goes up to approximately 50 (for men). I'm clarifying this because not all countries measure shoe sizes the same way.

The place where you try on clothes is called το δοκιμαστήριο (to do-kee-ma-stee-ree-o) (the fitting room). If you try on clothing or shoes that don't fit, you can say:

> Μου είναι μικρό. (moo ee-ne mee-kro) (It's too small for me.)

> Μου είναι μεγάλο. (moo ee-ne me-ga-lo) (It's too big for me.)

You can also ask Μήπως το έχετε σε **small/medium/large;** (*mee*-pos to *e*-he-te se small/medium/large): (*Do you perhaps have it in small/medium/large?*)

How do you say "it fits me" in Greek when you find that magic item? Easy: Μου κάνει (moo *ka*-nee).

Looking for the right style

Clothes and shoes, of course, come in different styles. Let's start with fabrics and patterns:

>> πουά (poo-*a*) (*polka dot*)

>> καρό (ka-*ro*) (*plaid*)

>> ριγέ (ree-*ye*) (*striped*)

>> τζιν (tzeen) (*denim*)

>> βαμβακερό (va-mva-ke-*ro*) (*cotton*)

>> βελούδινο (ve-*loo*-dee-no) (*velvet*)

>> μάλλινο (*ma*-lee-no) (*wool*)

Based on their use, clothes can be

>> καθημερινά (ka-thee-me-ree-*na*) (*casual*)

>> επίσημα (e-*pee*-see-ma) (*formal*)

>> αθλητικά (a-thlee-tee-*ka*) (*athletic*)

You may be looking for clothes in particular colors. Here are some basic ones:

>> πράσινο (*pra*-see-no) (*green*)

>> κίτρινο (*kee*-tree-no) (*yellow*)

>> μπλε (ble) (*blue*)

>> κόκκινα (*ko*-kee-no) (*red*)

>> μαύρο (*mav*-ro) (*black*)

>> άσπρο (*a*-spro) (*white*)

Here's vocabulary for different types of clothing in Greek, to help you choose clothes you like and that fit:

- παντελόνι (pa-de-*lo*-nee) (*pants*)

- φούστα (*foo*-sta) (*skirt*)

- πουκάμισο (poo-*ka*-mee-so) (*shirt*)

- μπλούζα (*bloo*-za) (*blouse*)

- φόρεμα (*fo*-re-ma) (*dress*)

- κουστούμι (koo-*stoo*-mee) (*suit*)

- παπούτσια (pa-poo-tsya) (*shoes*)

- καπέλο (ka-*pe*-lo) (*hat*)

- γραβάτα (gra-*va*-ta) (*tie*)

- κασκόλ (ka-*skol*) (*scarf*)

- σορτς (sorts) (*shorts*)

- σακάκι (sa-*ka*-kee) (*blazer, suit jacket*)

- κάλτσες (*ka*-ltses) (*socks*)

- γάντια (*ga*-dia) (*gloves*)

- παλτό (pa-*lto*) (*coat*)

- μπουφάν (boo-*fan*) (*jacket*)

Shoes come in different styles and here are their Greek versions:

- αθλητικά (a-thlee-tee-*ka*) (*sports shoes*)

- σανδάλια (sa-*nda*-lya) (*sandals*)

- μπότες (*bo*-tes) (*boots*)

- τακούνια (ta-*koo*-nya) (*high heels*)

Searching for sales

CULTURAL WISDOM

Every January and July, stores in Greece have sales. Sales in Greek are called εκπτώσεις (e-*kpto*-sees). This is your chance to buy products at a more affordable price.

Suppose you see a sign in a shop window that says "50 percent discount." How do you say this? In Greek, "percent" is translated as τοις εκατό (tees e-ka-*to*). For example: 20 percent is είκοσι τοις εκατό (*ee*-ko-see tees e-ka-*to*), and 50 percent is πενήντα τοις εκατό (pe-*nee*-nda tees e-ka-*to*). See Chapter 6 for an introduction to numbers in Greek.

CULTURAL WISDOM

Don't bargain! In Greece, haggling isn't part of the culture. Don't try to convince the shopkeeper to give you a better price than the one marked on the product. It's more likely to make them uncomfortable or annoyed rather than result in a discount.

Paying with ease

When you've found the product you like, you can ask the employee Πόσο κάνει; (*po*-so ka-nee), which means "How much is it?" or Πόσο κοστίζει; (po-so ko-*stee*-zee), which means "How much does it cost?"

The currency of Greece, like that of almost all European countries, is the ευρώ (ev-*ro*) (*euro*). Before that, Greece had the δραχμή (dra-*khmee*) (*drachma*). The ancient Greek currency had exactly the same name. Today, drachmas exist only as collector's items in specialty shops.

After completing your shopping, you go to the cashier. The employee may ask you Κάρτα ή μετρητά; (*ka*-rta *ee* me-tree-*ta*) (*Card or cash?*) and then you state your preferred payment method.

The cashier may also ask Θέλετε σακούλα; (*the*-le-te sa-*koo*-la) (*Do you want a bag?*). To this question you can answer Όχι, ευχαριστώ (*o*-hee ef-kha-ree-*sto*) (*no, thank you*) or Ναι, παρακαλώ (ne pa-ra-ka-*lo*) (*yes, please*).

After you pay and place the purchased items in a bag, the employee gives you the απόδειξη (a-*po*-dee-ksee) (*receipt*). Enjoy your purchase!

Talkin' the Talk

Dimitra is browsing in a clothing store. The store employee, Glykeria, approaches her.

Glykeria: Πώς μπορώ να βοηθήσω;
pos bo-*ro* na vo-ee-*thee*-so;
How can I help you?

Dimitra: Είδα ένα καρό πουκάμισο στη βιτρίνα.
ee-da e-na ka-*ro* poo-*ka*-mee-so stee vee-*tree*-na.
I saw a plaid shirt in the window.

Glykeria: Εννοείτε το βαμβακερό πουκάμισο στα δεξιά που είναι μπλε και άσπρο;
e-no-*ee*-te to va-mva-ke-*ro* poo-*ka*-mee-so sta de-ksee-*a* poo *ee*-ne ble ke *a*-spro;
Do you mean the cotton shirt on the right that's blue and white?

Dimitra: Μάλιστα. Μήπως το έχετε σε **small**;
ma-lee-sta. *mee*-pos to *e*-khe-te se small;
Yes. Do you have it in small?

Glykeria: Βεβαίως.
ve-*ve*-os.
Of course.

Dimitra: Ευχαριστώ. Εκείνη η μαύρη τζιν φούστα, πόσο κοστίζει;
ef-kha-ree-*sto*. e-*kee*-nee ee *mav*-ree tzeen *foo*-sta, *po*-so ko-*stee*-zee;
Thank you. How much is that black denim skirt?

Glykeria: Η φούστα κοστίζει **50** ευρώ, αλλά έχει έκπτωση, άρα η τελική τιμή είναι **25** ευρώ.
ee *foo*-sta ko-*stee*-zee pe-*nee*-nda ev-ro, a-*la* e-hee e-kpto-see, *a*-ra ee te-lee-*kee* tee-*mee* ee-ne ee-ko-see *pe*-nde ev-ro.
The skirt costs 50 euros, but it has a discount, so the final price is 25 euros.

Dimitra: Ωραία. Πού είναι το δοκιμαστήριο;
o-*re*-a. poo *ee*-ne to do-kee-ma-*stee*-ree-o;
Great. Where is the fitting room?

Glykeria: Από 'δω. Περάστε, παρακαλώ.
a-*po* do. pe-*ra*-ste, pa-ra-ka-*lo*.
This way, please.

WORDS TO KNOW

Πώς μπορώ να βοηθήσω;	pos bo-*ro* na vo-ee-*thee*-so	*How can I help you?*
καρό	ka-*ro*	*plaid*
πουκάμισο	poo-*ka*-mee-so	*shirt*
βιτρίνα	vee-*tree*-na	*store window*
βαμβακερό	va-mva-ke-*ro*	*cotton*
δεξιά	de-ksee-*a*	*right*
τζιν	tzeen	*denim*
φούστα	*foo*-sta	*skirt*
Πόσο κοστίζει . . .;	*po*-so ko-*stee*-zee . . .	*How much is . . .?*
τιμή	tee-*mee*	*price*
βεβαίως	ve-*ve*-os	*of course*
Πού είναι το δο κιμαστήριο;	poo *ee*-ne to do-kee-ma-*stee*-ree-o	*Where is the fitting room?*

Shopping for Groceries

In this section, I talk to you about shopping for food and other daily necessities at a supermarket. And how do you say "supermarket" in Greek? There is the Greek word υπεραγορά (ee-per-a-go-*ra*), but no one uses it. Everyone uses σούπερ μάρκετ (pronounced just like *supermarket*).

Discovering the supermarket sections

CULTURAL WISDOM

Greek supermarkets are somewhat like food malls because, beyond the sections with shelves, you also find sections that resemble small shops where you can buy fresh meat, fruits, fish, and cheese. Here I talk about the different sections of the supermarket and what you find in each one.

So, inside a supermarket, you can find a bakery, or αρτοποιείο (a-rto-pee-*ee*-o); a butcher, or κρεοπωλείο (kre-o-po-*lee*-o); and a greengrocer, or οπωροπωλείο (o-po-ro-po-*lee*-o) with fresh products. An employee is available to assist you as if you were in a small store.

Additionally, dairy products, or γαλακτοκομικά (ga-la-kto-ko-mee-*ka*), aren't taken from a refrigerator; instead, you go to the cheese section where you ask the employee to cut the quantity and type of cheese you want. In bigger supermarkets the same goes for fish and seafood, or ψάρια και θαλασσινά (*psa*-rya ke tha-la-see-*na*).

CULTURAL WISDOM

So, when you go to each specific section mentioned here, you can ask the employee for the product you want, just as you would in a small neighborhood shop. You can ask for information about the product and talk to the employee.

Of course, Greek supermarkets also have self-service sections, such as

>> Frozen food, or κατεψυγμένα τρόφιμα (ka-te-psee-*gme*-na *tro*-fee-ma)

>> Beverages, or ποτά (po-*ta*)

>> Household items, or είδη σπιτιού (*ee*-dee spee-*tyoo*)

>> Cleaning supplies, or είδη καθαρισμού (*ee*-dee ka-tha-ree-*smoo*)

>> Health and beauty, or υγεία και ομορφιά (ee-*yee*-a ke o-mo-*rfya*)

Buying fruits and vegetables

Since we're talking about supermarkets, this is a great opportunity to look at different food products, and I naturally start with fruits and vegetables.

Fruits include the following:

>> μήλο (*mee*-lo) (*apple*)

>> πορτοκάλι (po-rto-*ka*-lee) (*orange*)

>> μπανάνα (ba-*na*-na) (*banana*)

>> σταφύλι (sta-*fee*-lee) (*grape*)

>> φράουλα (*fra*-oo-la) (*strawberry*)

>> ροδάκινο (ro-*da*-kee-no) (*peach*)

>> αχλάδι (a-*khla*-dee) (*pear*)

>> κεράσι (ke-*ra*-see) (*cherry*)

>> καρπούζι (ka-*rpoo*-zee) (*watermelon*)

Vegetables include the following:

>> ντομάτα (do-*ma*-ta) (*tomato*)

>> αγγούρι (a-*goo*-ree) (*cucumber*)

>> καρότο (ka-*ro*-to) (*carrot*)

>> πατάτα (pa-*ta*-ta) (*potato*)

>> κρεμμύδι (kre-*mee*-dee) (*onion*)

>> σπανάκι (spa-*na*-kee) (*spinach*)

>> πιπεριά (pee-pe-*rya*) (*pepper*)

>> μαρούλι (ma-*roo*-lee) (*lettuce*)

>> κολοκύθι (ko-lo-*kee*-thee) (*zucchini*)

>> μπρόκολο (*bro*-ko-lo) (*broccoli*)

Meat and fish

Here, I want to look at the meats and some of the fish that you can find in the supermarket or in a local shop.

Meats you can buy include the following:

>> κοτόπουλο (ko-*to*-poo-lo) (*chicken*)

>> μοσχάρι (mo-*skha*-ree) (*beef*)

>> χοιρινό (hee-ree-*no*) (*pork*)

>> αρνί (a-*rnee*) (*lamb*)

>> γαλοπούλα (ga-lo-*poo*-la) (*turkey*)

Fish you can buy include the following:

>> **σολομός** (so-lo-*mos*) (*salmon*)

>> **τόνος** (*to*-nos) (*tuna*)

>> **σαρδέλα** (sa-*rde*-la) (*sardine*)

>> **μπακαλιάρος** (ba-ka-*lya*-ros) (*cod*)

>> **τσιπούρα** (tsee-*poo*-ra) (*gilthead seabream*)

>> **γαρίδα** (ga-*ree*-da) (*shrimp*)

>> **καλαμάρι** (ka-la-*ma*-ree) (*squid*)

>> **χταπόδι** (khta-*po*-dee) (*octopus*)

Other foods

Suppose you want to make a supermarket shopping list with your Greek room-mate. Do you know all the products you can find in the stores? No? Well, that's why I'm here! Here I share various other products you can find on the shelves of supermarkets and local shops:

>> **γαλακτοκομικά** (ga-la-kto-ko-mee-*ka*) (*dairy products*):

  ● **γάλα** (*ga*-la) (*milk*)

  ● **τυρί** (tee-*ree*) (*cheese*)

  ● **γιαούρτι** (ya-*oo*-rtee) (*yogurt*)

  ● **βούτυρο** (*voo*-tee-ro) (*butter*)

>> **αρτοποιείο** (a-rto-pee-*ee*-o) (*bakery*):

  ● **ψωμί** (pso-*mee*) (*bread*)

  ● **μπαγκέτες** (ba-*ge*-tes) (*baguettes*)

  ● **κρουασάν** (kroo-a-*san*) (*croissants*)

>> **κατεψυγμένα τρόφιμα** (ka-te-psee-*gme*-na tro-fee-ma) (*frozen foods*):

  ● **παγωτό** (pa-go-*to*) (*ice cream*)

  ● **κατεψυγμένα λαχανικά** (ka-te-psee-*gme*-na la-kha-nee-*ka*) (*frozen vegetables*)

>> σνακ (snak) (*snacks*):

- πατατάκια (pa-ta-*ta*-kya) (*chips*)

- σοκολάτα (so-ko-*la*-ta) (*chocolate*)

- μπισκότα (bee-*sko*-ta) (*cookies*)

>> ποτά (po-*ta*) (*beverages*):

- νερό (ne-*ro*) (*water*)

- αναψυκτικά (a-na-psee-ktee-*ka*) (*soft drinks*)

- χυμοί (hee-*mee*) (*juices*)

- τσάι (tsa-*ee*) (*tea*)

- καφές (ka-*fes*) (*coffee*)

- κρασί (kra-*see*) (*wine*)

- μπύρα (*bee*-ra) (*beer*)

Nonfood items

As in other grocery stores around the world, Greek supermarkets also carry plenty of nonfood items:

>> είδη καθαριότητας (*ee*-dee ka-tha-ree-*o*-tee-tas) (*cleaning supplies*)

>> απορρυπαντικά (a-po-ree-pa-dee-*ka*) (*detergents*)

>> προσωπική φροντίδα (pro-so-pee-*kee* fro-*dee*-da) (*personal care*):

- σαμπουάν (sa-boo-*an*) (*shampoo*)

- οδοντόκρεμα (o-do-*ndo*-kre-ma) (*toothpaste*)

- σαπούνι (sa-*poo*-nee) (*soap*)

>> χαρτικά (kha-rtee-*ka*) (*paper goods*):

- χαρτί υγείας (kha-*rtee* ee-*yee*-as) (*toilet paper*)

- χαρτοπετσέτες (kha-rto-pe-*tse*-tes) (*napkins*)

>> για μωρά (ya mo-*ra*) (*for babies*):

- πάνες (*pa*-nes) (*diapers*)

- μωρομάντηλα (mo-ro-*ma*-ndee-la) (*baby wipes*)

- γάλα σε σκόνη (*ga*-la se *sko*-nee) (*baby formula*)

Visiting a Greek supermarket

Let's see what a visit to the supermarket (σούπερ μάρκετ) is like. When you arrive there, you take a basket, or καλάθι (ka-*la*-thee), or a shopping cart, or καρότσι (ka-*ro*-tsee). Then, you proceed to the various τμήμα (*tmee*-ma) (*section*) and pick up different products. Naturally, as a smart consumer, you also look at the offers, or προσφορές (pro-sfo-*res*). When you finish your shopping, you go to the checkout counter, or ταμείο (ta-*mee*-o) and pay the bill, or λογαριασμός (lo-ga-rya-*smos*).

GRAMMATICALLY
SPEAKING

The word σούπερ μάρκετ isn't Greek, as you can tell! Like all foreign words, it has the same form in the plural. If you want to talk about many supermarkets, you simply use the plural article like this: το σούπερ μάρκετ (singular) and τα σούπερ μάρκετ (plural). This happens with all foreign words we use in Greek.

At the supermarket, you see plenty of different labels, logos, packaging types, and measurements. Packaging and quantity terms include the following:

>> συσκευασία (see-skev-a-*see*-a) (*packaging*)

>> κιλό (kee-*lo*) (*kilogram*)

>> γραμμάριο (gra-*ma*-ree-o) (*gram*)

>> μπουκάλι (boo-*ka*-lee) (*bottle*)

>> κουτί (koo-*tee*) (*box*)

>> σακούλα (sa-*koo*-la) (*bag*)

Now, let's take a look at some phrases that can help you when you're at a supermarket.

Πού μπορώ να βρω . . .; (poo bo-*ro* na vro) (*Where can I find . . .?*)

Μπορείτε να με βοηθήσετε; (bo-*ree*-te na me vo-ee-*thee*-se-te) (*Can you help me?*)

Πόσο κοστίζει; (*po*-so ko-*stee*-zee) (*How much does it cost?*)

Θέλω ένα . . . (*the*-lo e-na) (*I would like one . . .*)

Ευχαριστώ! (ef-kha-ree-*sto*) (*Thank you!*)

Talkin' the Talk

PLAY THIS

Evgenia is at the supermarket and needs assistance. She asks for help from an employee named Andreas. (Track 10)

Evgenia: Γεια σας, μπορείτε να μου πείτε πού είναι τα λαχανικά;
ya sas, bo-*ree*-te na moo *pee*-te poo *ee*-ne ta la-kha-nee-*ka*;
Hello, can you tell me where the vegetables are?

Andreas: Βεβαίως! Τα λαχανικά βρίσκονται στο τμήμα δίπλα από τα φρούτα.
ve-*ve*-os! ta la-kha-nee-*ka* *vree*-sko-de sto *tmee*-ma *dee*-pla a-*po* ta *froo*-ta.
Certainly! The vegetables are in the section next to the fruits.

Evgenia: Ευχαριστώ πολύ! Επίσης, πού μπορώ να βρω το γάλα και το τυρί;
ef-kha-ree-*sto* po-*lee*! e-*pee*-sees, poo bo-*ro* na vro to *ga*-la ke to tee-*ree*;
Thank you very much! Also, where can I find milk and cheese?

Andreas: Θα τα βρείτε στο τμήμα γαλακτοκομικών, στο τέλος του διαδρόμου δεξιά.
tha ta *vree*-te sto *tmee*-ma ga-la-kto-ko-mee-*kon*, sto *te*-los too dee-a-*dro*-moo de-ksee-*a*.
You'll find them in the dairy section, at the end of the aisle on the right.

Evgenia: Τέλεια! Μήπως έχετε προσφορές στα σνακ σήμερα;
te-lee-a! *mee*-pos e-he-te pro-sfo-*res* sta snak *see*-me-re;
Perfect! Do you happen to have offers on snacks today?

Andreas: Ναι, έχουμε προσφορές στα πατατάκια και στις σοκολάτες.
ne, *e*-khoo-me pro-sfo-*res* sta pa-ta-*ta*-kya ke stees so-ko-*la*-tes.
Yes, we have discounts on chips and chocolates.

Evgenia: Σας ευχαριστώ πολύ για τη βοήθεια!
sas ef-kha-tee-*sto* po-*lee* ya tee vo-*ee*-thee-a!
Thank you very much for your help!

Andreas: Παρακαλώ! Καλή σας ημέρα!
pa-ra-ka-*lo*! ka-*lee* sas ee-*me*-ra!
You're welcome! Have a great day!

WORDS TO KNOW

Μπορείτε να μου πείτε . . .	bo-*ree*-te na moo *pee*-te	*Can you tell me . . .*
τμήμα	*tmee*-ma	*section*
τμήμα γαλακτοκομικών	*tmee*-ma ga-la-kto-ko-mee-*kon*	*dairy section*
διάδρομος	dee-*a*-dro-mos	*aisle*
προσφορές	pro-sfo-*res*	*offers*
βοήθεια	vo-*ee*-thee-a	*help*
Καλή σας ημέρα!	ka-*lee* sas ee-*me*-ra!	*Have a great day!*

FUN & GAMES

Add each product to the cart of the store where you can purchase it.

- » κρασί
- » παλτό
- » ντομάτα
- » μαρούλι
- » φόρεμα
- » απορρυπαντικό
- » μπλούζα
- » αχλάδι
- » χαρτί υγείας
- » καφές
- » καπέλο
- » πορτοκάλι
- » γιαούρτι
- » καρότο

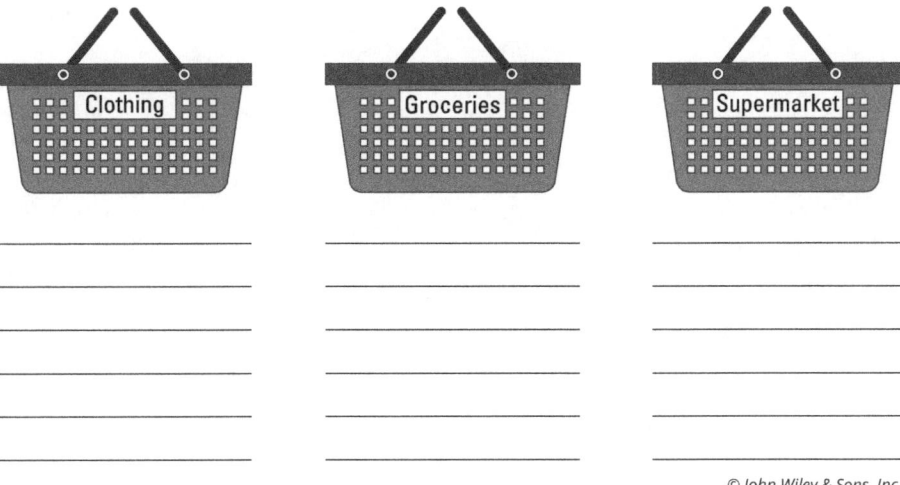

Clothing   Groceries   Supermarket

_____   _____   _____
_____   _____   _____
_____   _____   _____
_____   _____   _____
_____   _____   _____
_____   _____   _____

Chapter **10**

Days and Nights Out

I n the Tourism Ministry's campaigns to promote Greece, food and entertainment are always showcased. Greeks have developed an entire culture around dancing, celebration, and food. These are integral parts of the culture, and that's why visitors who come to Greece want to experience this side of the country as well. In this chapter, I focus on dining out and entertainment.

Eating Out

In Greece, you'll find many different places to dine, depending on how much you want to spend and the type of food you want to eat. And if you see the group next to you at the restaurant sharing all the dishes, don't be surprised. Greeks often order στη μέση (stee *me*-see) (*for the table*), meaning they place all the dishes in the middle, and everyone tries a bit of everything. It's a great way to sample all the specialties of the restaurant. Greek restaurateurs take pride in the fresh ingredients they use, the olive oil they serve, and the complementary treat they offer to their guests at the end of the meal.

CULTURAL WISDOM

If you visit people in a Greek home, the first thing they do is offer you food. This is because Greeks not only enjoy good homemade food, but they are also proud of it and love sharing it with their friends.

Knowing the best Greek recipes

In this section, I mention the names and descriptions of some basic Greek recipes. In Greek, "recipe" is συνταγή (see-da-*yee*). So, when you hold the menu at a restaurant, you'll have an idea of what to order.

>> μουσακάς (moo-sa-*kas*): Layers of eggplant, ground meat, and béchamel sauce, baked to golden perfection — a hearty comfort dish

>> τζατζίκι (tza-*tzee*-kee): A refreshing yogurt, cucumber, and garlic dip, perfect as an appetizer or sauce

>> σπανακόπιτα (spa-na-*ko*-pee-ta): A flaky phyllo pastry filled with spinach and feta cheese, baked until crispy

>> σουβλάκι (soo-*vla*-kee): Skewers of marinated meat (pork, chicken, or lamb), grilled and served with pita bread

>> ντολμαδάκια (do-lma-*da*-kya): Grape leaves stuffed with rice, herbs, and sometimes meat, served as a light and flavorful appetizer

>> χωριάτικη (kho-*rya*-tee-kee): A classic salad of tomatoes, cucumbers, olives, and feta cheese, drizzled with olive oil

>> γεμιστά (ye-mee-*sta*): Bell peppers or tomatoes stuffed with rice, herbs, and sometimes minced meat, baked until tender

>> φασολάδα (fa-so-*la*-da): A hearty bean soup with tomatoes, olive oil, and vegetables, considered Greece's national dish

>> κλέφτικο (*kle*-ftee-ko): Slow-cooked lamb marinated with garlic, lemon, and herbs, traditionally wrapped and baked in parchment

>> παστίτσιο (pa-*stee*-tsee-o): A classic Greek baked pasta dish layered with spiced ground meat, tubular noodles, and a rich, creamy béchamel sauce

TIP

Of course, there are many more Greek recipes, but if I had to discuss them all, this wouldn't be a book about the Greek language — it would be a cookbook! Nevertheless, if you come to Greece, a good food tour is one of the things you absolutely must do.

Looking at types of restaurants

Of course, depending on your food preferences and the type of entertainment you enjoy, you should choose the right type of restaurant. Not all establishments specialize in the same things.

>> **ταβέρνα** (ta-*ve*-rna): A traditional-style place that serves a variety of cooked and grilled dishes and is characterized by a warm and welcoming atmosphere

>> **ψαροταβέρνα** (psa-ro-ta-*ve*-rna): A fish tavern that serves fresh, perfectly grilled fish and seafood; usually found in coastal areas, where you can enjoy your meal while looking out at the sea

>> **μεζεδοπωλείο** (me-ze-do-po-*lee*-o): A traditional small eatery that serves *mezedes* — small dishes of food to be enjoyed while sipping on traditional drinks like tsipouro, ouzo, or raki

>> **σουβλατζίδικο** (soo-vla-*tzee*-dee-ko): The Greek version of fast food where you can enjoy souvlaki and gyros

>> **καφενείο** (ka-fe-*nee*-o): A traditional café where locals gather to enjoy their coffee in the morning or a drink in the evening

CULTURAL
WISDOM

Although these cafés were primarily frequented by older men in the past, younger generations have slowly started visiting them as well.

>> **μαγειρείο** (ma-yee-*ree*-o): A casual eatery that serves the kind of food you would eat in a Greek home — stews and oven-baked dishes accompanied by fresh bread

TIP

If you don't have a Greek grandmother, a **μαγειρείο** is the next best place for authentic homemade Greek food.

CULTURAL
WISDOM

In the courtyards of most restaurants, you'll find cats gathering around your table, trying to grab your attention in the hopes that you'll share some food with them. These are usually the neighborhood's stray cats, and they are well-fed because everyone gives them a little something from their meal.

Making reservations

When you want to dine out, you usually make a **κράτηση** (*kra*-tee-see) (*reservation*). You call the **εστιατόριο** (e-stee-a-*to*-ree-o) (*restaurant*) and ask to book a **τραπέζι** (tra-*pe*-zee) (*table*). You agree with the staff on the day and the time you'd like to dine (see Chapter 6 for details on days and times). Then, you specify the number of **άτομα** (*a*-to-ma) (*persons*) for the table and provide a name for the reservation.

Here are some basic phrases you'll need if you decide to make a reservation at a restaurant:

Θα ήθελα να κάνω μια κράτηση. (tha *ee*-the-la na *ka*-no mya *kra*-tee-see) (*I would like to make a reservation.*)

Θα ήθελα τραπέζι για τις 7:00 το απόγευμα. (tha *ee*-the-la tra-*pe*-zee ya tees e-*pta* to a-*po*-yev-ma) (*I would like a table for 7:00 p.m.*)

Έχετε διαθέσιμο τραπέζι; (*e*-he-te dya-*the*-see-mo tra-*pe*-zee) (*Do you have a table available?*)

The next question is usually:

Για πόσα άτομα; (ya *po*-sa *a*-to-ma) (*For how many people?*)

And then you state the number of people joining you for dinner:

Για δύο/τέσσερα/έξι άτομα, παρακαλώ. (ya *dee*-o/*te*-se-ra/*e*-ksee *a*-to-ma, pa-ra-ka-*lo*) (*For two/four/six people, please.*)

The following questions are also common:

Σε ποιο όνομα να γίνει η κράτηση; (se pyo *o*-no-ma na *yee*-nee ee *kra*-tee-see) (*Under which name should the reservation be made?*)

Για ποια μέρα; (ya pya *me*-ra) (*For which day?*)

TIP

Now, if your plans change for any reason, it's polite to call the restaurant and say:

Μπορώ να ακυρώσω την κράτησή μου; (bo-*ro* na a-kee-*ro*-so teen *kra*-tee-*see* moo) (*Can I cancel my reservation?*)

Ordering food

After you are seated at your table, **ο σερβιτόρος** (o se-rvee-*to*-ros) (*the waiter*) or **η σερβιτόρα** (ee se-rvee-*to*-ra) (*the waitress*) brings you **το μενού** (me-*noo*) (*the menu*). In Greek, the verb "to order" is **παραγγέλνω** (pa-ra-*ge*-lno). If you'd like to ask for the menu, you can say:

Θα ήθελα το μενού, παρακαλώ. (tha *ee*-the-la to me-*noo*, pa-ra-ka-*lo*) (*I would like the menu, please.*)

First, you order **τα ορεκτικά** (ta o-re-ktee-*ka*) (*the appetizers*). Next, you order **το κυρίως πιάτο** (to kee-*ree*-os pya-to) (*the main course*), and finally, **το επιδόρπιο** (to e-pee-*do*-rpee-o) (*the dessert*). You can ask for what you want by saying:

Θα ήθελα . . . (tha *ee*-the-la) (*I would like . . .*)

For example:

Θα ήθελα μουσακά. (tha *ee*-the-la moo-sa-*ka*) (*I would like moussaka.*)

Θα ήθελα ένα ποτήρι νερό/κρασί, παρακαλώ. (tha *ee*-the-la *e*-na po-*tee*-ree ne-*ro*/kra-*see*, pa-ra-ka-*lo*) (*I would like a glass of water/wine, please.*)

TIP

If you're unsure about what to order, you can ask the waiter for a recommendation by saying:

Μπορείτε να μου προτείνετε κάτι; (bo-*ree*-te na moo pro-*tee*-ne-te *ka*-tee) (*Can you recommend something?*)

Trying useful phrases in a restaurant

Although it's impossible to cover every possible phrase you might need in a restaurant, I try to provide as many as I can in the following list so you feel confident speaking Greek.

Ποιο είναι το πιάτο ημέρας; (pyo *ee*-ne to *pya*-to ee-*me*-ras) (*What's the dish of the day?*)

Το πιάτο ημέρας είναι γεμιστά. (to *pya*-to ee-*me*-ras *ee*-ne ye-mee-*sta*) (*The dish of the day is stuffed vegetables.*)

Είστε έτοιμοι να παραγγείλετε; (*ee*-ste *e*-tee-mee na pa-ra-*gee*-le-te) (*Are you ready to order?*)

Ναι, θα ήθελα έναν μουσακά. (ne, tha *ee*-the-la *e*-nan moo-sa-*ka*) (*Yes, I'd like a moussaka.*)

Μπορώ να παραγγείλω κάτι χορτοφαγικό; (bo-*ro* na pa-ra-*gee*-lo *ka*-tee kho-rto-fa-yee-*ko*) (*Can I order something vegetarian?*)

Βεβαίως. (ve-*ve*-os) (*Of course.*)

Θα θέλατε κάτι να πιείτε; (tha *the*-la-te *ka*-tee na *pyee*-te) (*Would you like something to drink?*)

Ένα ποτήρι νερό, παρακαλώ. (*e*-na po-*tee*-ree ne-*ro*, pa-ra-ka-*lo*) (*A glass of water, please.*)

Χρειάζεστε κάτι άλλο; (khree-*a*-ze-ste *ka*-tee *a*-lo) (*Do you need anything else?*)

Όχι, ευχαριστώ, όλα είναι τέλεια. (*o*-hee, ef-kha-ree-*sto*, *o*-la *ee*-ne *te*-lee-a) (*No, thank you, everything is perfect.*)

Θέλετε επιδόρπιο; (*the*-le-te e-pee-*do*-rpee-o) (*Would you like dessert?*)

Ναι, παρακαλώ. (ne, pa-ra-ka-*lo*) (*Yes, please.*)

After you finish your meal, ο λογαριασμός (o lo–ga–rya–*smos*) (*the bill*) arrives. You can ask for it by saying:

Τον λογαριασμό, παρακαλώ. (ton lo-ga-rya-*smo*, pa-ra-ka-*lo*) (*The bill, please.*)

You can also ask the waiter:

Δέχεστε πιστωτικές κάρτες; (*de*-he-ste pee-sto-tee-*kes ka*-rtes) (*Do you accept credit cards?*)

Or the waiter may ask you:

Θα πληρώσετε με κάρτα ή με μετρητά; (tha plee-*ro*-se-te me *ka*-rta ee me me-tree-*ta*) (*Will you pay by card or in cash?*)

TIP

When visiting a taverna, café, restaurant, or any place where you receive food and drink service, it's important to leave a tip for the waiter who gave their best effort to serve you.

If you're happy with your experience at the restaurant, as you leave, you can say:

Ευχαριστώ, όλα ήταν υπέροχα! (ef-kha-ree-*sto*, *o*-la *ee*-tan ee-*pe*-ro-kha) (*Thank you, everything was wonderful!*)

Talkin' the Talk

PLAY THIS

Zoe enters a Greek tavern and greets the waiter, Kostas. (Track 11)

Zoe: Καλησπέρα! Θα ήθελα ένα τραπέζι για δύο, παρακαλώ.
ka-lee-*spe*-ra! tha *ee*-the-la *e*-na tra-*pe*-zee ya *dee*-o, pa-ra-ka-*lo*.
Good evening! I would like a table for two, please.

Kostas: Βεβαίως, περάστε. Θέλετε να καθίσετε μέσα ή έξω;
ve-*ve*-os, pe-*ra*-ste. *the*-le-te na ka-*thee*-se-te *me*-sa ee e-kso;
Of course, please come in. Would you like to sit inside or outside?

Zoe: Έξω, παρακαλώ.
e-kso, pa-ra-ka-*lo*.
Outside, please.

Kostas: Ορίστε το μενού. Τι θα θέλατε;
o-*ree*-ste to me-*noo*. tee tha *the*-la-te;
Here's the menu. What would you like to order?

Zoe:	Θα θέλαμε μια χωριάτικη σαλάτα και ένα πιάτο γεμιστά.
	tha *the*-la-me mya kho-*rya*-tee-kee sa-*la*-ta ke *e*-na *pya*-to ye-mee-*sta*.
	We would like a Greek salad and a plate of stuffed vegetables.
Kostas:	Θέλετε κάτι να πιείτε;
	the-le-te *ka*-tee na *pyee*-te;
	Would you like something to drink?
Zoe:	Ναι, ένα ποτήρι λευκό κρασί και ένα νερό, παρακαλώ.
	ne, *e*-na po-*tee*-ree lef-*ko* kra-*see* ke *e*-na ne-*ro*, pa-ra-ka-*lo*.
	Yes, a glass of white wine and a water, please.
Kostas:	Έρχεται αμέσως!
	e-rhe-te a-*me*-sos!
	Coming right up!

WORDS TO KNOW

Καλησπέρα!	ka-lee-*spe*-ra	Good evening!
Θα ήθελα ένα τραπέζι.	tha *ee*-the-la *e*-na tra-*pe*-zee	I would like a table.
Περάστε.	pe-*ra*-ste	Come in.
μέσα ή έξω	*me*-sa ee *e*-kso	in or out
Ορίστε το μενού.	o-*ree*-ste to me-*noo*	Here is the menu.
Τι θα θέλατε;	tee tha *the*-la-te?	What would you like?
Θέλετε κάτι να πιείτε;	*the*-le-te *ka*-tee na *pyee*-te	Would you like something to drink?
αμέσως	a-*me*-sos	right away

Ordering Coffee

CULTURAL WISDOM

For most Greeks, going out for coffee means a long outing at a café. Coffee is a serious matter — it's not just a drink that helps us wake up but also a habit tied to socializing, communication, and leaving the house.

Coffee in Greek is καφές (ka-*fes*). Greeks love various types of coffee. Ελληνικός καφές (e-lee-nee-*kos* ka-*fes*) (*Greek coffee*) is the traditional coffee of Greece, brewed over low heat in a small pot called a briki — in Greek it's spelled μπρίκι (*bree*-kee).

More modern and definitely stronger coffees include frappé, freddo espresso, and freddo cappuccino. The last two are inspired by Italian espresso and cappuccino but differ as they are served cold.

Coffee can be enjoyed with ζάχαρη (za-kha-ree) (*sugar*) and γάλα (*ga*-la) (*milk*). If you prefer your coffee without sugar, you'd like it σκέτο (*ske*-to). If you want a little sugar, you'd say μέτριο (*me*-tree-o), and if you want it sweet, you'd say γλυκό (glee-*ko*). If you want milk, you'd say με γάλα (me *ga*-la). If you don't, you'd say χωρίς γάλα (kho-*rees ga*-la).

In a café, you can also enjoy τσάι (*tsa*-ee) (*tea*) or χυμός (hee-*mos*) (*juice*).

Useful phrases in a café include the following:

> **Έναν καφέ, παρακαλώ.** (*e*-nan ka-*fe,* pa-ra-ka-*lo*) (*One coffee, please.*)

> **Τι καφέ θέλετε;** (tee ka-*fe the*-le-te) (*What coffee would you like?*)

> **Θέλετε ζάχαρη στον καφέ σας;** (*the*-le-te *za*-kha-ree ston ka-*fe* sas) (*Do you want sugar in your coffee?*)

> **Θέλετε γάλα στον καφέ σας;** (*the*-le-te *ga*-la ston ka-*fe* sas) (*Do you want milk in your coffee?*)

> **Πώς πίνετε τον καφέ σας;** (pos *pee*-ne-te ton ka-*fe* sas) (*How do you take your coffee?*)

> **Μέτριο με γάλα.** (*me*-tree-o me *ga*-la) (*Medium sweet with milk.*)

> **Θέλω έναν διπλό καφέ.** (*the*-lo *e*-nan dee-*plo* ka-*fe*) (*I want a double coffee.*)

> **Μπορείτε να το κάνετε πακέτο;** (bo-*ree*-te na to *ka*-ne-te pa-*ke*-to) (*Can you make it to-go?*)

> **Ένα τσάι με μέλι, παρακαλώ.** (*e*-na *tsa*-ee me *me*-lee, pa-ra-ka-*lo*) (*One tea with honey, please.*)

Talkin' the Talk

PLAY THIS

Violeta is at a café and orders a coffee from the waiter, Vasili. (Track 12)

Violeta: Καλημέρα! Έναν καφέ, παρακαλώ;
ka-lee-*me*-ra! *e*-nan ka-*fe*, pa-ra-ka-*lo*;
Good morning! Can I order a coffee, please;

Vasili: Βεβαίως! Τι καφέ θέλετε;
ve-*ve*-os! tee ka-*fe* *the*-le-te;
Of course! What coffee would you like?

Violeta: Έναν φρέντο εσπρέσο μέτριο, με γάλα, παρακαλώ.
e-nan *fre*-do e-*spre*-so *me*-tree-o, me *ga*-la, pa-ra-ka-*lo*.
A freddo espresso, medium sweet, with milk, please.

Vasili: Θέλετε κάτι να φάτε;
the-le-te *ka*-tee na *fa*-te;
Would you like something to eat?

Violeta: Ναι, θα ήθελα ένα κομμάτι κέικ σοκολάτας.
ne, tha ee-*the*-la *e*-na ko-*ma*-tee *ke*-eek so-ko-*la*-tas.
Yes, I'd like a slice of chocolate cake.

Vasili: Έρχεται αμέσως!
e-rhe-te a-*me*-sos!
Coming right up!

WORDS TO KNOW		
παρακαλώ	pa-ra-ka-*lo*	*please*
βεβαίως	ve-*ve*-os	*of course*
Τι καφέ θέλετε;	tee ka-*fe* *the*-le-te	*What coffee would you like?*
μέτριος καφές	*me*-tree-os ka-*fes*	*medium sweet coffee*
με γάλα	me *ga*-la	*with milk*
Θέλετε κάτι να φάτε;	*the*-le-te *ka*-tee na *fa*-te	*Would you like something to eat?*
κομμάτι	ko-*ma*-tee	*piece*
κέικ	*ke*-eek	*cake*

Enjoying Entertainment

It's Saturday night, and you want to go out and have fun with your Greek friend Violeta. But what will you do? You have so many entertainment options, and you need to choose something that both of you will enjoy in order to have a wonderful evening together. Should you go to the cinema? Or perhaps stay up late at a club? Maybe tonight you could go and listen to your favorite singer's concert? Whatever way you decide to have fun, in this section, you'll find the vocabulary you need for entertainment in Greece. The word for "entertainment" in Greek is διασκέδαση (dee-a-*ske*-da-see).

CULTURAL WISDOM

Entertainment in Greece is often associated in the minds of many foreigners with the tradition of breaking plates while dancing. Indeed, this display of exuberance was popular as early as the 1960s. However, modern Greeks have abandoned this habit, and it's no longer part of their entertainment culture. It is, however, preserved by Greeks living abroad and is reproduced for tourism purposes in Greece's tourist destinations.

Cinema

In Greek, we use both the foreign word σινεμά (see-ne-*ma*) (*cinema*) and the Greek word κινηματογράφος (kee-nee-ma-to-*gra*-fos). So, when we go to the cinema, we watch a ταινία (te-*nee*-a) (*movie*). Naturally, to watch a film, we first need to buy a εισιτήριο (ee-see-*tee*-ree-o) (*ticket*). If the movie is foreign, then there are υπότιτλοι (ee-*po*-tee-tlee) (*subtitles*).

Before entering the αίθουσα προβολής (*e*-thoo-sa pro-vo-*lees*) (*screening room*), we can buy ποπ κορν (pop korn) (*popcorn*) and αναψυκτικά (a-na-psee-ktee-*ka*) (*soft drinks*) from the canteen.

Depending on our tastes, we can choose to watch a ταινία τρόμου (te-*nee*-a tro-moo) (*horror movie*), κωμωδία (ko-mo-*dee*-a) (*comedy*), or ταινία δράσης (te-*nee*-a dra-sees) (*action movie*).

Here are some common questions and phrases related to going to the movies:

> **Πότε αρχίζει η ταινία;** (*po*-te a-*rhee*-zee ee te-*nee*-a) (*When does the movie start?*)
>
> **Δύο εισιτήρια, παρακαλώ.** (*dee*-o ee-see-*tee*-ree-a, pa-ra-ka-*lo*) (*Two tickets, please.*)
>
> **Πού είναι η αίθουσα τρία;** (poo *ee*-ne ee *e*-thoo-sa *tree*-a) (*Where is screening room 3?*)

Clubbing

CULTURAL WISDOM

Most people, when they hear about partying in Greece, think of islands like Mykonos, Paros, and Ios. And indeed, these islands have been leaders in nightlife entertainment for years, although you can party in many other places.

In Greek, we use the foreign word **κλαμπ** (klab) (*club*), but there is also the Greek term **κέντρο διασκέδασης** (*ke*-dro dee-a-*ske*-da-sees). Many words related to clubbing are borrowed from other languages, like **κοκτέιλ** (ko-*kte*-eel) (*cocktail*) and **μπαρ** (*bar*). Here are some more Greek words and phrases associated with this form of entertainment:

» **μουσική** (moo-see-*kee*) (*music*)

» **πίστα** (*pee*-sta) (*dance floor*)

» **ρυθμός** (ree-*thmos*) (*rhythm*)

» **χορός** (kho-*ros*) (*dance*)

Phrases you can use in a club include the following:

Πάμε στο κλαμπ απόψε! (*pa*-me sto klab a-*po*-pse) (*Let's go to the club tonight!*)

Θα ήθελα ένα μοχίτο, παρακαλώ. (tha *ee*-the-la *e*-na mo-*hee*-to, pa-ra-ka-*lo*) (*I'd like a mojito, please.*)

Bouzoukia

There is, of course, the Greek version of a club, which is **τα μπουζούκια** (ta boo-*zoo*-kya). Do you know what that is? Bouzoukia are popular entertainment venues in Greece where customers typically enjoy live music performed by famous singers and bands. At **μπουζούκια**, the atmosphere is full of energy, with dancing and singing. If you ever visit Greece, make sure you spend an evening at a bouzoukia.

The type of music you hear during an evening at **μπουζούκια** is called **λαϊκή μουσική** (la-ee-*kee* moo-see-*kee*) (*popular folk music*). On stage, there's the **ορχήστρα** (o-*rhee*-stra) (*orchestra, band*), and the singers perform **τα τραγούδια** (ta tra-*goo*-dya) (*the songs*).

CULTURAL WISDOM

It's characteristic that when a singer performs at **μπουζούκια**, customers throw **λουλούδια** (loo-loo-dya) (*flowers*) to show their admiration and appreciation. Inside the venue, there are **λουλουδούδες** (loo-loo-*doo*-des) (*flower sellers*), who carry baskets of flowers that you can buy and then throw at the singer.

The Greek panigiri

The oldest and most traditional form of entertainment, however, is clearly the Greek πανηγύρι (pa-nee-*yee*-ree). This celebration takes place on the occasion of a saint's feast day in the Greek Orthodox Church or during a specific agricultural season. Most πανηγύρια happen during summer when the weather is good.

Η ορχήστρα (ee o-*rhee*-stra) (*the orchestra*) plays παραδοσιακή μουσική (pa-ra-do-see-a-*kee* moo-see-*kee*) (*traditional music*), and people dance παραδοσιακοί χοροί (pa-ra-do-see-a-*kee* kho-*ree*) (*traditional dances*).

CULTURAL WISDOM

These dances are usually danced in a circle, with people holding hands or placing their arms around each other's shoulders. It's a big γλέντι (*gle*-dee) (*celebration*), and people eat and drink until dawn.

CULTURAL WISDOM

A tradition of the πανηγύρι is the παραγγελιά (pa-ra-ge-*lya*) (*song request*). You can give money to the musicians and ask them to play a song you like. After paying for the song, you're the first to dance. In some places, when you pay for a song request, the entire orchestra comes to play music around you.

Making Plans with Friends

Good friends make the night special, and without good company, entertainment isn't as enjoyable. Let's explore some vocabulary and phrases related to making plans and going out:

>> έξοδος (*e*-kso-dos) (*going out*)

>> παρέα (pa-*re*-a) (*group of friends*)

>> σχέδια (*skhe*-dee-a) (*plans*)

>> Τι θα κάνουμε απόψε; (tee tha *ka*-noo-me a-*po*-pse) (*What are we doing tonight?*)

>> Πού θέλετε να πάμε; (poo *the*-le-te na *pa*-me) (*Where do you want to go?*)

>> Να κλείσουμε τραπέζι; (na *klee*-soo-me tra-*pe*-zee) (*Should we reserve a table?*)

CULTURAL WISDOM

One of the traits of Greeks is their spontaneity when it comes to entertainment. They don't need to plan something far in advance and put it on their agenda for it to happen. All it takes is for your friend to call you a few hours beforehand, and you're ready for a night out!

Talkin' the Talk

Eleni, Nikos, and Katerina are planning a night out.

Eleni: Θέλετε να βγούμε το Σάββατο;
the-le-te na *vgoo*-me to *sa*-va-to;
Do you want to meet up on Saturday?

Nikos: Ναι! Έχεις κάποια πρόταση; Θέλετε να πάμε μπουζούκια ή στο πανηγύρι που γίνεται στο χωριό;
ne! e-hees *ka*-pya *pro*-ta-see; *the*-le-te na *pa*-me boo-*zoo*-kya ee sto pa-nee-*yee*-ree poo *yee*-ne-te sto kho-*ryo*;
Yes! Do you have any suggestions? Should we go to the bouzoukia or the festival happening in the village?

Katerina: Τα μπουζούκια είναι καλή ιδέα αλλά το πανηγύρι έχει παραδοσιακούς χορούς και νόστιμο φαγητό! Δύσκολη απόφαση!
ta boo-*zoo*-kya *ee*-ne ka-*lee* ee-*de*-a a-*la* to pa-nee-*yee*-ree e-hee pa-ra-do-see-a-*koos* kho-*roos* ke *no*-stee-mo fa-yee-*to*! *dee*-sko-lee a-*po*-fa-see!
Bouzoukia is a great idea, but the festival has traditional dances and delicious food! Tough decision!

Eleni: Θέλετε να πάμε σε μία ταβέρνα και μετά στο πανηγύρι;
the-le-te na *pa*-me se mya ta-*ve*-rna ke me-*ta* sto pa-nee-*yee*-ree;
How about going to a tavern and then heading to the festival?

Nikos: Μου αρέσει αυτό το σχέδιο.
moo a-*re*-see af-*to* to *skhe*-dee-o.
I like that plan.

Eleni: Ωραία! Κλείνω τραπέζι στην ταβέρνα. Στο πανηγύρι μπορούμε να βρούμε τραπέζι εύκολα.
o-*re*-a! *klee*-no tra-*pe*-zee steen ta-*ve*-rna. sto pa-nee-*yee*-ree bo-*roo*-me na *vroo*-me tra-*pe*-zee *ef*-ko-la.
Great! I'll reserve a table at the tavern. At the festival, we can easily find a table.

Katerina: Τι ώρα;
tee *o*-ra;
What time?

(continued)

(continued)

Nikos: Στις επτά είναι καλά;
stees e-pta *ee*-ne ka-*la;*
Is 7:00 okay?

Eleni: Καλύτερα στις οκτώ.
ka-*lee*-te-ra stees o-*kto.*
Better make it 8.

Katerina: Τέλεια! Ανυπομονώ!
te-lee-a! A-nee-po-mo-*no!*
Perfect! I can't wait!

WORDS TO KNOW

Θέλετε να βγούμε;	*the*-le-te na *vgoo*-me	*Do you want to meet up?*
πρόταση	*pro*-ta-see	*suggestion*
χωριό	kho-*ryo*	*village*
ιδέα	ee-*de*-a	*idea*
νόστιμο φαγητό	*no*-stee-mo fa-yee-*to*	*tasty food*
απόφαση	a-*po*-fa-see	*decision*
σχέδιο	*skhe*-dee-o	*plan*
Ανυπομονώ!	a-nee-po-mo-*no*	*I can't wait!*

FUN & GAMES

Can you much the words that go together?

κυρίως	διασκέδασης
ελληνικός	μουσική
ταινία	πιάτο
κέντρο	καφές
λαϊκή	χοροί
παραδοσιακοί	τρόμου

Chapter **11**

Your Body and Your Health

magine you're on vacation in Greece, and for some reason, you have to visit a doctor. You'll need to talk about your body and health. This chapter contains essential Greek vocabulary on these topics.

Naming Body Parts

In Greek, the word for "body" is σώμα (*so*-ma). For a tour of the body, let's start from the top — το κεφάλι (to ke-*fa*-lee) (*the head*) — and move downward (see Figure 11-1):

>> μαλλιά (ma-*lya*) (*hair*)

>> μέτωπο (*me*-to-po) (*forehead*)

>> φρύδι (*free*-dee) (*eyebrow*)

>> μάτι (*ma*-tee) (*eye*)

>> μύτη (*mee*-tee) (*nose*)

>> μάγουλο (*ma*-goo-lo) (*cheek*)

- » αυτί (af-tee) (*ear*)

- » χείλια (*hee*-lya) (*lips*)

- » δόντια (*do*-dya) (*teeth*)

- » γλώσσα (*glo*-sa) (*tongue*)

- » πιγούνι (pee-*goo*-nee) (*chin*)

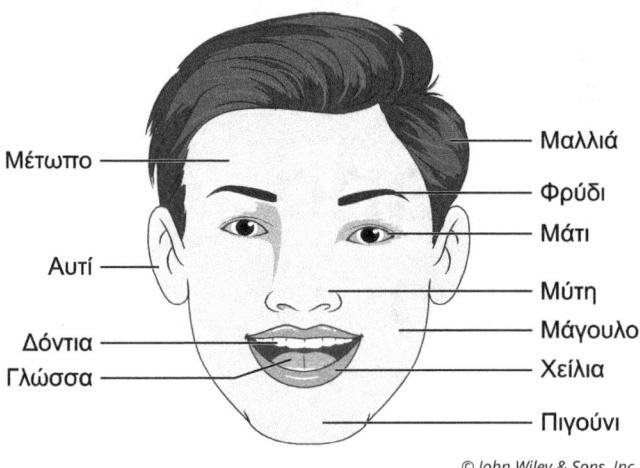

Μέτωπο — Μαλλιά
Φρύδι
Μάτι
Αυτί — Μύτη
Μάγουλο
Δόντια — Χείλια
Γλώσσα —
Πιγούνι

FIGURE 11-1:
The head.

© *John Wiley & Sons, Inc.*

Now let's look at the rest of the body (see Figure 11–2):

- » λαιμός (le-*mos*) (*neck*)

- » στήθος (*stee*-thos) (*chest*)

- » κοιλιά (kee-*lya*) (*belly*)

- » πλάτη (*pla*-tee) (*back*)

- » γλουτοί (gloo-*tee*) (*glutes*)

- » οπίσθια (o-*pee*-sthee-a) (*butt*)

- » μπράτσο (*bra*-tso) (*arm*)

- » αγκώνας (a-*go*-nas) (*elbow*)

- » χέρι (*he*-ree) (*hand*)

- » παλάμη (pa-*la*-mee) (*palm*)

- » δάχτυλα (*da*-khtee-la) (*fingers*)

» γεννητικά όργανα (ye-nee-tee-*ka* o-rga-na) (*genitals*)

» μπούτι (*boo*-tee) (*thigh*)

» γόνατο (*go*-na-to) (*knee*)

» γάμπα (*ga*-mba) (*calf*)

» πατούσα (pa-*too*-sa) (*foot*)

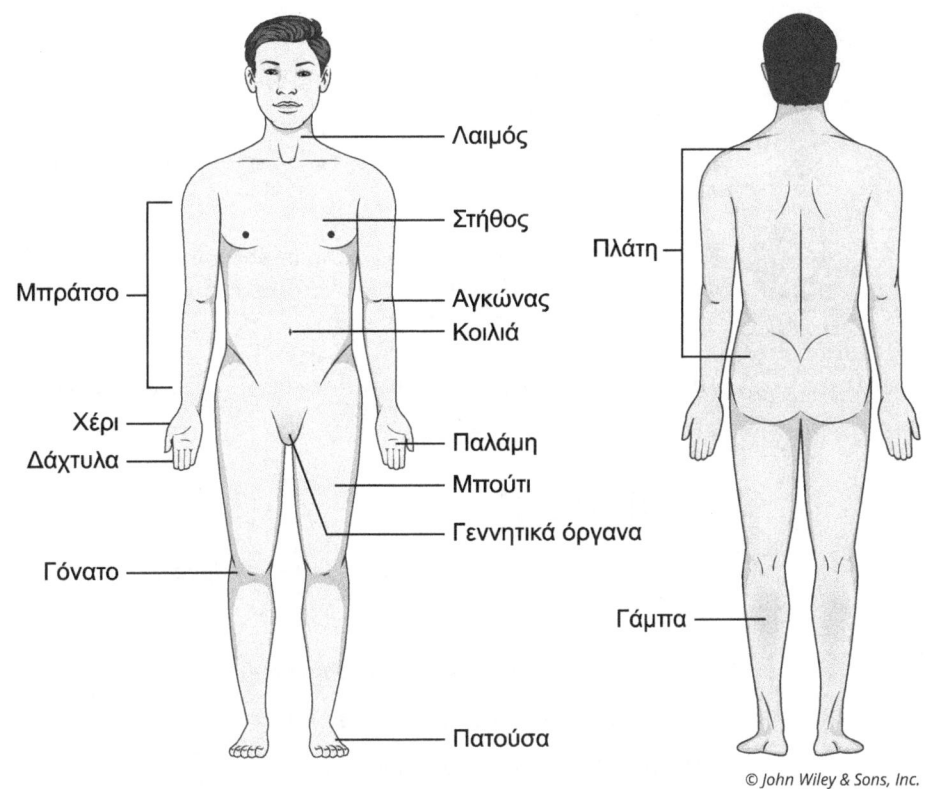

Λαιμός

Στήθος

Πλάτη

Μπράτσο

Αγκώνας

Κοιλιά

Χέρι

Παλάμη

Δάχτυλα

Μπούτι

Γεννητικά όργανα

Γόνατο

Γάμπα

FIGURE 11-2:
The body.

Πατούσα

© *John Wiley & Sons, Inc.*

Discussing Health

The ancient Greeks had a wise saying: Νους υγιής εν σώματι υγιεί (noos e-yee-*ees* en *so*-ma-tee ee-yee-*ee*), which means "A healthy mind in a healthy body." With this phrase, they meant that the health of the mind and body are interconnected and influence each other. Let's look at some words and phrases related to our health.

The word "health" in Greek is υγεία (ee–*yee*–a). When someone is healthy, they can say είμαι υγιής (ee–me ee–*yee*–ees) (*I am healthy*).

The adjective υγιής remains the same for both masculine and feminine forms, so you can say ο υγιής άνδρας (o ee–yee–ees a–ndras) (*the healthy man*) or η υγιής γυναίκα (ee ee–yee–ees yee–ne–ka) (*the healthy woman*).

There's also the adjective υγιεινός, υγιεινή, υγιεινό (ee–yee–ee–*nos*, ee–yee–ee–*nee*, ee–yee–ee–*no*) which is used to describe not people but habits, foods, and so on. For example:

> Ο Γιώργος κάνει υγιεινή διατροφή. (o yo-rgos ka-nee ee-yee-ee-*nee* dee-a-tro-*fee*) (*George follows a healthy diet.*)

> Τα λαχανικά είναι υγιεινά. (Ta la-kha-nee-ka ee-ne ee-yee-ee-*na*) (*Vegetables are healthy.*)

For the ancient Greeks, health was so important that they established worship for the goddess Hygeia, and you can even see a statue of the goddess at the National Archaeological Museum of Athens.

The following sections discuss various terms related to illness, pain, recovery, and accidents.

Feeling sick

When we start to get sick, certain symptoms appear that may make daily activities difficult for us:

>> το συνάχι (to see-*na*-hee) (*the runny nose*)

>> Φυσάω τη μύτη μου. (fee-*sa*-o tee *mee*-tee moo) (*I blow my nose.*)

>> Φτερνίζομαι. (fte-*rnee*-zo-me) (*I sneeze.*)

>> Βήχω. (*vee*-kho) (*I cough.*)

Here are examples of these phrases in use:

> Η Ειρήνη είναι συναχωμένη και φυσάει τη μύτη της. (ee ee-*ree*-nee *ee*-ne see-na-kho-*me*-nee ke fee-*sa*-ee tee *mee*-tee tees) (*Irene has a runny nose and blows her nose.*)

> Είμαι άρρωστος, φτερνίζομαι, και βήχω όλη μέρα. (*ee*-me a-ro-stos, fte-*rnee*-zo-me, ke *vee*-kho o-lee *me*-ra) (*I'm sick, I sneeze, and I cough all day.*)

We may have these symptoms because we have a virus or the flu. However, some people show these symptoms because they have allergies. For example: Έχω αλλεργία στη γύρη, και την άνοιξη, έχω συνάχι. (*e*-kho a-le-*ryee*-a stee *yee*-ree, ke teen *a*-nee-ksee, *e*-kho see-*na*-hee) (*I have an allergy to pollen, and in spring, I have a runny nose.*)

If I have something more serious, then I may have a fever, or έχω πυρετό (*e*-kho pee-re-*to*), and vomit, or κάνω εμετό (*ka*-no e-me-*to*).

When the fever rises, we say Ο πυρετός ανεβαίνει (o pee-re-*tos* a-ne-*ve*-nee) (*the fever rises*), and when it drops, we say Ο πυρετός πέφτει (o pee-re-*tos* pe-ftee) (*the fever drops*). For example:

> Το μωρό είχε πυρετό όλη νύχτα, αλλά το πρωί έπεσε. (to mo-*ro* ee-he pee-re-*to* o-*lee* *nee*-khta, a-*la* to pro-*ee* e-pe-se) (*The baby had a fever all night, but in the morning it dropped.*)

Having pain

When we're sick, it's also possible to feel pain. The word for pain in Greek is πόνος (*po*-nos). To talk about it, you can say one of the following:

> Πονάω. (po-*na*-o) (*I hurt.*)

> Νιώθω πόνο. (*nyo*-tho *po*-no) (*I feel pain.*)

Depending on which body part hurts, you can use the verb πονάω in the third person and the body part. For example, you can say πονάει (po-*na*-ee)

- » ο λαιμός μου (o le-*mos* moo) (*my throat*)

- » το κεφάλι μου (to ke-*fa*-lee moo) (*my head*)

- » το στομάχι μου (to sto-*ma*-hee moo) (*my stomach*)

- » η κοιλιά μου (ee kee-*lya* moo) (*my belly*)

- » το δόντι μου (to *do*-ndee moo) (*my tooth*)

Another way to say the same thing is to use the verb έχω (*e*-kho) (*I have*) and the type of pain. For example, Έχω

- » πονόδοντο (po-*no*-do-do) (*a toothache*)

- » στομαχόπονο (sto-ma-*kho*-po-no) (*a stomachache*)

>> πονόκοιλο (po-*no*-kee-lo) (*a bellyache*)

>> πονοκέφαλο (po-no-*ke*-fa-lo) (*a headache*)

Talkin' the Talk

PLAY THIS

Anna checks on her younger brother, Nikos, in the morning. (Track 13)

Anna: Καλημέρα, Νίκο. Πώς είσαι;
ka-lee-*me*-ra, *nee*-ko. pos *ee*-se;
Good morning, Nikos. How are you?

Nikos: Καλημέρα, Άννα. Δεν νιώθω καλά.
ka-lee-*me*-ra, *A*-na. den *nyo*-tho ka-*la*.
Good morning, Anna. I don't feel well.

Anna: Τι έχεις; Έχεις πονοκέφαλο; Πυρετό; Πονάει η κοιλιά σου;
tee *e*-hees; *e*-hees po-no-*ke*-fa-lo; pee-re-*to*; po-*na*-ee ee
kee-*lya* soo;
*What's wrong? Do you have a headache? A fever? Does your
stomach hurt?*

Nikos: Έχω πυρετό και συνάχι. Επίσης, ο λαιμός μου πονάει.
e-kho pee-re-*to* ke see-*na*-hee. e-*pee*-sees, o le-*mos* moo
po-*na*-ee.
I have a fever and a runny nose. Also, my throat hurts.

Anna: Ωχ, φαίνεται σαν να έχεις κρυώσει. Πρέπει να ξεκουραστείς.
Έχεις πάρει φάρμακο;
okh, *fe*-ne-te san na *e*-hees kree-*o*-see. *pre*-pee na kse-koo-
ra-*stees*. *e*-hees *pa*-ree *fa*-rma-ko;
*Oh, it looks like you have a cold. You need to rest. Have you
taken any medicine?*

Nikos: Όχι ακόμη. Σκεφτόμουν να πάρω κάτι από το φαρμακείο.
o-hee a-*ko*-mee. ske-*fto*-moon na *pa*-ro *ka*-tee a-*po* to
fa-rma-*kee*-o.
Not yet. I was thinking of getting something from the pharmacy.

Anna: Πηγαίνω εγώ στο φαρμακείο να σου φέρω ένα παυσίπονο.
pee-*ye*-no e-*go* sto fa-rma-*kee*-o na soo *fe*-ro *e*-na
paf-*see*-po-no.
I'll go to the pharmacy and bring you a painkiller.

WORDS TO KNOW

Νιώθω.	nyo-tho	I feel.
Νιώθω καλά.	nyo-tho ka-la	I feel well.
πονοκέφαλος	po-no-ke-fa-los	headache
πυρετός	pee-re-tos	fever
Πονάει η κοιλιά σου;	po-na-ee ee kee-lya soo	Does your stomach hurt?
συνάχι	see-na-hee	runny nose
επίσης	e-pee-sees	also, additionally
λαιμός	le-mos	throat
Έχω κρυώσει.	e-kho kree-o-see	I have caught a cold.
Ξεκουράζομαι	kse-koo-ra-zo-me	I rest; I am resting.
Παίρνω φάρμακο.	pe-rno fa-rma-ko	I take medicine.
φαρμακείο	fa-rma-kee-o	pharmacy

Taking care when you're sick

If you're sick, you need special care. You can do some things at home to feel better, but sometimes you may need to go to the doctor. (I cover visiting the doctor later in this chapter.)

It helps to drink a warm beverage, which we call ρόφημα (ro-fee-ma), like tea. Also, if you have a headache or fever, you can take a παυσίπονο (paf-see-po-no) (painkiller). When you want to say you're taking a painkiller in Greek, you use the verb παίρνω (pe-rno) (I take):

> Παίρνω παυσίπονο. (pe-rno paf-see-po-no) (I take a painkiller.)

If you have something more serious, then you need to take a stronger medicine, or φάρμακο (fa-rma-ko). So, you go to the doctor, and they prescribe an αντιβιωτικό (a-dee-vee-o-tee-ko) (antibiotic). The antibiotic can be a χάπι (kha-pee) (pill) or σιρόπι (see-ro-pee) (syrup).

After staying in bed for a few days and following the appropriate treatment, you'll get better. Then you can say είμαι καλά (ee-me ka-la) (I'm well) or έγινα καλά (e-yee-na ka-la) (I got well).

Having an accident

An accident is certainly not pleasant, but sometimes we need to deal with such a situation. Here are some useful phrases:

> Είχα ένα ατύχημα. (*ee*-kha *e*-na a-*tee*-hee-ma) (*I had an accident.*)
>
> Χτύπησα το χέρι μου, το πόδι μου. (*khtee*-pee-sa to *he*-ree moo, to *po*-dee moo) (*I hurt my hand, my leg.*)
>
> Τράκαρα. (*tra*-ka-ra) (*I crashed.*)
>
> Έπεσα. (*e*-pe-sa) (*I fell.*)
>
> Καλέστε ένα ασθενοφόρο. (ka-*le*-ste *e*-na a-sthe-no-*fo*-ro) (*Call an ambulance.*)
>
> Υπάρχει κάποιος γιατρός εδώ; (ee-*pa*-rhee *ka*-pyos ya-*tros* e-*do*) (*Is there a doctor here?*)
>
> Χρειάζεστε βοήθεια; (khree-*a*-ze-ste vo-*ee*-thee-a) (*Do you need help?*)

TIP

In case you need immediate help, you can shout Βοήθεια! (vo-*ee*-thee-a) (*Help!*).

If you ever have an accident in Greece, note that the number for ambulances is 166.

REMEMBER

Visiting the Doctor's Office

Young and old alike fear visits to the γιατρός (ya-*tros*) (*doctor*). However, such visits are also a part of life, and that's why I can't skip this topic.

GRAMMATICALLY SPEAKING

The word γιατρός is one of the professions that don't change based on the gender of the doctor. You can change only the article to specify the gender: ο γιατρός (male) and η γιατρός (female).

CULTURAL WISDOM

And since I am a Greek mythology nerd, I want to tell you that the first doctor in Greek mythology was Asclepius, who held a staff wrapped with a snake. That's why in many health-related services, such as hospitals, doctor's offices, and pharmacies, you'll often see the symbol of the staff with the snake.

Arranging your appointment

We go to the doctor's office, or ιατρείο (ee-a-*tree*-o), when we have a health/medical issue, or πρόβλημα υγείας (*pro*-vlee-ma ee-*yee*-as). Then we must make an appointment, or ραντεβού (ra-de-*voo*), by calling or sending an email. What can you say when arranging the appointment?

Θα ήθελα να κλείσω ένα ραντεβού. (tha ee-the-la na *klee*-so e-na ra-de-*voo*) (*I would like to book an appointment.*)

Είναι διαθέσιμος ο γιατρός [μέρα/ώρα]; (*ee*-ne dee-a-*the*-see-mos o ya-*tros* [*me*-ra/o-ra]) (*Is the doctor available on [day/time]?*)

Μπορώ να δω τον γιατρό σήμερα; (bo-*ro* na do ton ya-*tro see*-me-ra) (*Can I see the doctor today?*)

Χρειάζομαι ένα ραντεβού το συντομότερο δυνατόν. (khree-*a*-zo-me e-na ra-de-*voo* to see-do-*mo*-te-ro dee-na-*ton*) (*I need an appointment as soon as possible.*)

Ποιος γιατρός θα με δει; (pyos ya-*tros* tha me dee) (*Which doctor will see me?*)

If plans change, you need to inform the doctor's office:

Θέλω να ακυρώσω το ραντεβού μου. (*the*-lo na a-kee-*ro*-so to ra-de-*voo* moo) (*I need to cancel my appointment.*)

Μπορώ να αλλάξω το ραντεβού μου; (bo-*ro* na a-*la*-kso to ra-de-*voo* moo) (*Can I reschedule my appointment?*)

Based on your condition you need to visit different doctors. Here are some basic types:

>> γενικός ιατρός (ye-nee-*kos* ya-*tros*) (*general practitioner*)

>> παιδίατρος (pe-*dee*-a-tros) (*pediatrician*)

>> χειρουργός (hee-roo-*rgos*) (*surgeon*)

>> καρδιολόγος (ka-rdee-o-*lo*-gos) (*cardiologist*)

>> δερματολόγος (de-rma-to-*lo*-gos) (*dermatologist*)

>> γυναικολόγος (yee-ne-ko-*lo*-gos) (*gynecologist*)

>> ψυχίατρος (psee-*hee*-a-tros) (*psychiatrist*)

>> οφθαλμίατρος (o-ftha-*lmee*-a-tros) (*ophthalmologist*)

>> οδοντίατρος (o-do-*dee*-a-tros) (*dentist*)

Speaking with the doctor

As the doctor examines you, they may ask you questions and give you various instructions to understand what you're feeling and to be able to examine you properly.

Πώς αισθάνεστε; (pos e-*stha*-ne-ste) (*How are you feeling?*)

Πού πονάτε; (poo po-*na*-te) (*Where does it hurt?*)

Πότε ξεκίνησε το πρόβλημα; (*po*-te kse-*kee*-nee-se to *pro*-vlee-ma) (*When did the problem start?*)

Έχετε αλλεργίες; (*e*-he-te a-le-*ryee*-es) (*Do you have any allergies?*)

Παίρνετε φάρμακα; (*pe*-rne-te *fa*-rma-ka) (*Are you taking any medications?*)

Μπορώ να σας εξετάσω; (bo-*ro* na sas e-kse-*ta*-so) (*May I examine you?*)

Ανοίξτε το στόμα σας. (a-*nee*-kste to *sto*-ma sas) (*Open your mouth.*)

Πάρτε βαθιά ανάσα. (*pa*-rte va-*thya* a-*na*-sa) (*Take a deep breath.*)

Ξαπλώστε εδώ, παρακαλώ. (ksa-*plo*-ste e-*do*, pa-ra-ka-*lo*) (*Lie down here, please.*)

After the doctor examines you, they may give you instructions for the next steps. They may prescribe medication or additional tests.

Σας γράφω εξετάσεις. (sas *gra*-fo e-kse-*ta*-sees) (*You need to do some tests.*)

Σας γράφω φάρμακα. (sas *gra*-fo *fa*-rma-ka) (*I'll prescribe you some medication.*)

Δεν είναι κάτι σοβαρό. (den *ee*-ne *ka*-tee so-va-*ro*) (*It's nothing serious.*)

Πρέπει να ξεκουραστείτε. (*pre*-pee na kse-koo-ra-*stee*-te) (*You'll need to rest.*)

Talkin' the Talk

PLAY THIS

Panagiotis isn't feeling well and goes to his doctor, Dr. Papadimitriou. (Track 14)

Panagiotis: Καλημέρα. Δεν νιώθω καλά.
ka-lee-*me*-ra. den *nyo*-tho ka-*la*.
Good morning. I don't feel well.

Dr. Papadimitriou: Καλημέρα! Πώς αισθάνεστε;
ka-lee-*me*-ra! pos e-*stha*-ne-ste
Good morning! How do you feel?

Panagiotis:	Έχω πυρετό, βήχα, και νιώθω αδύναμος. Επίσης, έχω πονοκέφαλο. e-kho pee-re-*to*, *vee*-kha, ke *nyo*-tho a-*dee*-na-mos. e-*pee*-sees, e-kho po-no-*ke*-fa-lo. *I have a fever, a cough, and I feel weak. Also, I have a headache.*
Dr. Papadimitriou:	Καταλαβαίνω. Θα σας εξετάσω τώρα. Πάρτε βαθιά ανάσα. ka-ta-la-*ve*-no. tha sas e-kse-*ta*-so *to*-ra. *pa*-rte va-*thya* a-*na*-sa. *I see. I will examine you now. Please take a deep breath.*
Panagiotis:	Ναι, φυσικά. ne, fee-see-*ka*. *Yes, of course.*
Dr. Papadimitriou:	Ο λαιμός σας είναι λίγο κόκκινος. Θα σας γράψω κάποια φάρμακα. o le-*mos* sas *ee*-ne *lee*-go ko-kee-nos. tha sas *gra*-pso *ka*-pya *fa*-rma-ka. *Your throat is a bit red. I will prescribe some medication for you.*
Panagiotis:	Είναι σοβαρό; *ee*-ne so-va-*ro*; *Is it serious?*
Dr. Papadimitriou:	Όχι, δεν είναι κάτι σοβαρό, αλλά πρέπει να ξεκουραστείτε. o-hee, den *ee*-ne *ka*-tee so-va-*ro*, a-*la pre*-pee na kse-koo-ra-*stee*-te. *It's nothing serious, but you need to rest.*
Panagiotis:	Ευχαριστώ, γιατρέ. ef-kha-ree-*sto*, ya-*tre*. *Thank you, doctor.*
Dr. Papadimitriou:	Περαστικά! pe-ra-stee-*ka*! *Get well soon!*

• •

WORDS TO KNOW

Πώς αισθάνεστε;	pos e-*stha*-ne-ste	*How do you feel?*
Νιώθω αδύναμος.	*nyo*-tho a-*dee*-na-mos	*I feel weak.*
Θα σας εξετάσω τώρα.	tha sas e-kse-*ta*-so *to*-ra	*I will examine you now.*
ανάσα	a-*na*-sa	*breath*
φυσικά	fee-see-*ka*	*of course, naturally*
Γράφω φάρμακα.	*gra*-fo *fa*-rma-ka	*I prescribe medication.*
Είναι σοβαρό;	*ee*-ne so-va-*ro*	*Is it serious?*
Πρέπει να ξεκουραστείτε.	*pre*-pee na kse-koo-ra-*stee*-te	*You need to rest.*
Περαστικά.	pe-ra-stee-*ka*	*Get well soon.*

Going to the Hospital

If something more serious happens to our health, we may end up at the hospital, or νοσοκομείο (no-so-ko-*mee*-o), and if it requires immediate treatment, we go to the emergency room, or επείγοντα (e-*pee*-go-da). In such a case, an ambulance, or ασθενοφόρο (a-sthe-no-*fo*-ro), will take us to the hospital.

Here's the essential vocabulary for a hospital:

» ιατρός or γιατρός (ee-a-*tros* or ya-*tros*) (*doctor*)

» νοσηλευτής/νοσηλεύτρια (no-see-lef-*tees*/no-see-*lef*-tree-a) (*nurse* [male/female])

» ασθενής (a-sthe-*nees*) (*patient*)

» ιατρική περίθαλψη (ee-a-tree-*kee* pe-*ree*-tha-lpsee) (*medical care*)

» θάλαμος (*tha*-la-mos) (*hospital ward*)

» χειρουργείο (hee-roo-*ryee*-o) (*operating room*)

Every hospital has departments or clinics specializing in different medical cases. Here are some key ones:

>> **παιδιατρική κλινική** (pe-dee-a-tree-*kee* klee-nee-*kee*) (*pediatrics department*)

>> **παθολογικό τμήμα** (pa-tho-lo-yee-*ko* tmee-ma) (*internal medicine department*)

>> **ορθοπεδική κλινική** (o-rtho-pe-dee-*kee* klee-nee-*kee*) (*orthopedics department*)

>> **ακτινολογικό τμήμα** (a-ktee-no-lo-yee-*ko* tmee-ma) (*radiology*)

>> **μονάδα εντατικής θεραπείας (ΜΕΘ)** (mo-*na*-da e-da-tee-*kees* the-ra-*pee*-as) (*intensive care unit [ICU]*)

When we are admitted to the hospital, we call it **εισαγωγή στο νοσοκομείο** (ee-sa-go-*yee* sto no-so-ko-*mee*-o) (*hospital admission*), and when we recover and leave, we receive a hospital discharge, or **εξιτήριο από το νοσοκομείο** (e-ksee-*tee*-ree-o a-*po* to no-so-ko-*mee*-o).

While in the hospital, we may have to undergo these treatments:

>> **χειρουργική επέμβαση** (hee-roo-ryee-*kee* e-*pe*-mva-see) (*surgical procedure*)

>> **αιματολογικές εξετάσεις** (e-ma-to-lo-yee-*kes* e-kse-*ta*-sees) (*blood tests*)

>> **ακτινογραφία** (a-ktee-no-gra-*fee*-a) (*x-ray*)

Eating Healthy

From a young age, even in elementary school, we learn about the importance of a healthy diet, or **υγιεινή διατροφή** (ee-yee-ee-*nee* dee-a-tro-*fee*), meaning a diet that provides all the **θρεπτικά συστατικά** (thre-ptee-*ka* see-sta-tee-*ka*) (*nutrients*) our body needs. To maintain a balanced diet, or **ισορροπημένη διατροφή** (ee-so-ro-pee-*me*-nee dee-a-tro-*fee*), we must eat healthy foods.

So, what foods does someone who eats healthily prefer?

>> **φρέσκα φρούτα και λαχανικά** (*fre*-ska *froo*-ta ke la-kha-nee-*ka*) (*fresh fruits and vegetables*)

>> **δημητριακά** (dee-mee-tree-a-*ka*) (*whole grains*)

>> **πρωτεῖνη** (pro-te-*ee*-nee) (*lean protein*)

>> **φυτικές ίνες** (fee-tee-*kes* ee-nes) (*foods rich in fiber*)

CULTURAL WISDOM

In Greece, packaged fruits and vegetables aren't very popular. At the local market stalls, fruits are displayed openly, and customers can touch them, squeeze them, and choose which ones to put in their bags.

If you want to say that you eat healthily, you can say:

Τρώω υγιεινά. (*tro*-o ee-yee-ee-*na*) (*I eat healthy.*)

Another important healthy habit is drinking plenty of water:

Πίνω πολύ νερό. (*pee*-no po-*lee ne*-ro) (*I drink a lot of water.*)

Additionally, you may want to use these phrases:

Αποφεύγω τα επεξεργασμένα τρόφιμα. (a-po-*fev*-go ta e-pe-kse-rga-*sme*-na tro-fee-ma) (*I avoid processed foods.*)

Μειώνω τη ζάχαρη. (mee-o-no tee *za*-kha-ree) (*I limit sugar.*)

Τρώω μικρά και συχνά γεύματα. (*tro*-o mee-*kra* ke see-*khna gev*-ma-ta) (*I eat small and frequent portions.*)

Αποφεύγω τα λιπαρά. (a-po-*fev*-go ta lee-pa-*ra*) (*I avoid fats.*)

Many times, if we struggle to organize our healthy habits ourselves, it's a good idea to visit a διατροφολόγος (dee–a–tro–fo–*lo*–gos) (*nutritionist*) who can create a διατροφή (dee–a–tro–*fee*) (*meal plan*) tailored to our body's needs.

··············· Talkin' the Talk ···············

PLAY THIS

Elli and Nikos talk about healthy eating when they run into each other at a café for lunch. (Track 15)

Elli: Γεια σου, Νίκο! Τι θα φας για μεσημεριανό σήμερα;
ya soo, *nee*-ko! tee tha fas ya me-see-me-rya-*no see*-me-ra;
Hi, Nikos! What are you having for lunch today?

Nikos: Γεια σου, Έλλη! Θα φάω μια σαλάτα με κοτόπουλο και αβοκάντο. Προσπαθώ να τρώω υγιεινά.
ya soo, *e*-lee! tha *fa*-o mya sa-*la*-ta me ko-*to*-poo-lo ke a-vo-*ka*-do. pro-spa-*tho* na *tro*-o ee-yee-ee-*na*.
Hi, Elli! I'm having a salad with chicken and avocado. I'm trying to eat healthily.

Elli:	Τέλεια! Κι εγώ προσπαθώ να τρώω περισσότερα φρέσκα φρούτα και λαχανικά.
	te-lee-a! kee e-*go* pro-spa-*tho* na *tro*-o pe-ree-*so*-te-ra *fre*-ska *froo*-ta ke la-kha-nee-*ka*.
	Great! I'm also trying to eat more fresh fruits and vegetables.
Nikos:	Τα φρούτα και τα λαχανικά έχουν πολλές βιταμίνες. Επίσης, πίνω πολύ νερό κάθε μέρα.
	ta *froo*-ta ke ta la-kha-nee-*ka* e-khoon po-*les* vee-ta-*mee*-nes. e-*pee*-sees, *pee*-no po-*lee* ne-*ro* ka-the me-ra.
	Fruits and vegetables have lots of vitamins. I also drink plenty of water every day.
Elli:	Εγώ προσπαθώ να αποφεύγω τη ζάχαρη και τα επεξεργασμένα τρόφιμα.
	e-*go* pro-spa-*tho* na a-po-*fev*-go tee *za*-kha-ree ke ta e-pe-kse-rga-*sme*-na *tro*-fee-ma.
	I try to avoid sugar and processed foods.
Nikos:	Κι εγώ!
	kee e-*go*!
	Me too!
Elli:	Πολύ ωραία! Η υγιεινή διατροφή είναι σημαντική για την ευεξία μας.
	po-*lee* o-*re*-a! ee ee-yee-ee-*nee* dee-a-tro-*fee* *ee*-ne see-ma-dee-*kee* ya teen ev-e-*ksee*-a mas.
	Awesome! A healthy diet is important for our well-being.

• •

WORDS TO KNOW

μεσημεριανό	me-see-me-rya-*no*	*lunch*
προσπαθώ	pro-spa-*tho*	*I try, I attempt*
βιταμίνη	vee-ta-*mee*-nee	*vitamin*
κάθε μέρα	*ka*-the me-ra	*every day*
η υγιεινή διατροφή	ee ee-gee-ee-*nee* dee-a-tro-*fee*	*a healthy diet*
ευεξία	ev-e-*ksee*-a	*well-being*

Fitting in Exercise

Apart from diet, η σωματική άσκηση (ee so-ma-tee-*kee* a-skee-see) (*physical exercise*) plays a crucial role in our health. It helps us achieve ευεξία (ev-e-*ksee*-a) (*well-being*) and maintain καλή φυσική κατάσταση (ka-*lee* fee-see-*kee* ka-*ta*-sta-see) (*good physical condition*).

Let's look at some vocabulary related to exercising:

>> άσκηση (*a*-skee-see) (*exercise*)

>> γυμναστική (yee-mna-stee-*kee*) (*workout*)

>> προπόνηση (pro-*po*-nee-see) (*training*)

>> ενδυνάμωση (en-dee-*na*-mo-see) (*strengthening*)

If you exercise every day, you can say:

Κάνω γυμναστική κάθε μέρα. (*ka*-no yee-mna-stee-*kee* ka-the *me*-ra) (*I work out every day.*)

Τρέχω στο πάρκο κάθε πρωί. (*Tre*-kho sto *pa*-rko *ka*-the pro-ee) (*I run in the park every morning.*)

Προσπαθώ να βελτιώσω την αντοχή μου. (Pro-spa-*tho* na ve-ltee-*o*-so teen a-do-*hee* moo) (*I'm trying to improve my endurance.*)

You can exercise alone or with a προπονητής (pro-po-nee-*tees*) (*personal trainer, coach*). You can train in different ways, either by yourself at a γυμναστήριο (yee-mna-*stee*-ree-o) (*gym*), or by doing an άθλημα (*a*-thlee-ma) (*sport*).

Want to learn how to say some basic sports in Greek?

>> ποδόσφαιρο (po-*do*-sfe-ro) (*football, soccer*)

>> μπάσκετ (*ba*-sket) (*basketball*)

>> τένις (*te*-nees) (*tennis*)

>> βόλεϊ (*vo*-le-ee) (*volleyball*)

>> στίβος (*stee*-vos) (*track and field*)

>> κολύμβηση (ko-*lee*-mve-see) (*swimming*)

>> ποδηλασία (po-dee-la-*see*-a) (*cycling*)

>> πυγμαχία (pee-gma-*hee*-a) (*boxing*)

>> χειμερινά σπορ (hee-me-ree-*na* spor) (*winter sports*)

Talkin' the Talk

Irini and Niki talk about exercising when they see each other at the gym.

Irini: Πώς πάει η γυμναστική;
pos *pa*-ee ee yee-mna-stee-*kee;*
How's your workout going?

Niki: Τα πάω καλά! Προσπαθώ να γυμνάζομαι τουλάχιστον τρεις φορές την εβδομάδα.
ta *pa*-o ka-*la!* pro-spa-*tho* na yee-*mna*-zo-me too-*la*-hee-ston trees fo-*res* teen ev-do-*ma*-da.
I'm doing well! I try to exercise at least three times a week.

Irini: Μπράβο! Εγώ προσπαθώ να τρέχω κάθε πρωί, αλλά μερικές φορές νιώθω κουρασμένη.
bra-vo! e-*go* pro-spa-*tho* na *tre*-kho *ka*-the pro-*ee,* a-*la* me-ree-*kes* fo-*res* *nyo*-tho koo-ra-*sme*-nee.
Good job! I try to run every morning, but sometimes I feel tired.

Niki: Το καταλαβαίνω.
to ka-ta-la-*ve*-no.
I understand.

Irini: Τι άσκηση κάνεις συνήθως;
tee *a*-skee-see *ka*-nees see-*nee*-thos;
What kind of exercises do you usually do?

Niki: Μου αρέσουν πολύ οι αερόβιες ασκήσεις, όπως το τρέξιμο και το σχοινάκι. Επίσης, κάνω διατάσεις για ευελιξία.
moo a-*re*-soon po-*lee* ee a-e-*ro*-vee-es a-*skee*-sees, o-pos to *tre*-ksee-mo ke to skhee-*na*-kee. e-*pee*-sees, *ka*-no dee-a-*ta*-sees ya ev-e-lee-*ksee*-a.
I really like aerobic exercises like running and jump rope. I also do stretching for flexibility.

Irini: Κάνεις καθόλου ενδυνάμωση;
ka-nees ka-*tho*-loo en-dee-*na*-mo-see;
Do you do any strength training?

Niki: Όχι. Πριν έξη μήνες πήγαινα σε ένα γυμναστήριο και έκανα βάρη. Τώρα θα μου άρεσε να ξεκινήσω ένα ομαδικό άθλημα.
o-hee. preen *e*-ksee *mee*-nes *pee*-ye-na se *e*-na yee-mna-*stee*-ree-o ke *e*-ka-na *va*-ree. *to*-ra tha moo *a*-re-se na kse-kee-*nee*-so *e*-na o-ma-dee-*ko* *a*-thlee-ma.
No. Six months ago, I used to go to the gym and lift weights. Now, I'd like to start a team sport.

(continued)

(continued)

Irini:	**Τι άθλημα;**	
	tee *a*-thlee-ma;	
	What sport?	
Niki:	**Μου αρέσει το μπάσκετ.**	
	moo a-*re*-see to *ba*-sket.	
	I like basketball.	
Irini:	**Καλή ιδέα!**	
	ka-*lee* ee-*de*-a!	
	Good idea!	

WORDS TO KNOW

γυμναστική	gee-mna-stee-*kee*	*workout*
Τα πάω καλά.	ta *pa*-o ka-*la*	*I do well, I get along well.*
τουλάχιστον	too-*la*-hee-ston	*at least*
μερικές φορές	me-ree-*kes* fo-*res*	*sometimes*
συνήθως	see-*nee*-thos	*usually*
αερόβιες ασκήσεις	a-e-*ro*-vee-es a-*skee*-sees	*aerobic exercises*
το τρέξιμο	to *tre*-ksee-mo	*running*
το σχοινάκι	to skhee-*na*-kee	*jumping rope*
η διάταση	ee dee-*a*-ta-see	*stretching*
η ενδυνάμωση	ee e-ndee-*na*-mo-see	*strength training*
τα βάρη	ta *va*-ree	*weights*
ομαδικό άθλημα	o-ma-dee-*ko* *a*-thlee-ma	*team sport*

FUN & GAMES

Match the words with the corresponding part of the body.

» **κεφάλι**

» **στήθος**

» **κοιλιά**

» **παλάμη**

» **μπούτι**

» **γόνατο**

» **πατούσα**

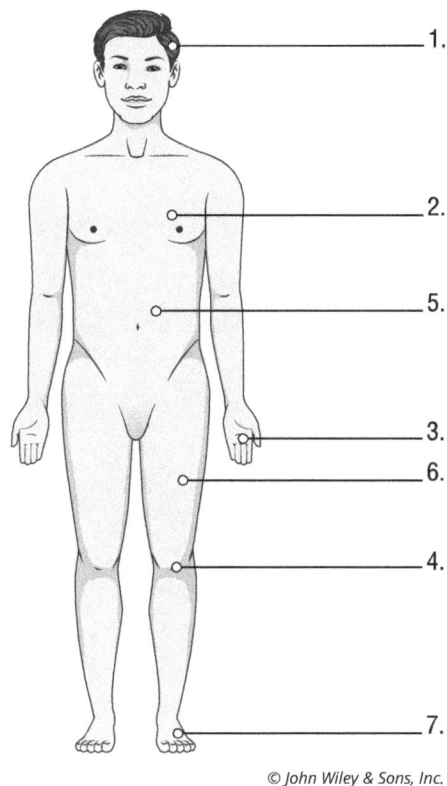

1.

2.

5.

3.

6.

4.

7.

© *John Wiley & Sons, Inc.*

Chapter **12**

Let's Talk About Business

Suppose you've decided to look for a job at a Greek company. Even though your colleagues speak English, and you can have conversations with them, you would surely impress them if you could throw in a few Greek words here and there. In this chapter, I look at relevant business vocabulary.

Working in an Office

The word for "office" in Greek is γραφείο (gra-*fee*-o), while εταιρεία (e-te-*ree*-a) means "company." Here are some essential concepts related to work and employment in a company:

» επιχείρηση (e-pee-*hee*-ree-see) (*business*)

» διοίκηση (dee-*ee*-kee-see) (*management*)

» οργανισμός (o-rga-nee-*smos*) (*organization*)

» τμήμα (*tmee*-ma) (*department*)

Here are some items you see in an office:

» γραφείο (gra-*fee*-o) (*office, desk*)

» καρέκλα γραφείου (ka-*re*-kla gra-*fee*-oo) (*office chair*)

>> υπολογιστής (ee-po-lo-gee-*stees*) (*computer*)

>> εκτυπωτής (e-ktee-po-*tees*) (*printer*)

>> τηλέφωνο (tee-*le*-fo-no) (*telephone*)

>> αρχεία (a-rhee-a) (*files, documents*)

>> κινητό τηλέφωνο (kee-nee-*to* tee-*le*-fo-no) (*mobile phone*)

And here are some helpful verbs, phrases, and sentences to know:

Εργάζομαι. (e-*rga*-zo-me) (*I work.*)

Δουλεύω. (doo-*lev*-o) (*I work.*)

Επικοινωνώ. (e-pee-kee-no-*no*) (*I communicate.*)

Συνεργάζομαι. (see-ne-*rga*-zo-me) (*I collaborate.*)

Δουλεύω σε ένα γραφείο. (doo-*lev*-o se e-na gra-*fee*-o) (*I work in an office.*)

Έχω πολλή δουλειά σήμερα. (e-kho po-*lee* doo-*lya* see-me-ra) (*I have a lot of work today.*)

Μου στέλνετε το αρχείο; (moo ste-lne-te to a-*rhee*-o) (*Can you send me the file?*)

Πού είναι το γραφείο του διευθυντή; (poo ee-ne to gra-*fee*-o too dee-ef-thee-*dee*) (*Where is the manager's office?*)

Κάθε μέρα κάνουμε μίτινγκ. (*ka*-the *me*-ra *ka*-noo-me *mee*-teeng) (*Every day, we have a meeting.*)

GRAMMATICALLY
SPEAKING

The word for "meeting" (μίτινγκ) isn't Greek, but in corporate terminology, many foreign words are used, like "manager" (μάνατζερ) and "deadline" (ντεντλάιν). This is due to globalization, in which English functions as the lingua franca, meaning the universal language of corporate terminology.

Talking About Colleagues

Anyone who works in an office as an employee is called an υπάλληλος (ee–*pa*–lee–los). All employees in a company are colleagues; a colleague in Greek is a συνάδελφος (see–*na*-de–lfos).

Different roles and hierarchy levels are within a company. Some key roles are as follows:

- δ διευθυντής/διευθύντρια (dee-ef-thee-*dees*/dee-ef-*thee*-dree-a) (*manager, director*) (*male/female*)

- δ ιδρυτής/ιδρύτρια (ee-dree-*tees*/ee-*dree*-tree-a) (*founder*) (*male/female*)

- δ επενδυτής/επενδύτρια (e-pe-ndee-*tees*/e-pe-*ndee*-tree-a) (*investor*) (*male/female*)

- δ νομικός σύμβουλος (no-mee-*kos* see-mvoo-los) (*legal advisor*)

- δ γραμματέας (gra-ma-*te*-as) (*secretary*)

Discussing Responsibilities

Every employee in a company has a role that fulfills specific needs. Everyone works with the goal of making the business function like a well-tuned clock.

Here are some fundamental words related to corporate tasks:

- δ εργασία (e-rga-*see*-a) (*work*)

- δ συνάντηση (see-*na*-dee-see) (*meeting*)

- δ ημερολόγιο (ee-me-ro-*lo*-yee-o) (*calendar*)

- δ πρόγραμμα (*pro*-gra-ma) (*schedule*)

- δ διορία (dee-o-*ree*-a) (*deadline*)

- δ υπευθυνότητα (ee-pef-thee-*no*-tee-ta) (*responsibility*)

- δ λήψη αποφάσεων (*lee*-psee a-po-*fa*-se-on) (*decision-making*)

Each department of a company has a different role:

- δ έρευνα αγοράς (*e*-rev-na a-go-*ras*) (*market research*)

- δ προώθηση προϊόντων (pro-*o*-thee-see pro-ee-o-don) (*product promotion*)

- δ εξυπηρέτηση πελατών (e-ksee-pee-*re*-tee-see pe-la-*ton*) (*customer service*)

- δ οικονομικός έλεγχος (ee-ko-no-mee-*kos* e-le-nkhos) (*financial control*)

- δ ανάλυση δεδομένων (a-*na*-lee-see de-do-*me*-non) (*data analysis*)

Of course, the list of work-related terms is vast, but I focus on some basic ones in this section.

Talkin' the Talk

It's time for a morning meeting in a company. Niko and Elias are employees who are speaking with their manager, Dimitris.

Dimitris: Ας ξεκινήσουμε. Ευχαριστώ που ήρθατε. Πώς πάει το καινούργιο πρότζεκτ, Νίκο;

as kse-kee-*nee*-soo-me. ef-kha-ree-*sto* poo *ee*-rtha-te. pos *pa*-ee to ke-*noo*-ryo *pro*-tzekt, *nee*-ko;

Let's start. Thanks for coming. How is the new project going, Niko?

Niko: Έχουμε πρόοδο. Μίλησα με τους πελάτες και είναι χαρούμενοι. Χρειάζεται όμως βελτίωση στο σύστημα.

e-khoo-me *pro*-o-do. *mee*-lee-sa me toos pe-*la*-tes ke *ee*-ne kha-*roo*-me-nee. hree-*a*-ze-te *o*-mos ve-*ltee*-o-see sto *see*-stee-ma.

We have progress. I spoke with the customers, and they are happy. But the system needs improvement.

Dimitris: Εντάξει, Νίκο. Ηλία, μπορείς να βοηθήσεις τον Νίκο με το σύστημα;

e-*da*-ksee, *nee*-ko. ee-*lee*-a, bo-*rees* na vo-ee-*thee*-sees ton *nee*-ko me to *see*-stee-ma;

Okay, Niko. Elias, can you help Niko with the system?

Elias: Μάλιστα.

ma-lee-sta.

Yes.

Dimitris: Ωραία, προχωράμε! Πότε είναι η προθεσμία;

o-*re*-a, pro-kho-*ra*-me! *po*-te *ee*-ne ee pro-the-*smee*-a;

Great, let's move forward! When is the deadline?

Elias: Σε δύο μήνες.

se *dee*-o *mee*-nes.

In two months.

Dimitris: Εντάξει, έχετε χρόνο. Καλή δουλειά, ομάδα! Ευχαριστώ για τον χρόνο σας.

e-*da*-ksee, *e*-he-te *khro*-no. ka-*lee* doo-lee-*a*, o-*ma*-da! ef-kha-ree-*sto* ya ton *khro*-no sas.

Okay, you have time. Good job, team! Thanks for your time.

WORDS TO KNOW

Ξεκινάω	kse-kee-*na*-o	*I start.*
καινούργιο	ke-*noo*-ryo	*new (neutral)*
πρόοδος	*pro*-o-dos	*progress*
πελάτης	pe-*la*-tees	*customer*
σύστημα	*see*-stee-ma	*system*
μάλιστα	*ma*-lee-sta	*indeed, yes*
Προχωράω	pro-kho-*ra*-o	*I move forward.*
προθεσμία	pro-the-*smee*-a	*deadline*
η ομάδα	ee o-*ma*-da	*the team*
Ευχαριστώ για τον χρόνο σας.	ef-ha-ree-*sto* ya ton *khro*-no sas	*Thank you for your time.*

Going for an Interview

The job market today is challenging, and to secure a position, you must prove that you're the right fit through a series of interviews. When you attend an interview, you are an υποψήφιος (ee-po-*psee*-fee-os) (*candidate for the position*). The Greek word for "interview" is συνέντευξη (see-*ne*-def-ksee).

You can say this when you're interviewing for a job:

Δίνω συνέντευξη. (*dee*-no see-*ne*-def-ksee) (*I am giving an interview.*)

Έχω συνέντευξη. (*e*-kho see-*ne*-def-ksee) (*I have an interview.*)

While the employer says this:

Παίρνω συνέντευξη. (*pe*-rno see-*ne*-def-ksee) (*I am conducting an interview.*)

When looking for a job, you send your βιογραφικό σημείωμα (vee-o-gra-fee-*ko* see-*mee*-o-ma) (*résumé, CV*). In it, you include these items:

>> δεξιότητες (de-ksee-*o*-tee-tes) (*skills*)

>> προσόντα (pro-*so*-da) (*qualifications*)

>> προϋπηρεσία (pro-ee-pee-re-*see*-a) (*work experience*)

If the company finds you suitable, they will offer you a συμβόλαιο (see-*mvo*-le-o) (*contract*). The person or organization offering the job is the εργοδότης (e-rgo-*do*-tees) (*employer*).

Here are some classic interview questions:

Μπορείτε να μας πείτε λίγα λόγια για τον εαυτό σας; (bo-*ree*-te na mas *pee*-te *lee*-ga *lo*-ya ya ton e-a-*fto* sas) (*Can you tell us a little about yourself?*)

Γιατί θέλετε να εργαστείτε στην εταιρεία μας; (ya-*tee the*-le-te na e-rga-*stee*-te steen e-te-*ree*-a mas) (*Why do you want to work at our company?*)

Ποιες είναι οι δυνατότητες και οι αδυναμίες σας; (pyes *ee*-ne ee dee-na-*to*-tee-tes ke ee a-dee-na-*mee*-es sas) (*What are your strengths and weaknesses?*)

Πού βλέπετε τον εαυτό σας σε πέντε χρόνια; (Poo *vle*-pe-te ton e-af-*to* sas se *pe*-nde *khro*-nya) (*Where do you see yourself in five years?*)

Some answers you can offer include the following:

Θέλω να εργαστώ στην εταιρία σας γιατί . . . (*the*-lo na e-rga-*sto* steen e-te-*ree*-a sas ya-*tee*) (*I would like to work at your company because . . .*)

Είμαι καλός/καλή σε . . . (*ee*-me ka-*los*/ka-*lee* se) (*I am good at . . .*)

Έχω εμπειρία σε . . . (*e*-kho e-bee-*ree*-a se) (*I have experience in . . .*)

Talkin' the Talk

PLAY THIS

Victoria goes to an interview for a position she really wants. She speaks with the interviewer, Evangelos. (Track 16)

Evangelos: Καλημέρα. Ευχαριστώ που ήρθες σήμερα.
ka-lee-*me*-ra. ef-kha-ree-*sto* poo *ee*-rthes *see*-me-ra.
Good morning. Thank you for coming today.

Victoria:	Καλημέρα σας! Εγώ ευχαριστώ.
	ka-lee-*me*-ra sas! e-*go* ef-kha-re-*sto*.
	Good morning! Thank you.
Evangelos:	Μπορείς να μας πεις λίγα λόγια για τον εαυτό σου;
	bo-*rees* na mas pees *lee*-ga *lo*-ya ya ton e-af-*to* soo;
	Can you tell us a little about yourself?
Victoria:	Βεβαίως! Σπούδασα οικονομικά και εργάστηκα για πέντε χρόνια σε ένα μεγάλο λογιστικό γραφείο στον Πειραιά.
	ve-*ve*-os! *spoo*-da-sa ee-ko-no-mee-*ka* ke e-*rga*-stee-ka ya *pe*-nde *khro*-nya se *e*-na me-*ga*-lo lo-yee-stee-*ko* gra-*fee*-o ston pee-re-*a*.
	Certainly! I studied economics and worked for five years in a large accounting office in Piraeus.
Evangelos:	Γιατί θέλεις να εργαστείς στην εταιρεία μας;
	ya-*tee the*-lees na e-rga-*stees* steen e-te-*ree*-a mas;
	Why do you want to work at our company?
Victoria:	Θαυμάζω την εταιρεία σας για τις καινοτομίες της και θέλω κι εγώ να είμαι μέρος αυτού του έργου.
	thav-*ma*-zo teen e-te-*ree*-a sas ya tees ke-no-to-*mee*-es tees ke *the*-lo kee e-*go* na *ee*-me *me*-ros af-*too* too e-*rgoo*.
	I admire your company for its innovations, and I want to be part of this vision.
Evangelos:	Ευχαριστώ. Θα επικοινωνήσουμε σύντομα μαζί σου.
	ef-kha-ree-*sto*. tha e-pee-kee-no-*nee*-soo-me *see*-do-ma ma-*zee* soo.
	Thank you. We will contact you soon.
Victoria:	Ευχαριστώ πολύ! Ανυπομονώ να συνεργαστούμε.
	ef-kha-ree-*sto* po-*lee*! a-nee-po-mo-*no* na see-ne-rga-*stoo*-me.
	Thank you very much! I look forward to working together.

WORDS TO KNOW

ο εαυτός	o e-af-*tos*	*self*
οικονομικά	ee-ko-no-mee-*ka*	*economics*
λογιστικό γραφείο	lo-yee-stee-*ko* gra-*fee*-o	*accounting office*

εταιρεία	e-te-*ree*-a	*company*
θαυμάζω	thav-*ma*-zo	*I admire*
καινοτομία	ke-no-to-*mee*-a	*innovation*
Θα επικοινωνήσουμε σύντομα μαζί σου.	tha e-pee-kee-no-*nee*-soo-me *see*-do-ma ma-*zee* soo.	*We will contact you soon.*
ανυπομονώ	a-nee-po-mo-*no*	*I look forward to*

FUN & GAMES

Can you match the words with the objects you see in the figure?

>> τηλέφωνο

>> εκτυπωτής

>> γραφείο

>> αρχεία

>> υπολογιστής

>> καρέκλα γραφείου

3._____

6._____

2._____

4._____

5._____

1._____

3

Greek on the Go

IN THIS PART . . .

Plan a trip to Greece.

Travel around Greece via plane, train, taxi, and more.

Enjoy Greek art and cultural sights.

Discover beautiful Greek traditions.

Chapter **13**
Planning a Trip

Y ou're sitting at your desk; it's raining outside; you have 30 unread emails; and the phone won't stop ringing. And suddenly, you start dreaming that you're lying on the beach, the sea splashing at your feet, and your kids are swimming and playing happily . . . wait a moment! Maybe it's time to book your tickets for a vacation in Greece? Probably so . . . especially now that you have this book and know basic Greek! In this chapter, I look at some vocabulary related to travel.

A Tourist's Dream: Traveling to Greece

Greece has been a beloved tourist destination for many years, and rightly so. It's a country full of charm. It has an incredible history, strong religious significance, dreamlike beaches, picturesque villages and islands, majestic mountains, and a mild climate. Tourism is one of the main pillars of the Greek economy, and the services offered are of a high standard.

CULTURAL WISDOM

Greeks have a tradition of hospitality dating back to ancient times. In fact, one of Zeus's titles was "Xenios," meaning protector of strangers and hospitality. The Greek word for hospitality is φιλοξενία (fee-lo-kse-*nee*-a), which comes from two words: φίλος (*fee*-los) (*friend*) and ξένος (*kse*-nos) (*stranger*), and it means the friendly and welcoming behavior toward foreigners.

So, here are some words related to tourism in Greece:

>> **το νησί** (to nee-*see*) (*the island*)

>> **το βουνό** (to voo-*no*) (*the mountain*)

>> **το χωριό** (to kho-*ryo*) (*the village*)

>> **η πόλη** (ee *po*-lee) (*the city*)

>> **η παραλία** (ee pa-ra-*lee*-a) (*the beach*)

>> **το κοσμοπολίτικο μέρος** (to ko-smo-po-*lee*-tee-ko *me*-ros) (*the cosmopolitan place*)

>> **το εξωτερικό** (to e-kso-te-ree-*ko*) (*abroad*)

>> **ο τουρίστας** (o too-*ree*-stas) (*the tourist*)

>> **ο ντόπιος** (o *do*-pyos) (*the local*)

>> **ο προορισμός** (o pro-o-ree-*smos*) (*the destination*)

>> **οι διακοπές** (ee dya-ko-*pes*) (*the vacation*)

Some useful sentences include the following:

Ταξιδεύω στο εξωτερικό. (ta-ksee-*dev*-o sto e-kso-te-ree-*ko*) (*I travel abroad.*)

Προγραμματίζω ένα ταξίδι. (pro-gra-ma-*tee*-zo *e*-na ta-*ksee*-dee) (*I am planning a trip.*)

Preparing for Your Trip

Once you decide to take a trip to Greece, it's time to prepare.

If you want to travel abroad, you need **το διαβατήριο** (to dya-va-*tee*-ree-o) (*the passport*) and sometimes a **βίζα** (*vee*-za) (*visa*).

You can choose to organize your trip yourself or through a travel agency, or **το ταξιδιωτικό γραφείο** (to ta-ksee-dyo-tee-*ko* gra-*fee*-o). You may also want to hire a tour guide, or **ξεναγός** (kse-na-*gos*).

Of course, many people prefer to travel completely alone, having a map, or **χάρτης** (*kha*-rtees), and a **τουριστικός οδηγός** (too-ree-stee-*kos* o-dee-*gos*) (*tourist guide*).

Essential items for traveling include the following:

>> η βαλίτσα (ee va-*lee*-tsa) (*the suitcase*)

>> το αεροπορικό εισιτήριο (to a-e-ro-po-ree-*ko* ee-see-*tee*-ree-o) (*the plane ticket*)

>> η φωτογραφική μηχανή (ee fo-to-gra-fee-*kee* mee-kha-*nee*) (*the camera*)

When you're packing, you may say Ετοιμάζω τη βαλίτσα μου (e-tee-*ma*-zo tee va-*lee*-tsa moo) (*I am packing my suitcase*). Depending on where you're going, you'll pack different things. If you're heading to the mountains, you need παπούτσια πεζοπορίας (pa-*poo*-tsya pe-zo-po-*ree*-as) (*hiking shoes*), whereas if you're going to the sea, you'll pack a μαγιό (ma-*yo*) (*swimsuit*). Find Greek words for different types of clothing in Chapter 9.

CULTURAL WISDOM

Greece may be famous for its beaches, but it also has beautiful tall mountains. Actually, 80 percent of Greece is covered by mountains or hilly terrain. Many people prefer them for their cool climate and natural beauty. The highest mountain in Greece is ο Όλυμπος (o o-lee-mbos) (*Mount Olympus*). The ancient Greeks believed that their gods lived on Olympus.

Booking Your Accommodations

Before you go to your destination, you think about where you'll stay — you plan your accommodation and arrange all the details. Here are some useful vocabulary words and phrases:

>> η κράτηση (ee *kra*-tee-see) (*the booking*)

>> Κάνω κράτηση. (*ka*-no *kra*-tee-see) (*I am making a reservation.*)

>> η τιμή (ee tee-*mee*) (*the price*)

>> το ξενοδοχείο (to kse-no-do-*hee*-o) (*the hotel*)

>> Κλείνω ξενοδοχείο. (*klee*-no kse-no-do-*hee*-o) (*I am booking a hotel.*)

>> η υποδοχή (ee ee-po-do-*hee*) (*the reception*)

>> το κλειδί (to klee-*dee*) (*the key*)

>> το δωμάτιο (to do-*ma*-tee-o) (*the room*)

Hotel rooms can be any of the following:

>> μονόκλινο (mo-*no*-klee-no) (*single room, with one bed*)

>> δίκλινο (*dee*-klee-no) (*double room, with two beds*)

>> τρίκλινο (*tree*-klee-no) (*triple room*)

>> τετράκλινο (te-*tra*-klee-no) (*quadruple room*)

>> δωμάτιο με θέα (do-*ma*-tee-o me *the*-a) (*room with a view*)

>> ενοικιαζόμενο δωμάτιο (e-nee-kee-a-*zo*-me-no do-*ma*-tee-o) (*rental room*)

Some people prefer adventurous vacations and choose to stay in η κατασκήνωση (ee ka-ta-*skee*-no-see) (*the campsite*), also known as το κάμπινγκ (to *cam*-ping). Others prefer independence and opt for το τροχόσπιτο (to tro-*kho*-spee-to) (*the caravan*).

And in case you need any help from the staff of your hotel, you can say these phrases:

Θα ήθελα να κλείσω ένα δωμάτιο. (tha *ee*-the-la na *klee*-so e-na do-*ma*-tee-o) (*I'd like to book a room.*)

Υπάρχουν διαθέσιμα δωμάτια; (ee-*pa*-rkhoon dya-*the*-see-ma do-*ma*-tee-a) (*Are there available rooms?*)

Τι ώρα είναι το τσεκ-ιν/τσεκ-αουτ; (tee *o*-ra *ee*-ne to tsek-in/tsek-aoot) (*What time is check-in/check-out?*)

Έχω κράτηση στο όνομα . . . (e-kho *kra*-tee-see sto o-no-ma) (*I have a reservation under the name [your name].*)

Υπάρχει δωρεάν **Wi-Fi** στο δωμάτιο; (ee-*pa*-rkhee do-re-*an* Wi-Fi sto do-*ma*-tee-o) (*Is there free Wi-Fi in the room?*)

TIP

The term "Wi-Fi" is spoken and written in English, even in Greece.

Talkin' the Talk

Beatrice wants to book a room in a hotel in Crete. She approaches the receptionist, Emmelia.

Emmelia: Καλησπέρα! Πώς μπορώ να βοηθήσω;
ka-lee-*spe*-ra! pos bo-*ro* na vo-ee-*thee*-so;
Good evening! How can I help you?

Beatrice: Θα ήθελα ένα δωμάτιο για δύο νύχτες.
tha *ee*-the-la e-na do-*ma*-tee-o ya *dee*-o *nee*-khtes.
I would like a room for two nights.

Emmelia: Βεβαίως! Θέλετε μονόκλινο ή δίκλινο δωμάτιο;
ve-*ve*-os! *the*-le-te mo-*no*-klee-no ee *dee*-klee-no
do-*ma*-tee-o;
Of course! Would you like a single or a double room?

Beatrice: Δίκλινο, παρακαλώ. Πόσο κοστίζει η διαμονή ανά βράδυ;
dee-klee-no, pa-ra-ka-*lo*. *po*-so ko-*stee*-zee ee dya-mo-*nee*
a-*na vra*-dee;
*A double room, please. How much does the stay cost
per night?*

Emmelia: Η τιμή είναι ογδόντα ευρώ τη βραδιά με πρωινό.
ee tee-*mee* ee-ne o-*gdo*-nda ev-*ro* tee vra-*dya* me
pro-ee-*no*.
The price is 80 euros per night and includes breakfast.

Beatrice: Έχετε δωμάτια με θέα στη θάλασσα;
e-he-te do-*ma*-tee-a me *the*-a stee *tha*-la-sa;
Are there rooms with a sea view?

Emmelia: Ναι, έχουμε ένα δωμάτιο με θέα. Να το κλείσω για εσάς;
ne, *e*-khoo-me *e*-na do-*ma*-tee-o me *the*-a. na to *klee*-so
ya e-*sas*;
*Yes, there is an available room with a view. Shall I book it
for you?*

Beatrice: Ναι, παρακαλώ!
ne, pa-ra-ka-*lo*!
Yes, please!

Emmelia: Χρειάζομαι το όνομά σας για την κράτηση.
hree-*a*-zo-me to *o*-no-*ma* sas ya teen *kra*-tee-see.
I need your name for the reservation.

Beatrice: Το όνομά μου είναι Βεατρίκη Μαύρου.
to *o*-no-*ma* moo *ee*-ne ve-a-*tree*-kee *mav*-roo.
My name is Beatrice Mavrou.

Emmelia: Η κράτησή σας επιβεβαιώθηκε. Καλή διαμονή!
ee *kra*-tee-*see* sas e-pee-ve-ve-*o*-thee-ke. ka-*lee* dya-
mo-*nee*!
Your reservation has been confirmed. Enjoy your stay!

WORDS TO KNOW

δωμάτιο	do-*ma*-tee-o	*room*
βεβαίως	ve-*ve*-os	*of course*
μονόκλινο	mo-*no*-klee-no	*single room*
δίκλινο	*dee*-klee-no	*double room*
ανά βράδυ	a-*na vra*-dee	*per night*
πρωινό	pro-ee-*no*	*breakfast*
με θέα	me *the*-a	*with a view*
κράτηση	*kra*-tee-see	*reservation*
Καλή διαμονή!	ka-*lee* dya-mo-*nee*	*Enjoy your stay!*

Speaking with Locals

Καλώς ήρθατε! (ka-*los ee*-rtha-te) (*Welcome!*)

The locals will probably say this to you when you arrive at your destination. Then you can respond like so: **Καλώς σας βρήκαμε** (ka-*los* sas *vree*-ka-me), which means "Nice to meet you."

Greeks love helping visitors. You can ask for whatever you need:

> **Μπορείτε να μας προτείνετε ένα εστιατόριο;** (bo-*ree*-te na mas pro-*tee*-ne-te *e*-na e-stee-a-*to*-ree-o) (*Can you recommend a restaurant?*)

> **Πού είναι το κέντρο;** (poo *ee*-ne to *ke*-dro) (*Where is the city center?*)

> **Πού είναι το μουσείο;** (poo *ee*-ne to moo-*see*-o) (*Where is the museum?*)

> **Μπορείτε να με βοηθήσετε;** (bo-*ree*-te na me vo-ee-*thee*-se-te) (*Can you help me?*)

It's very likely that you'll be asked this: **Από πού είστε;** (a-*po* poo *ee*-ste) (*Where are you from?*)

REMEMBER

To answer this question, you use what you read in Chapter 5: **Είμαι από τον/την/το [χώρα].** (*Ee*-me a-*po* ton/teen/to [country]) (*I am from [country].*) The article τον/την/το depends on the gender of the country.

Using Money in Greece

Money is essential when traveling. Not only do you need the local currency, but you also spend quite a bit.

Greece's currency is το ευρώ (to ev-ro) (*the euro*). Other currencies, used in other countries, include το δολάριο (to do-*la*-ree-o) (*the dollar*), η κορόνα (ee ko-*ro*-na) (*the koruna*), το δηνάριο (to dee-*na*-ryo) (*the dinar*), η λίρα (ee *lee*-ra) (*the pound*), and το φράγκο (to *fra*-go) (*the franc*). Anyone visiting Greece with one of these currencies must exchange their money.

Here are some words related to money:

- ▶ χρήματα (*khree*-ma-ta) (*money*)
- ▶ μετρητά (me-tree-*ta*) (*cash*)
- ▶ νόμισμα (*no*-mee-sma) (*currency, coin*)
- ▶ χαρτονόμισμα (kha-rto-*no*-mee-sma) (*banknote*)
- ▶ πορτοφόλι (po-rto-*fo*-lee) (*wallet*)
- ▶ συναλλαγή (see-na-la-*yee*) (*transaction*)
- ▶ ανταλλάσσω (a-da-*la*-so) (*exchange*)

To exchange currency when traveling, you can go to the τράπεζα (*tra*-pe-za) (*bank*). Of course, if you're uncertain, you can ask a local: Πού μπορώ να αγοράσω συνάλλαγμα; (poo bo-*ro* na a-go-*ra*-so see-*na*-la-gma) (*Where can I exchange currency?*)

If you want to go shopping as a tourist in Greece, these phrases will be useful (see Chapter 9 for more details):

Πόσο κοστίζει; (*po*-so ko-*stee*-zee) (*How much does it cost?*)

Είναι ακριβό! (*ee*-ne a-kree-*vo*) (*It's expensive!*)

Είναι φθηνό. (*ee*-ne fthee-*no*) (*It's cheap.*)

Δέχεστε πιστωτική κάρτα; (*de*-he-ste pee-sto-tee-*kee ka*-rta) (*Do you accept credit cards?*)

Μπορώ να πληρώσω με μετρητά; (bo-*ro* na plee-*ro*-so me me-tree-*ta*) (*Can I pay in cash?*)

Μπορείτε να μου δώσετε απόδειξη; (bo-*ree*-te na moo *do*-se-te a-*po*-dee-ksee) (*Can you give me a receipt?*)

Ποια είναι η ισοτιμία ευρώ-δολαρίου; (pya *ee*-ne ee ee-so-tee-*mee*-a ev-*ro* do-la-*ree*-oo) (*What is the exchange rate for euros to dollars?*)

Μπορείτε να μου κάνετε καλύτερη τιμή; (bo-*ree*-te na moo *ka*-ne-te ka-*lee*-te-ree tee-*mee*) (*Can you give me a better price?*)

Έχετε κάποια έκπτωση για τουρίστες; (*e*-he-te *ka*-pya *e*-kpto-see ya too-*ree*-stes) (*Do you have a tourist discount?*)

Something indirectly related to money is το φιλοδώρημα (to fee–lo–*do*–ree–ma) (*the tip*). It's a monetary amount given to the waiter who serves you at a restaurant or café. It is usually about 10 percent of the bill.

In Greece, not leaving a tip is considered very rude toward the waiter.

Talkin' the Talk

PLAY THIS

Charlotte is a tourist in Santorini and goes to a currency exchange to buy euros. She speaks to an employee named Joseph. (Track 17)

Charlotte: Καλημέρα! Θα ήθελα να ανταλλάξω κάποια χρήματα.
ka-lee-*me*-ra! tha *ee*-the-la na a-da-*la*-kso *ka*-pya *khree*-ma-ta.
Good morning! I would like to exchange some money.

Joseph: Καλημέρα σας! Τι ποσό θέλετε να ανταλλάξετε και από ποιο νόμισμα;
ka-lee-*me*-ra sas! tee po-*so the*-le-te na a-da-*la*-kse-te ke a-*po* pyo *no*-mee-sma;
Good morning! What amount would you like to exchange and from which currency?

Charlotte: Έχω πεντακόσια δολάρια Αμερικής και θα ήθελα να τα αλλάξω σε ευρώ.
e-kho pe-nda-*ko*-sya do-*la*-ree-a a-me-ree-*kees* ke tha *ee*-the-la na ta a-*la*-kso se ev-*ro*.
I have 500 U.S. dollars, and I would like to exchange them for euros.

Joseph:	Μάλιστα. Σήμερα η ισοτιμία είναι ένα δολάριο προς μηδέν κόμμα ενενήντα δύο ευρώ. Το σύνολο είναι τετρακόσια εξήντα ευρώ.

ma-lee-sta. *see*-me-ra ee ee-so-tee-*mee*-a *ee*-ne e-na do-*la*-ree-o pros mee-*den ko*-ma e-ne-*nee*-nda *dee*-o ev-*ro*. to *see*-no-lo *ee*-ne te-tra-*ko*-sya e-*ksee*-nda ev-*ro*.
Certainly. Today the exchange rate is 1 dollar to 0.92 euros. The total is 460 euros.

Charlotte: Ευχαριστώ πολύ! Καλή σας μέρα!
ef-kha-ree-*sto* po-*lee*! ka-*lee* sas *me*-ra!
Thank you very much! Have a great day!

Joseph: Ευχαριστούμε. Καλή διαμονή στην Ελλάδα!
ef-kha-ree-*stoo*-me. ka-*lee* dya-mo-*nee* steen e-*la*-da!
Thank you. Have a great stay in Greece!

WORDS TO KNOW

χρήματα	*khree*-ma-ta	*money*
ποσό	po-*so*	*amount*
ανταλλάσσω	a-da-*la*-so	*exchange*
νόμισμα	*no*-mee-sma	*currency*
μάλιστα	*ma*-lee-sta	*certainly*
ισοτιμία	ee-so-tee-*mee*-a	*exchange rate*

FUN & GAMES

In this box there are six words from this chapter's vocabulary. Can you find them?

Δ	Ι	Α	Κ	Ο	Π	Ε	Σ
Α	Θ	Ο	Φ	Ν	Δ	Ν	Β
Κ	Ρ	Α	Τ	Η	Σ	Η	Ο
Β	Π	Ι	Ε	Σ	Γ	Χ	Υ
Ρ	Σ	Κ	Υ	Θ	Μ	Α	Ν
Η	Χ	Ω	Ρ	Ι	Ο	Ε	Ο
Υ	Τ	Γ	Ω	Λ	Ζ	Ψ	Β
Δ	Ι	Α	Μ	Ο	Ν	Η	Ξ

Chapter **14**

Getting Around: Planes, Trains, Taxis, and More

When you travel, you need to use various means of transportation. Planes, trains, cars, taxis . . . In Greece, besides these classic options, ferries are available to take you to the islands. In this chapter, I discuss words and phrases that will help you communicate when using these kinds of transportation.

Flying to Greece

Greek airports are packed every summer with tourists coming to enjoy their vacations. The largest airport in Greece is Eleftherios Venizelos in Athens, but many others are available — not only on the mainland but also on the islands.

So, when you want to take a πτήση (*ptee*-see) (*flight*), you go to the αεροδρόμιο (a-e-ro-*dro*-mee-o) (*airport*) and board the αεροπλάνο (a-e-ro-*pla*-no) (*airplane*).

What vocabulary do you need related to flights?

>> **η αεροπορική εταιρεία** (ee a-e-ro-po-ree-*kee* e-te-*ree*-a) (*the airline*)

>> **το εισιτήριο** (to ee-see-*tee*-ree-o) (*the ticket*)

>> **η επιβίβαση** (ee e-pee-*vee*-va-see) (*the boarding*)

>> **η απογείωση** (ee a-po-*yee*-o-see) (*the takeoff*)

>> **η προσγείωση** (ee pros-*yee*-o-see) (*the landing*)

>> **η πύλη** (ee *pee*-lee) (*the gate*)

>> **οι αναχωρήσεις** (ee a-na-kho-*ree*-sees) (*the departures*)

>> **οι αφίξεις** (ee a-*fee*-ksees) (*the arrivals*)

>> **το τσεκ-ιν** (to tsek-een) (*the check-in*)

>> **η χειραποσκευή** (ee hee-ra-po-skev-*ee*) (*the carry-on luggage*)

>> **η αποσκευή** (ee a-po-skev-*ee*) (*the checked luggage*)

>> **ο έλεγχος ασφαλείας** (o *e*-le-nkhos a-sfa-*lee*-as) (*the security check*)

>> **το διαβατήριό** (to dya-va-*tee*-ree-o) (*the passport*)

>> **ο έλεγχος διαβατηρίων** (o *e*-le-nkhos dya-va-tee-*ree*-on) (*passport control*)

>> **η καθυστέρηση πτήσης** (ee ka-thee-*ste*-ree-see *ptee*-sees) (*the flight delay*)

>> **η ακύρωση πτήσης** (ee a-*kee*-ro-see *ptee*-sees) (*the flight cancellation*)

Other useful phrases at the airport include the following:

Κάνω τσεκ-ιν. (*ka*-no tsek-een) (*I check in.*)

Πού είναι το τσεκ-ιν; (poo *ee*-ne to tsek-een) (*Where is the check-in?*)

Πού είναι η πύλη . . .; (poo *ee*-ne ee *pee*-lee) (*Where is gate [number]?*)

Η πτήση μου έχει καθυστέρηση. (ee *ptee*-see moo *e*-hee ka-thee-*ste*-ree-see) (*My flight is delayed.*)

Πότε αρχίζει η επιβίβαση; (*po*-te a-*rhee*-zee ee e-pee-*vee*-va-see) (*When does boarding start?*)

Θέλω μία θέση δίπλα στο παράθυρο. (*the*-lo *mee*-a *the*-see *dee*-pla sto pa-*ra*-thee-ro) (*I want a window seat.*)

Talkin' the Talk

Anna speaks with an airport staff member, Magdalene, about her flight.

Anna:	**Καλημέρα! Έχω μία πτήση για Παρίσι και θέλω να κάνω τσεκ-ιν.** ka-lee-*me*-ra! *e*-kho *mee*-a *ptee*-see ya pa-*ree*-see ke *the*-lo na *ka*-no tsek-een. *Good morning! I have a flight to Paris, and I would like to check in.*
Magdalene:	**Βεβαίως! Μπορώ να δω το εισιτήριό σας και το διαβατήριό σας, παρακαλώ;** ve-*ve*-os! bo-*ro* na do to ee-see-*tee*-ree-*o* sas ke to dya-va-*tee*-ree-*o* sas, pa-ra-ka-*lo;* *Certainly! May I see your ticket and passport, please?*
Anna:	**Ορίστε!** o-*ree*-ste! *Here you go!*
Magdalene:	**Έχετε αποσκευές για έλεγχο;** *e*-he-te a-po-skev-*es* ya *e*-le-nkho; *Do you have checked luggage?*
Anna:	**Ναι, έχω μία μεγάλη βαλίτσα.** ne, *e*-kho *mee*-a me-*ga*-lee va-*lee*-tsa. *Yes, I have one large suitcase.*
Magdalene:	**Το επιτρεπόμενο βάρος είναι είκοσι τρία κιλά. Η βαλίτσα σας φαίνεται εντάξει.** to e-pee-tre-*po*-me-no *va*-ros *ee*-ne *ee*-ko-see *tree*-a kee-*la*. ee va-*lee*-tsa sas *fe*-ne-te e-*da*-ksee. *The allowed weight is 23 kilograms. Your suitcase looks fine.*
Anna:	**Τέλεια! Ευχαριστώ.** *te*-lee-a! ef-kha-tee-*sto*. *Great! Thank you.*
Magdalene:	**Καλή πτήση!** ka-*lee ptee*-see! *Have a great flight!*

WORDS TO KNOW

πτήση	*ptee*-see	*flight*
Θέλω να κάνω τσεκ-ιν.	*the*-lo na *ka*-no tsek-een	*I would like to check in.*
εισιτήριό	ee-see-*tee*-ree-o	*ticket*
διαβατήριό	dya-va-*tee*-ree-o	*passport*
Ορίστε.	o-*ree*-ste	*Here you go.*
βαλίτσα	va-*lee*-tsa	*suitcase*
το επιτρεπόμενο βάρος	to e-pee-tre-*po*-me-no *va*-ros	*the allowed weight*
Καλή πτήση.	ka-*lee ptee*-see	*Have a great flight.*

Traveling by Train

If you're someone who prefers trains over planes, then this section is for you! Let's say you want to travel from Athens to Thessaloniki by train — here's the most important vocabulary to know:

>> ο σταθμός (o sta-*thmos*) (*the station*)

>> το τρένο (to *tre*-no) (*the train*)

>> η πλατφόρμα (ee pla-*tfo*-rma) (*the platform*)

>> η γραμμή (ee gra-*mee*) (*the track, the line*)

>> το δρομολόγιο (to dro-mo-*lo*-yee-o) (*the route, the schedule*)

>> το βαγόνι (to va-*go*-nee) (*the wagon, the carriage*)

>> η θέση (ee *the*-see) (*the seat*)

>> το εισιτήριο (to ee-see-*tee*-ree-o) (*the ticket*)

>> η κράτηση θέσης (ee *kra*-tee-see *the*-sees) (*the seat reservation*)

>> η πρώτη/δεύτερη θέση (ee *pro*-tee/*def*-te-ree *the*-see) (*first/second class*)

When you arrive at the station, you may need to ask the following:

Πού είναι το εκδοτήριο εισιτηρίων; (poo *ee*-ne to e-kdo-*tee*-ree-o ee-see-tee-*ree*-on) (*Where is the ticket office?*)

Πόσο κοστίζει ένα εισιτήριο για . . . ; (*po*-so ko-*stee*-zee *e*-na ee-see-*tee*-ree-o ya) (*How much is a ticket to [destination]?*)

Πότε φεύγει το τρένο για . . .; (*po*-te *fev*-yee to *tre*-no ya) (*When does the train leave for [destination]?*)

Taxi, Please!

Taking a taxi in Greece can be an experience in itself! Greek taxi drivers, when they start talking (if they're in the mood, of course), will tell you all sorts of stories, political opinions, and complaints, and they may even ask many, sometimes intrusive, questions. But beyond how entertaining these conversations can be, they're also a great chance to practice your Greek!

In Athens, taxis are yellow, but in other cities the colors vary. In Thessaloniki, taxis are dark blue; in Patras burgundy; and in other towns, gray or other colors.

The word used in Greek is the English word "taxi," or το ταξί (to ta-*ksee*). The taxi driver is called ο οδηγός ταξί (o o-dee-*gos* ta-*ksee*) or more commonly, ο ταξιτζής (o ta-ksee-*tzees*).

When you call a taxi, it comes to pick you up. You take the ride and upon arriving at your destination, you pay the fare, or η ταρίφα (ee ta-*ree*-fa), which is displayed on the taximeter, or το ταξίμετρο (to ta-*ksee*-me-tro). If you take a taxi after midnight, you pay a double fare, or διπλή ταρίφα (dee-*plee* ta-*ree*-fa).

If you're walking on the street looking for a taxi, you may ask:

Πού μπορώ να βρω ταξί; (poo bo-*ro* na vro ta-*ksee*) (*Where can I find a taxi?*)

There are specific spots where you can catch a taxi. The taxi stand is called η πιάτσα (ee *pya*-tsa). If you're at a hotel reception desk, you may ask:

Μπορείτε να καλέσετε ταξί; (bo-*ree*-te na ka-*le*-se-te ta-*ksee*) (*Can you call me a taxi?*)

Θα ήθελα ένα ταξί για το αεροδρόμιο. (tha *ee*-the-la *e*-na ta-*ksee* ya to a-e-ro-*dro*-mee-o) (*I would like a taxi to the airport.*)

Χρειάζομαι ταξί για . . . (khree-*a*-zo-me ta-ksee ya) (*I need a taxi to [address/destination].*)

When you're inside the taxi, you may say:

Θέλω να πάω στον/στη(ν)/στο . . . (*the*-lo na *pa*-o ston/stee[n]/sto) (*I want to go to [destination].*)

Πόσο θα κοστίσει η διαδρομή; (*po*-so tha ko-*stee*-see ee dya-dro-*mee*) (*How much will the trip cost?*)

Πόση ώρα θα πάρει; (*po*-see *o*-ra tha *pa*-ree) (*How long will it take?*)

And if the taxi driver is playing loud music, you could politely ask this:

Μπορείτε να χαμηλώσετε τη μουσική; (bo-*ree*-te na kha-mee-*lo*-se-te teen moo-see-*kee*) (*Can you lower the music?*)

.... Talkin' the Talk ....

PLAY THIS

Jovanna is taking a taxi to her hotel and having a conversation with the driver, Christos. (Track 18)

Jovanna: Καλησπέρα! Μπορείτε να με πάτε στο ξενοδοχείο «Ακρόπολη»;
ka-lee-*spe*-ra! bo-*ree*-te na me *pa*-te sto kse-no-do-*hee*-o a-*cro*-po-lee;
Good evening! Can you take me to the Acropolis hotel?

Christos: Βεβαίως! Η διαδρομή κρατάει περίπου είκοσι λεπτά.
ve-*ve*-os! ee dya-dro-*mee* kra-*ta*-ee pe-*ree*-poo *ee*-ko-see le-*pta*.
Of course! The ride will take about 20 minutes.

Jovanna: Τέλεια! Πόσο κοστίζει περίπου;
te-lee-a! *po*-so ko-*stee*-zee pe-*ree*-poo;
Great! How much will it cost approximately?

Christos: Η ταρίφα είναι περίπου δεκαπέντε ευρώ, αλλά εξαρτάται από την κίνηση.
ee ta-*ree*-fa *ee*-ne pe-*ree*-poo de-ka-*pe*-nde ev-ro, a-*la* e-ksa-*rta*-te a-*po* teen *kee*-nee-see.
The fare is about 15 euros, but it depends on the traffic.

Jovanna: Μπορώ να πληρώσω με κάρτα;
bo-*ro* na plee-*ro*-so me *ka*-rta;
Can I pay by credit card?

Christos:	Ναι, φυσικά!
	ne, fee-see-*ka*!
	Yes, of course!
Jovanna:	Ωραία, σας ευχαριστώ.
	o-*re*-a, sas ef-kha-ree-*sto*.
	Great, thank you.

WORDS TO KNOW

το ξενοδοχείο	to kse-no-do-*hee*-o	*the hotel*
η διαδρομή	ee dya-dro-*mee*	*the route, the journey*
περίπου	pe-*ree*-poo	*approximately*
η ταρίφα	ee ta-*ree*-fa	*the fare*
εξαρτάται	e-ksa-*rta*-te	*depends*
η κίνηση	ee *kee*-nee-see	*the traffic*
Μπορώ να πληρώσω με κάρτα;	bo-*ro* na plee-*ro*-so me *kar*-ta	*Can I pay by credit card?*

Taking the Ferry

During the summer, passenger ships are filled with people traveling to the islands of the Aegean and Ionian Seas. The journey on the ferry feels like a small festival — you see children, animals, groups of young people with guitars, sleepy passengers, and people taking photos, admiring the sea, and sipping their coffee. From the moment the ship leaves the port, you feel like you're leaving all your worries behind.

Here are some useful vocabulary words related to taking the ferry:

>> το πλοίο (to *plee*-o) (*the ship*)

>> το φεριμπότ (to fe-ree-*bot*) (*the ferry*)

>> το λιμάνι (to lee-*ma*-nee) (*the port*)

- » η αποβάθρα (ee a-po-*va*-thra) (*the dock*)

- » το κατάστρωμα (to ka-*ta*-stro-ma) (*the deck*)

- » η καμπίνα (ee ka-*bee*-na) (*the cabin*)

- » το ναύλο (to *nav*-lo) (*the fare*)

- » η κράτηση (ee *kra*-tee-see) (*the reservation*)

Before taking the ferry, you first need to buy a ticket, and you can say "I buy a ticket," or Αγοράζω εισιτήριο (a-go-*ra*-zo ee-see-*tee*-ree-o).

You can buy a ticket online, at εκδοτήρια εισιτηρίων (e-kdo-*tee*-ree-a ee-see-tee-ree-on) (*ticket offices*), or at a ταξιδιωτικό γραφείο (ta-ksee-dyo-tee-*ko* gra-*fee*-o) (*travel agency*). When speaking with the ticket agent, you can ask for details about your ticket:

> Υπάρχουν εισιτήρια για . . .; (ee-*pa*-rkhoon ee-see-*tee*-ree-a ya) (*Are there tickets available for [destination]?*)

> Θέλω ένα εισιτήριο με επιστροφή. (*the*-lo *e*-na ee-see-*tee*-ree-o me e-pee-stro-*fee*) (*I want a round-trip ticket.*)

> Μπορώ να κλείσω καμπίνα; (bo-*ro* na *klee*-so ka-*bee*-na) (*Can I book a cabin?*)

> Πόσο κοστίζει το εισιτήριο; (*po*-so ko-*stee*-zee to ee-see-*tee*-ree-o) (*How much does the ticket cost?*)

WARNING

It's crucial to arrive at the port on time, because *ferries do not wait for anyone* — you definitely don't want to be waving goodbye to your ferry as it departs for Mykonos without you!

FUN & GAMES

Here is a table with four types of transportation. Sort the words from the word bank into the correct category.

- » πλατφόρμα
- » αεροδρόμιο
- » ταρίφα
- » λιμάνι
- » απογείωση
- » κατάστρωμα
- » ταξιτζής
- » σταθμός
- » αφίξεις
- » ταξίμετρο
- » καμπίνα
- » πτήση
- » βαγόνι

© John Wiley & Sons, Inc.

Chapter **15**

Enjoying the Sights

G reece is renowned for its ancient and Byzantine civilization. Its historical significance has been so profound for centuries that today entire university departments around the world are dedicated to studying Greek antiquity. Greece's rich history and art act as a magnet, drawing tourists eager to admire firsthand the masterpieces left behind by Greek ancestors.

In this chapter I focus on vocabulary related to sightseeing in Greece. Let's start!

Appreciating Ancient Greece

The ancient Greeks had a deep appreciation for beauty, which they studied not only through philosophy but also through art.

Many words you use today originate from Greek. For example, consider the word δημοκρατία (dee-mo-kra-*tee*-a) (*democracy*). Did you know that democracy as a political system first appeared in Greece and, over the centuries, became known across the civilized world?

Another ancient Greek word still in use today is φιλοσοφία (fee-lo-so-*fee*-a) (*philosophy*). Some of the most famous Greek philosophers include

>> **Σωκράτης** (so-*kra*-tees) (*Socrates*)

>> **Πλάτων** (*pla*-ton) (*Plato*)

>> **Αριστοτέλης** (a-ree-sto-*te*-lees) (*Aristotle*)

The ancient Greeks believed in 12 gods who, according to mythology, resided atop Mount Olympus, the highest mountain in Greece. It's likely that you've heard some of their names through school, literature, or various movies and series. Some of these gods include

>> **Δίας** (*dee*-as) (*Zeus*)

>> **Αθηνά** (a-thee-*na*) (*Athena*)

>> **Απόλλων** (a-*po*-lon) (*Apollo*)

>> **Αφροδίτη** (a-fro-*dee*-tee) (*Aphrodite*)

>> **Ποσειδώνας** (po-see-*do*-nas) (*Poseidon*)

>> **Άδης** (*a*-dees) (*Hades*)

The Greeks also created outstanding theatrical works. Many tragedies and comedies continue to inspire audiences to this day.

>> **τραγωδία** (tra-go-*dee*-a) (*tragedy*)

>> **κωμωδία** (ko-mo-*dee*-a) (*comedy*)

>> **θέατρο** (*the*-a-tro) (*theater*)

All of these elements — history, mythology, philosophy, and art — make Greece a fascinating destination for travelers.

Visiting Historical Sites and Landmarks

CULTURAL WISDOM

Some of the most famous archaeological monuments of the ancient world, visited by thousands of people every year, include

>> **η Ακρόπολη** (ee a-*kro*-po-lee) (*the Acropolis*): The Acropolis is located in Athens on a hilltop. At its center stands the Parthenon, an iconic symbol of ancient Greek civilization. If you visit Athens, make sure not to miss a trip there.

>> **το Θέατρο του Διονύσου** (to *the*-a-tro too dyo-*nee*-soo) (*the Theatre of Dionysus*): Situated beneath the Acropolis, the ancient Theatre of Dionysus is one of the oldest theaters in Greece. Every summer, it hosts performances of theater, opera, and remarkable concerts.

>> **το Μαντείο των Δελφών** (to ma-*dee*-o ton de-*lfon*) (the *Oracle of Delphi*): This was one of the most significant religious centers of antiquity, dedicated to Apollo. Today, the archaeological site welcomes hundreds of visitors annually.

>> **η Ολυμπία** (ee o-lee-*bee*-a) (*Olympia*): Olympia was the birthplace of the Olympic Games, held every four years just as they are today but in honor of Zeus.

>> **οι Μυκήνες** (ee mee-*kee*-nes) (*Mycenae*): Mycenae is located in the Peloponnese. It flourished during the Bronze Age, making its civilization and architecture all the more impressive — including its massive fortifications.

>> **η Κνωσός** (Ee Kno-*sos*) (*Knossos*): Knossos was the center of Minoan civilization and is located on Crete. Today, the magnificent palace, adorned with stunning frescoes, still stands and is a must-visit.

Discovering the Greek Orthodox Christian Tradition

Greece is also an important center of religious tourism. Its connection to Christianity dates back to when Christ's Apostles traveled to Greece to spread their teachings.

The official religion of Greece is Orthodox Christianity. As a center of Orthodoxy, Greece is renowned for its churches, Byzantine iconography, Byzantine music, and the many saints and fathers of the Church. Interest in this aspect of Greece extends beyond Orthodox Christians — people of all faiths and ideologies appreciate Greek architecture and history.

CULTURAL WISDOM

Here are a few key religious sites:

>> **η Παναγία της Τήνου** (ee pa-na-*yee*-a tees *tee*-noo): The Church of Panagia on the island of Tinos. Inside the church stands the miraculous **εικόνα** (ee-*ko*-na)

(*icon*) of the Virgin Mary, and people from all over the world come to venerate it. On August 15, when the Virgin Mary is celebrated, thousands of faithful gather on the island of Tinos.

» **το Σπήλαιο της Αποκάλυψης** (to *spee*-le-o tees a-po-*ka*-lee-psees): The Cave of the Apocalypse on the island of Patmos. It's the place where, according to tradition, Saint John received his visions and wrote the **Βιβλίο της Αποκάλυψης** (vee-*vlee*-o tees a-po-*ka*-lee-psees) (*Book of Revelation*) in 95 AD. Today, the cave is protected as a UNESCO World Heritage Site.

» **τα βυζαντινά προσκυνήματα της Θεσσαλονίκης** (ta vee-za-dee-*na* pro-skee-*nee*-ma-ta tees the-sa-lo-*nee*-kees): The Byzantine pilgrimage sites of Thessaloniki. This city flourished during the Byzantine era, and many monuments reflect this rich heritage, such as the **Ναός του Αγίου Δημητρίου** (na-*os* too a-*yee*-oo dee-me-*tree*-oo) (*Church of Saint Demetrios*), the **Ναός της Αγίας Σοφίας** (na-*os* tees a-*yee*-as so-*fee*-as) (*Church of Saint Sophia*), and the **Ροτόντα** (ro-*to*-nda) (*Rotunda*).

» **Άθως** (*a*-thos): Mount Athos, a monastic community in northern Greece, where only male monks reside. It serves as a spiritual retreat for visitors seeking renewal. The area has 20 Orthodox monasteries and is accessible only to men. The reason is that, according to tradition, the area is dedicated to the **Παναγία** (pa-na-*yee*-a) (*Virgin Mary*), and she is the only female figure who belongs there.

» **Μονή Αγίου Νεκταρίου** (mo-*nee* a-*yee*-oo ne-kta-*ree*-oo): Saint Nektarios Monastery. Saint Nektarios is a modern saint of the Orthodox Church who founded a monastery on Aegina, where his tomb is also located. Because he was a great scholar and theologian with an admirable life, people from every corner of the world visit the monastery and venerate his tomb.

Greece for Art Lovers

Something worth seeing when visiting a place is called αξιοθέατο (a-ksee-o-*the*-a-to) in Greek, meaning "landmark" or "attraction." In Greece, you can enjoy all forms of art, depending on your interests. Let's look at some vocabulary related to various forms of art and expression:

» **τέχνη** (*te*-khnee) (*art*)

» **ζωγραφική** (zo-gra-fee-*kee*) (*painting*)

» **γλυπτική** (glee-ptee-*kee*) (*sculpture*)

- » μουσείο (moo-*see*-o) (*museum*)

- » έκθεση (*e*-kthe-see) (*exhibition*)

- » καλλιτέχνης (ka-lee-*te*-khnees) (*artist*)

- » πίνακας (*pee*-na-kas) (*painting, as in a framed artwork*)

- » αρχιτεκτονική (a-rhee-te-kto-nee-*kee*) (*architecture*)

- » θέατρο (*the*-a-tro) (*theater*)

- » φωτογραφία (fo-to-gra-*fee*-a) (*photography*)

- » ποίηση (*pee*-ee-see) (*poetry*)

- » κινηματογράφος (kee-nee-ma-to-*gra*-fos) (*cinema*)

- » χορός (kho-*ros*) (*dance*)

- » κεραμική (ke-ra-mee-*kee*) (*ceramics*)

When watching or experiencing a form of art, you use the verb παρακολουθώ (pa–ra–ko–loo–*tho*), meaning "to watch" or "to attend." Here are some examples of its usage:

Παρακολουθώ μία παράσταση. (pa-ra-ko-loo-*tho mee*-a pa-*ra*-sta-see) (*I watch a performance.*)

Παρακολουθώ θέατρο. (pa-ra-ko-loo-*tho the*-a-tro) (*I watch theater.*)

Παρακολουθώ χορό. (pa-ra-ko-loo-*tho* kho-*ro*) (*I watch dance.*)

To express your preferences for art, use μου αρέσει (moo a–*re*–see), meaning "I like." Here are some examples:

Μου αρέσει το θέατρο. (moo a-*re*-see to *the*-a-tro) (*I like theater.*)

Μου αρέσει η φωτογραφία. (moo a-*re*-see ee fo-to-gra-*fee*-a) (*I like photography.*)

Μου αρέσει η ποίηση. (moo a-*re*-see ee *pee*-ee-see) (*I like poetry.*)

Visiting Museums

As a tourist, you'll likely visit museums — or at least that's what most people do. So, you'll need some words and phrases to help you navigate your visit.

In a μουσείο (moo-*see*-o) (*museum*), there is always an έκθεση (*e*-kthe-see) (*exhibition*) related to the museum's theme. If you take a ξενάγηση (kse-*na*-yee-see) (*guided tour*), the tour guide will provide information about the exhibition. You can also take a guided tour when visiting an αρχαιολογικός χώρος (a-rhe-o-lo-yee-*kos kho*-ros) (*archaeological site*), though it's not mandatory.

If you want to discover more details about the museum, you can ask someone at your hotel or a tourist information center:

Τι ώρα ανοίγει/κλείνει το μουσείο; (tee *o*-ra a-*nee*-yee/klee-nee to moo-*see*-o) (*What time does the museum open/close?*)

Πόσο κοστίζει το εισιτήριο; (*po*-so ko-*stee*-zee to ee-see-*tee*-ree-o) (*How much is the ticket?*)

Ποιος είναι ο καλλιτέχνης αυτού του έργου; (pyos *ee*-ne o ka-lee-*te*-khnees af-*too* too e-rgoo) (*Who is the artist of this piece?*)

Going Wine Tasting

CULTURAL WISDOM

Greece's Mediterranean climate is ideal for cultivating vineyards. In Greek, αμπελώνας (a-be-*lo*-nas) refers to a vineyard. The country produces high-quality κρασί (kra-*see*) (*wine*), so visiting a winery, or οινοποιείο (ee-no-pee-*ee*-o), for a tasting, or γευσιγνωσία (yef-see-gno-*see*-a), is highly recommended!

You can describe wine in various ways. Here are some examples:

>> ξηρό κρασί (ksee-*ro* kra-*see*) (*dry wine*)

>> γλυκό κρασί (glee-*ko* kra-*see*) (*sweet wine*)

>> φρουτώδες κρασί (froo-*to*-des kra-*see*) (*fruity wine*)

>> αρωματικό κρασί (a-ro-ma-tee-*ko* kra-*see*) (*aromatic wine*)

When visiting a restaurant or winery, you may say:

Ποιο κρασί προτείνετε; (pyo kra-*see* pro-*tee*-ne-te) (*Which wine do you recommend?*)

Μπορώ να δοκιμάσω αυτό το κρασί; (bo-*ro* na do-kee-*ma*-so af-*to* to kra-*see*) (*Can I taste this wine?*)

Από ποια περιοχή είναι αυτό το κρασί; (a-*po* pya pe-ree-o-*hee* ee-ne af-*to* to kra-*see*) (*Where is this wine from?*)

Πώς παράγεται αυτό το κρασί; (pos pa-*ra*-ye-te af-*to* to kra-*see*) (*How is this wine produced?*)

Έχετε κρασί από . . . ; (e-he-te kra-*see* a-po) (*Do you have wine from [location]?*)

Vineyards across Greece offer guided tours — some even have restaurants and hotels, so you can stay overnight.

REMEMBER

However, if you go wine tasting, make sure you won't need to drive afterward. It's always best to take a taxi — never drive after drinking!

Talkin' the Talk

PLAY THIS

Nikos and Eleni are in Thessaloniki, and they are ready to explore the city. They are making their plans for the day. (Track 19)

Nikos: Καλημέρα, Ελένη! Ανυπομονώ να εξερευνήσουμε τη Θεσσαλονίκη σήμερα. Πού θα πάμε;
ka-lee-*me*-ra, e-*le*-nee! a-nee-po-mo-*no* na e-kse-rev-*nee*-soo-me tee the-sa-lo-*nee*-kee *see*-me-ra. poo tha *pa*-me;
Good morning, Eleni! I'm excited to explore Thessaloniki today. Where should we go?

Eleni: Στον Λευκό Πύργο! Είναι το πιο εμβληματικό σημείο της πόλης και η θέα από την κορυφή είναι εκπληκτική.
ston lef-*ko pee*-rgo! *ee*-ne to pyo e-mvlee-ma-tee-*ko* see-*mee*-o tees *po*-lees ke ee *the*-a a-*po* teen ko-ree-*fee ee*-ne e-kplee-ktee-*kee*.
To the White Tower! It's the city's most iconic landmark, and the view from the top is amazing.

Nikos: Και μπορούμε να επισκεφτούμε και το μουσείο μέσα στον πύργο για να μάθουμε για την ιστορία της Θεσσαλονίκης.
ke bo-*roo*-me na e-pee-ske-*ftoo*-me ke to moo-*see*-o *me*-sa ston *pee*-rgo ya na *ma*-thoo-me ya teen ee-sto-*ree*-a tees the-sa-lo-*nee*-kees.
We can also visit the museum inside the tower to learn more about Thessaloniki's history.

Eleni: Σωστά! Μετά μπορούμε να κάνουμε μία βόλτα στην παραλία.
so-*sta!* me-*ta* bo-*roo*-me na *ka*-noo-me *mee*-a *vo*-lta steen pa-ra-*lee*-a.
Exactly! After that, we can take a stroll along the seafront.

(continued)

(continued)

Nikos:	**Συμφωνώ! Και μετά από λίγο περπάτημα, μπορούμε να επισκεφτούμε τη Ρωμαϊκή Αγορά ή την Αψίδα του Γαλέριου.**
	see-mfo-*no*! ke me-*ta* a-*po* lee-go pe-*rpa*-tee-ma, bo-*roo*-me na e-pee-ske-*ftoo*-me tee ro-ma-ee-*kee* a-go-*ra* ee teen a-*psee*-da too ga-*le*-ree-oo.
	I agree! And after a bit of walking, we could visit the Roman Agora or Galerius' Arch.

Eleni:	**Πολύ καλή ιδέα! Μπορούμε να δούμε και τη Ροτόντα — έχει εκπληκτική αρχιτεκτονική.**
	po-lee ka-*lee* ee-*de*-a! bo-*roo*-me na *doo*-me ke tee ro-*to*-da — e-hee e-kplee-ktee-*kee* a-rhee-te-kto-nee-*kee*.
	That's a great idea! We can also check out the Rotunda — it has stunning architecture.

Nikos:	**Τέλειο! Και για το απόγευμα;**
	te-lee-o! ke ya to a-*po*-yev-ma;
	Perfect! What about the afternoon?

Eleni:	**Μπορούμε να επισκεφτούμε το Μουσείο Βυζαντινού Πολιτισμού ή να εξερευνήσουμε την Άνω Πόλη.**
	bo-*roo*-me na e-pee-ske-*ftoo*-me to moo-*see*-o vee-za-dee-*noo* po-lee-tee-*smoo* ee na e-kse-rev-*nee*-soo-me teen *a*-no *po*-lee.
	We could visit the Museum of Byzantine Culture or explore Ano Poli (Upper Town).

Nikos:	**Προτιμώ να περπατήσουμε στην Άνω Πόλη.**
	pro-tee-*mo* na pe-rpa-*tee*-soo-me steen *a*-no *po*-lee.
	I'd rather walk around Ano Poli.

Eleni:	**Αυτό ακούγεται σαν η τέλεια ημέρα στη Θεσσαλονίκη! Πάμε να ξεκινήσουμε!**
	af-*to* a-*koo*-ye-te san ee *te*-lee-a ee-*me*-ra stee the-sa-lo-*nee*-kee! *pa*-me na kse-kee-*nee*-soo-me!
	That sounds like the perfect day in Thessaloniki! Let's get started!

• •

WORDS TO KNOW

ανυπομονώ	a-nee-po-mo-*no*	*I'm excited, I look forward to.*
εξερευνώ	e-kse-rev-*no*	*I explore.*
εκπληκτικός, -η, -ο	e-kplee-ktee-*kos*, -ee, -o	*amazing, stunning, incredible (masculine, feminine, neutral)*
επισκέπτομαι	e-pee-*ske*-pto-me	*I visit.*
το μουσείο	to moo-*see*-o	*the museum*
η ιστορία	ee ee-sto-*ree*-a	*the history, the story*
σωστά	so-*sta*	*exactly*
η παραλία	ee pa-ra-*lee*-a	*the beach, the seafront*
συμφωνώ	see-mfo-*no*	*I agree.*
το περπάτημα	to pe-*rpa*-tee-ma	*walking, the walk*
ξεκινάω	kse-kee-*na*-o	*I start, I begin.*

FUN & GAMES

Let's say you're a tourist in Athens. Prioritize the activities you would do, putting a 1 next to your top choice and a 5 next to your last choice.

» Επισκέπτομαι την Ακρόπολη.

» Πηγαίνω στο αρχαιολογικό μουσείο.

» Πηγαίνω στο οινοποιείο.

» Πηγαίνω στην παραλία.

» Παρακολουθώ μία παράσταση.

Chapter **16**

Understanding Greek Traditions

The more you explore Greece and make Greek friends, the more you realize that there are different aspects of Greek culture that are fascinating. You may be invited to a Greek wedding, a dinner with dancing, or an Easter service. These experiences, which may not be readily available to someone visiting the country for the first time, hold their own charm and, of course, provide a golden opportunity to practice Greek!

Having a Big Fat Greek Wedding

Ο γάμος (o *ga*-mos) (*a wedding*) is a central event in a family's life. A wedding brings joy but also requires many preparations and expenses. Also, a Greek wedding isn't something that only the bride and groom organize. Parents, siblings, and friends also get involved and help. So, from the moment you say "I do," a whole team of people mobilizes!

Let's see how it all begins . . . Usually, there is a **πρόταση γάμου** (*pro*-ta-see *ga*-moo) (*marriage proposal*):

> **Θέλεις να με παντρευτείς;** (*the*-lees na me pa-ndref-*tees*) (*Will you marry me?*)

> **Με παντρεύεσαι;** (me pa-n*drev*-e-se) (*Would you like to marry me?*)

And if the answer is yes, then the preparations for the couple begin.

While the couple is engaged, they say **Αρραβωνιαζόμαστε** (a-ra-vo-nya-*zo*-ma-ste) (*We are engaged*), and when the time comes for the wedding, they say **Παντρευόμαστε** (pa-ndrev-*o*-ma-ste) (*We are getting married*). A woman who is getting married is called a **νύφη** (*nee*-fee) (*bride*), and a man is called a **γαμπρός** (ga-*bros*) (groom). Together, they are referred to as a **ζευγάρι** (zev-*ga*-ree) (*couple*).

Let's look at some words and phrases related to wedding preparations: First, the **γαμπρός** must find a **κουστούμι** (koo-*stoo*-mee) (*suit*), and the **νύφη** must find a **νυφικό** (nee-fee-*ko*) (*wedding dress*).

The couple must also decide on the following:

» **προσκλητήρια** (pro-sklee-*tee*-ree-a) (*invitations*)

» **λίστα καλεσμένων** (*lee*-sta ka-le-*sme*-non) (*guest list*)

» **στολισμός** (sto-lee-*smos*) (*decorations*)

» **χώρος δεξίωσης** (*kho*-ros de-*ksee*-o-sees) (*reception venue*)

» **φωτογράφος** (fo-to-*gra*-fos) (*photographer*)

» **μουσική** (moo-see-*kee*) (*music*)

» **μενού** (me-*noo*) (*menu*)

If the couple has a **θρησκευτικός γάμος** (three-skef-tee-*kos ga*-mos) (*religious wedding*), they must decide in which **εκκλησία** (e-klee-*see*-a) (*church*) the ceremony will take place. If they have a **πολιτικός γάμος** (po-lee-tee-*kos ga*-mos) (*civil wedding*), then it happens at the **δημαρχείο** (dee-ma-*rhee*-o) (*town hall*).

When arranging the venue for the ceremony, you say:

> **Κλείνουμε εκκλησία.** (*klee*-noo-me e-klee-*see*-a) (*We are booking a church.*)

> **Κλείνουμε δημαρχείο.** (*klee*-noo-me dee-ma-*rhee*-o) (*We are booking the town hall.*)

CULTURAL WISDOM

Do you know what **κουφέτα** (koo-*fe*-ta) are? They are small white sugar-coated candies with an almond in the center. This is the traditional treat given at the end of a wedding. The **κουφέτα** are placed inside **μπομπονιέρες** (bo-mbo-*nye*-res), which are decorative tulle-wrapped packages, and each guest receives one at the end of the wedding. Additionally, in various regions of Greece, traditional wedding sweets are offered to guests outside the church.

The wedding day

After the couple, their family, and their friends have prepared all the details, the wedding day finally arrives. Let's look at some key vocabulary related to the wedding day (in addition to those words and phrases I mention previously):

» **οι νιόπαντροι** (ee *nyo*-pa-dree) (*the newlyweds*)

» **τα στέφανα** (ta *ste*-fa-na) (*the wedding crowns used in a Greek Orthodox ceremony*)

» **οι καλεσμένοι** (ee ka-le-*sme*-nee) (*the guests*)

» **οι βέρες** (ee *ve*-res) (*the wedding rings*)

CULTURAL WISDOM

Every wedding has one or more **κουμπάρος/κουμπάρα** (koo-*ba*-ros/koo-*ba*-ra), who are the best man/maid of honor. They are close friends of the couple. Symbolically, their role is to support the couple through difficulties in their marriage. In reality, the role is mostly ceremonial, reinforcing the bond of friendship.

CULTURAL WISDOM

At the end of the wedding, it's customary to throw **ρύζι** (ree-zee) (*rice*) at the couple. This has a symbolic meaning. Rice is a seed that has the power to take root and bear fruit. Similarly, the wish is that the couple's relationship has deep roots, meaning it will remain stable and will bear fruit — children.

Wedding wishes

When a couple is about to get married, people say **Η ώρα η καλή!** (ee *o*-ra ee ka-*lee*). This is a wish that their wedding day is fortunate and blessed.

After the wedding, people offer congratulations by saying:

Βίον ανθόσπαρτον! (*vee*-on a-*ntho*-spa-rton) (*Wishing a life full of flowers* [symbolizing happiness and prosperity]).

Να ζήσετε! (na zee-se-te) (*May you live long and happily!*)

Να ευτυχίσετε! (na ef-tee-*hee*-se-te) (*May you be happy!*)

For young unmarried guests, people say **Και στα δικά σας!** (ke sta dee-*ka* sas). This is a wish that we will also celebrate their wedding one day!

For the **κουμπάροι** (koo-*ba*-ree), people say **Πάντα άξιοι!** (*pa*-da *a*-ksee-ee). This is a wish that they will always be worthy of such an honor.

The wedding reception

After all the traditions, the couple and guests go to the wedding banquet. This is where the party begins!

The night starts with **παραδοσιακή μουσική** (pa-ra-do-see-a-*kee* moo-see-*kee*) (*traditional Greek music*) and ends with modern Greek or foreign songs. Some couples prefer **ζωντανή μουσική** (zo-da-*nee* moo-see-*kee*) (*live music*), while others hire a DJ.

CULTURAL WISDOM

The first dances are performed by the couple and their family, in a circular formation, with everyone holding hands. The parents, best man, maid of honor, siblings, and couple lead the dance. Then, the guests join in. So, if you want to practice Greek dance steps, wait until it's the guests' turn!

.... Talkin' the Talk ....

PLAY THIS

Yorgos and Maria are preparing for their wedding and thinking about the final details. (Track 20)

Yorgos: **Μαρία, είναι όλα έτοιμα για τον γάμο; Θέλω να είναι τέλειος!**
ma-*ree*-a, *ee*-ne *o*-la *e*-tee-ma ya ton *ga*-mo; *the*-lo na *ee*-ne *te*-lee-os!
Maria, is everything ready for the wedding? I want it to be perfect!

Maria: **Νομίζω πως ναι, αλλά πρέπει να αποφασίσουμε για τη μουσική. Θέλεις παραδοσιακά τραγούδια ή κάτι πιο μοντέρνο;**
no-*mee*-zo pos ne, a-*la pre*-pee na a-po-fa-*see*-soo-me ya tee moo-see-*kee*. *the*-lees pa-ra-do-see-a-*ka* tra-*goo*-dya ee *ka*-tee pyo mo-*de*-rno;
I think so, but we need to decide on the music. Do you want traditional songs or something more modern?

Yorgos: Λίγη παράδοση δεν βλάπτει! Φαντάζομαι ένα μεγάλο γλέντι! Αχ, Μαρία, ανυπομονώ να σε δω με το νυφικό! Θα είσαι πανέμορφη!

lee-yee pa-*ra*-do-see den *vla*-ptee! fa-*da*-zo-me *e*-na me-*ga*-lo *gle*-dee! akh, ma-*ree*-a, a-nee-po-mo-*no* na se do me to nee-fee-*ko*! tha *ee*-se pa-*ne*-mo-rfee!

A little tradition never hurts! I imagine a big celebration! Oh, Maria, I can't wait to see you in your wedding dress! You will be gorgeous!

Maria: Και εγώ ανυπομονώ να αρχίσουμε τη νέα μας ζωή μαζί!

ke e-go a-nee-po-mo-*no* na a-*rhee*-soo-me tee *ne*-a mas zo-*ee* ma-*zee*!

And I can't wait for us to start our new life together!

• •

WORDS TO KNOW

έτοιμος, -η, -ο	e-tee-mos, -ee, -o	ready
γάμος	*ga*-mos	wedding
νομίζω	no-*mee*-zo	I think; I believe.
παραδοσιακά τραγούδια	pa-ra-do-see-a-*ka* tra-*goo*-dya	traditional songs
Δεν βλάπτει.	den *vla*-ptee	It doesn't hurt; it's harmless.
γλέντι	*gle*-dee	celebration
ανυπομονώ	A-nee-po-mo-*no*	I can't wait; I am looking forward.
νυφικό	nee-fee-*ko*	wedding dress
πανέμορφος, -η, -ο	pa-*ne*-mo-rfos, -ee, -o	gorgeous, very beautiful

Celebrating a Name Day

Greeks celebrate their ονομαστική γιορτή (o-no-ma-stee-*kee* yo-*rtee*) (*name day*). What is this? It's the day when the Greek Orthodox Church honors the saint whose name you have taken. For example, my name is Irene, after Saint Irene the Great Martyr, who is celebrated on May 5. So, that day is my name day.

What does this mean in practice? I treat my friends, I have a celebration at my house, I receive gifts, and people wish me well.

> » η γιορτή (ee yo-*rtee*) (*celebration*)

> » Είναι η γιορτή μου. (*ee*-ne ee yo-*rtee* moo) (*It's my name day.*)

> » Κερνάω τους φίλους μου. (ke-*rna*-o toos *fee*-loos moo) (*I treat my friends.*)

> » το δώρο (to *do*-ro) (*the gift*)

> » η ευχή (ee ef-*hee*) (*the wish*)

What kind of wishes might my friends give me?

> Χρόνια πολλά! (*khro*-nya po-*la*) (*Happy name day!*)

> Να χαίρεσαι το όνομά σου. (na *he*-re-se to *o*-no-*ma* soo) (*Enjoy your name!*)

CULTURAL WISDOM

If the saint being celebrated is also the patron of a village or city, then a πανηγύρι (pa-nee-*yee*-ree) (*festival*) takes place. I talk about festivals in Chapter 10 — they are public celebrations with music, food, and drinks open to everyone.

Celebrating Greek Orthodox Easter

Easter is the most important religious celebration in Greece. Even those who are less religious take part in the festivities.

Πάσχα (*pa*-skha) (*Easter*) is accompanied by many traditions, with the peak of the celebrations occurring on Sunday, when people celebrate the Resurrection of Christ, or η Ανάσταση του Χριστού (ee a-*na*-sta-see too khree-*stoo*). However, preparations begin in the days leading up to this event. The week before Easter Sunday is called Μεγάλη Εβδομάδα (me-*ga*-lee e-vdo-*ma*-da) (*Holy Week*). Here are some preparations:

>> **η νηστεία** (ee nee-*stee*-a) (*fasting*): Forty days before Easter, many Orthodox Christians follow a strict fast, avoiding all animal products — no meat, dairy, or fish.

>> **Holy Thursday:** Families dye **κόκκινα αυγά** (*ko*-kee-na av-*ga*) (*red eggs*) and bake **τσουρέκι** (tsoo-*re*-kee), a soft and sweet braided bread. Various regions in Greece also prepare other traditional sweets and dishes for the grand Sunday feast.

>> **Holy Saturday:** In the evening, Greeks gather at church holding **λαμπάδες** (la-*ba*-des) (*decorated candles*). At midnight, the Resurrection is celebrated with hugs, kisses, fireworks, and crackers to mark the joyous occasion. After church, families return home to eat **μαγειρίτσα** (ma-yee-*ree*-tsa), a traditional lamb offal soup.

>> **Easter Sunday:** Instead of saying "Good morning," people greet each other with **Χριστός Ανέστη!** (khree-*stos* a-*ne*-stee!) (*Christ is Risen*) And the answer is **Αληθώς Ανέστη!** (a-lee-*thos* a-*ne*-stee) (*Truly, He is Risen!*)

>> **Egg cracking game:** If someone offers you a red Easter egg, you must crack it by tapping the tips against someone else's egg. The person whose egg doesn't break is the winner — though, of course, you can eat it afterward! Here are some useful phrases for this game:

- **Τσουγκρίζω αυγά.** (tsoo-*gree*-zo av-*ga*) (*I crack eggs.*)

- **Σπάει το αυγό μου.** (*spa*-ee to av-*go* moo) (*My egg cracks.*)

On Easter Sunday, families slow–roast a lamb on a spit over hot coals, making the meat tender and incredibly flavorful. Try these handy phrases:

>> **το αρνί** (to a-*rnee*) (*the lamb*)

>> **η ψησταριά** (ee psee-sta-*rya*) (*the grill*)

>> **η σούβλα** (ee *soo*-vla) (*the roasting spit*)

>> **Σουβλίζω το αρνί.** (soo-*vlee*-zo to a-*rnee*) (*I spit-roast the lamb.*)

Talkin' the Talk

Vasilis and Manos prepare the final details for the celebration of Easter.

Vasilis: Μάνο, είσαι έτοιμος για το Πάσχα; Έχουμε τόσα πράγματα να ετοιμάσουμε!

ma-no, ee-se e-tee-mos ya to pa-skha; e-khoo-me to-sa pra-gma-ta na e-tee-ma-soo-me!

Manos, are you ready for Easter? We have so many things to prepare!

Manos: Σχεδόν! Αύριο πρέπει να βάψουμε τα κόκκινα αυγά. Εσύ αγόρασες το αρνί για τη σούβλα;

skhe-don! av-ree-o pre-pee na va-psoo-me ta ko-kee-na av-ga. e-see a-go-ra-ses to a-rnee ya tee soo-vla;

Almost! Tomorrow, we need to dye the red eggs. Did you buy the lamb for the spit?

Vasilis: Ναι, το πήρα από τον χασάπη.

ne, to pee-ra a-po ton kha-sa-pee.

Yes, I got it from the butcher.

Manos: Θα πάμε στη βραδινή Ανάσταση, σωστά;

tha pa-me stee vra-dee-nee a-na-sta-see, so-sta;

We're going to the midnight Resurrection service, right?

Vasilis: Εννοείται!

e-no-ee-te!

Of course!

WORDS TO KNOW

Πάσχα	*pa*-skha	*Easter*
σχεδόν	skhe-*don*	*almost*
κόκκινα αυγά	*ko*-kee-na av-*ga*	*red eggs*
αρνί	a-*rnee*	*lamb*
σούβλα	*soo*-vla	*spit*
χασάπης	kha-*sa*-pees	*butcher*
βραδινός, -ή, -ό	vra-dee-*nos*, -ee, -o	*evening, night-related (depending on context)*
εννοείται	e-no-*ee*-te	*of course*

Dancing Like a Greek

As you may know, Greeks dance at every opportunity — weddings, religious celebrations, festivals, and feasts. Everything is an occasion for dancing until the morning!

CULTURAL WISDOM

Each region of Greece has its own songs, unique musical style, and traditional dances. Folklorists have documented around 10,000 dances across Greece. Impressive, right?

There are circular dances and paired dances. Here is some dance-related vocabulary:

» **Χορεύω.** (kho-*rev*-o) (*I dance.*)

» **οι παραδοσιακοί χοροί** (ee pa-ra-do-see-a-*kee* kho-*ree*) (*the traditional dances*)

» **ο κυκλικός χορός** (o kee-klee-*kos* kho-*ros*) (*the circular dance*)

» **ο ζευγαρωτός χορός** (o zev-ga-ro-*tos* kho-*ros*) (*the paired dance*)

» **οι χορευτές** (ee kho-ref-*tes*) (*the dancers*)

In many countries around the world, Greek dances are taught at cultural associations. These are usually connected to the Greek community or the Greek church. So, if you join one of these associations, you're likely to start with one of the following dances: **Συρτός** (see-*rtos*), **Μπάλος** (*ba*-los), **Καλαματιανός** (ka-la-ma-tya-*nos*), and **Χασάπικο** (kha-*sa*-pee-ko).

FUN & GAMES

Match the words from the first column with those from the second to create meaningful phrases.

σουβλίζω	άξιοι
κερνάω	καλεσμένων
λίστα	το αρνί
Μεγάλη	γάμου
πάντα	Εβδομάδα
πρόταση	τους φίλους μου

4

The Part of Tens

Find practical tips for picking up Greek.

Learn a few popular Greek words.

Talk about love like a Greek.

Translate the untranslatable from Greek.

Speak like a local with phrases that make you sound fluent.

Chapter **17**

Ten Ways to Pick Up Greek Quickly

Naturally, no matter how much theory, grammar, and vocabulary you learn, the most important thing is being able to use the Greek language in your daily life and engage in conversations. In this chapter, I suggest ways in which you can easily and freely practice.

TIP

Apart from the ways to pick up Greek that I recommend here, you can try my online Greek language school, Greek Learning Hub. We offer group and individual lessons. The lessons are live and interactive, so you can talk with your classmates, ask questions, and practice your Greek on a weekly basis. You can tailor the lessons to your schedule and your local time zone, while learning from the comfort of your own home. If you want to try it, email us at info@greeklearninghub.com or visit https://greeklearninghub.com/.

Watch TV Series and Movies

Watching TV series and movies in the language you're learning is an easy and fun way to practice your listening skills — that is, your ability to understand native speakers speaking at a natural pace.

TIP

If you're a fan of classic children's cartoons, you can watch them dubbed in Greek. These movies are a great way to practice the language because the story is already familiar, allowing you to focus more on the language itself. Try searching for such cartoons on YouTube.

If you prefer regular television series and movies, you can use the public Greek television platform called ERTFLIX. The website is `www.ert.gr/international/ertflix-en/`, and you get free access by signing in.

You also can sign up for subscription-based Greek TV channels. By paying a monthly fee, you gain access to every Greek television channel. Here are some links:

>> Antenna: `www.antenna.gr/live`

>> Mega: `www.megatv.com/`

>> Skai: `www.skai.gr/tv/`

>> Cosmote TV: `www.cosmotetvott.gr/`

Read Articles and Books

Reading articles and books in Greek strengthens your vocabulary because you not only revisit words you've learned but you also discover new ones. It's especially helpful if, while reading, you look up unknown words in a dictionary.

It's easy to find many articles online covering a variety of interesting topics. You can focus more on articles that align with your interests, such as sports, music, or travel. News articles may be a bit more challenging as they use more formal and serious language.

I recommend checking out these online magazines:

>> `www.lifo.gr/`

>> `www.athensvoice.gr/`

You can also follow news about Greece and the world here:

» www.in.gr/

» The Greek edition of Google News (https://news.google.com/home?hl=el &gl=GR&ceid=GR:el)

Books are also incredibly helpful. You can choose short stories written in simplified language, specifically designed for Greek learners, with vocabulary adjusted to different levels.

TIP

Additionally, classic children's fairy tales in Greek can be a great resource. The language is simple, and the stories are familiar, allowing you to improve your reading skills.

If you don't live in Greece and can't visit a local bookstore, you can easily order books online and have them delivered to your home. Apart from Amazon, various Greek online bookstores worldwide can assist you. You can check the US-based The Greek Bookstore (https://thegreekbookstore.com/) or the Politeia bookstore, which is one of the biggest bookshops in Greece and which delivers internationally: https://www.politeianet.gr.

Listen to Greek Radio and Podcasts

If you can't look at a screen or read something, you can still practice Greek easily by listening to the radio or podcasts. For example, you can go for your morning run, drive to work, or shop at the supermarket while having someone speak Greek in your headphones.

Radio is a great option because, besides listening to hosts discuss and comment on various topics, you can also enjoy plenty of Greek music. Songs are a fun way to learn a language or at least pick up some words.

Many Greek radio stations covering all genres of music are available, as well as stations focusing on sports, news, and the arts. You can also listen to all these stations online. The website https://live24.gr/ has all Greek radio stations, so you can tune in no matter where you are.

Podcasts cover all kinds of topics and allow you to listen to the Greek language for hours. Some podcasts are specifically designed for learners and feature slow and clear speech on simple, everyday subjects. Search for "Greek podcasts" on your favorite podcast app.

REMEMBER

In general, beginners in Greek may feel overwhelmed when listening to the language at its natural pace. You may feel like you don't understand anything and that everything is spoken too quickly. This is completely normal. When you start learning a language, you're not yet able to follow native speakers, especially when they speak quickly among themselves. However, listening to the language helps you familiarize yourself with its sounds, improve your pronunciation, and gradually understand more. So my advice is: Don't be discouraged, and don't give up! You're on the right track.

Look for Greeks Online

Let me tell you the story of one of my students, Helen from the Netherlands. Helen was at an intermediate level and wanted to speak Greek to practice. However, she didn't know any Greeks in her city.

So, she decided to post in a Facebook group for Greeks living in the Netherlands and ask whether anyone would be interested in speaking Greek with her. The response was overwhelming — many Greeks reached out to her, and they started scheduling online meetings during which they would chat in Greek while enjoying their coffee.

Helen's story is just one example of how you can find Greeks to practice with. If you live in Greece or travel often to Greece, things are much simpler. But if you live in another country, the internet can be a great solution.

Try a Language Exchange Program

Language exchange programs are another option. For example, if you speak English and want to practice Greek, you can join a language exchange program and connect with a Greek speaker who wants to practice English. In your meetings, you can speak both languages, benefiting from the experience together. If you search for "language exchange" online, you'll find many websites that help you connect with native speakers.

Visit Your Local Greek Community

If you want to socialize in your city and meet Greeks in your neighborhood, look for the nearest Greek community or church. Greeks often gather there to catch up, meet new people, and participate in various activities. It's an ideal place for someone who wants to speak Greek. You can take part in community events and activities, which will help you learn more about the culture while practicing the language.

Of course, it may take some time to get to know the regular members and establish communication. But once you overcome the initial challenge, everything will become much easier. You'll become part of the community, and everyone will be happy to see you and share their news with you.

Pick a Greek Hobby

Another way to practice the language is through a hobby. For example:

» You could take Greek dance lessons. Many schools — not just in Greece — offer classes. These schools are usually, but not necessarily, connected to Greek schools, communities, or churches.

» Greek cooking classes are also very popular, and you can even take them online.

Build Connections with Greeks

Although this is something you can't force and usually happens naturally, forming close relationships with Greeks helps — whether it's making good friends or having a romantic partner. Spending time with them will definitely give you more opportunities to practice Greek. Nearly half of my students start learning Greek because they are in a relationship with a Greek person and want to be able to communicate with them and their family.

In such cases, you get the chance to learn much more because you discuss all kinds of everyday topics and sometimes find yourself exposed to the language in a way that pushes you out of your comfort zone. This process can feel a bit overwhelming at first, but it helps you make great leaps in your language skills.

Take Part in a Student Exchange Program

If you're a student, you have an incredible opportunity ahead. Many Greek universities collaborate with foreign universities and welcome international students through exchange programs. Often, these programs include free Greek language lessons.

This means you can come to Greece with a small scholarship and study for one or two semesters. University courses will be in English, but you'll be in Greece — surrounded by the language daily, making Greek friends, traveling to the islands, and living an unforgettable experience. To get started, visit https://studyingreece.edu.gr/international-strategic-partnerships/ and https://erasmus-plus.ec.europa.eu/.

Label Objects Around You

TIP

This is a tip I always give my students. Grab small, colorful sticky notes and use them to learn vocabulary more effectively. You can stick them onto objects in your home with their Greek names. That way, every time you approach your refrigerator, you'll read the Greek word for it: ψυγείο (psee-*yee*-o).

Beyond that, you can create sticky notes with difficult words from your weekly vocabulary list, place them in a visible spot in your house, and repeat them whenever you pass by. This method may take time, but it guarantees fast and effective word learning.

Chapter **18**

Ten Popular Greek Words

Some words are directly linked to the culture of Greek people. You hear these words within the first few hours of being in Greece. This chapter explains the meaning behind ten popular Greek words.

Ώπα

Imagine you're at a Greek celebration, and everyone is dancing. Suddenly, an elderly man with a mustache shouts Ώπα! (*o*-pa) and jumps up to dance. What does it mean? Absolutely nothing! It's an exclamation of excitement, a word you can shout when watching someone dance or when you yourself feel an abundance of joy.

But ώπα has other uses, too. This word has several different meanings, and its interpretation changes not only based on tone but also on context:

» If you say Έχω στα ώπα ώπα (*e*-kho sta *o*-pa *o*-pa), it means that you take great care or you spoil someone. For example: Οι γονείς έχουν την κόρη τους στα ώπα ώπα. (ee go-*nees* e-khoon teen *ko*-ree toos sta *o*-pa *o*-pa) (*Parents take excellent care of their daughter.*)

>> It can also be used to interrupt or stop someone's behavior. For instance, if a child is crying persistently, their mother may say **Ωπα ώπα, για σταμάτα σε παρακαλώ.** (*o*-pa *o*-pa, ya sta-*ma*-ta se pa-ra-ka-*lo*) (*Opa, opa, stop, please.*)

Γεια Μας

You're sitting at a table with a Greek family. Suddenly, everyone raises their glasses and says Γεια μας! (ya mas). You immediately understand that this phrase means "Cheers!"

The full phrase is Στην υγειά μας (steen ee-*ya* mas), which translates to "to our health." So, when drinking, Greeks wish good health to their fellow diners.

Holding your drink, you may say:

>> **Γεια μας!** (ya mas) (*Cheers!*)

>> **Στην υγειά μας!** (steen ee-*ya* mas) (*To our health!*)

>> Or simply, **Υγεία!** (ee-*yee*-a) (*Health!*)

Then, you clink glasses with others.

CULTURAL WISDOM

However, be careful: Don't clink glasses if your glass contains water! A superstition in Greek culture is that clinking glasses with water is bad luck. Why? No one knows for sure! Personally, I wouldn't worry too much about these superstitions, but it's fun to know them from a cultural perspective.

Γείτσες

It's spring, the flowers are blooming, and pollen allergies have hit you hard. If you're in Greece, every time you sneeze, you'll hear people around you say Γείτσες! (*yee*-tses) (*Bless you!*). This is a wish given when someone sneezes, derived from the word υγεία (ee-*yee*-a) (*health*), meaning "may you be healthy." You can simply respond with ευχαριστώ (ef-kha-ree-*sto*) (*thank you*).

Μαλάκας

If you've ever been to Greece or have a Greek family, it's almost impossible not to have heard the word μαλάκας (ma-*la*-kas). In dictionaries, you'll find translations like asshole, jerk, or jackass. The feminine form of the word is μαλακισμένη (ma-la-kee-*sme*-nee).

This word can be used aggressively as an insult:

Είσαι μεγάλος μαλάκας. (*ee*-se me-*ga*-los ma-*la*-kas) (*You're a huge jerk.*)

Ο Νίκος είναι μαλάκας. (o *nee*-kos *ee*-ne ma-*la*-kas) (*Nikos is a jerk.*)

Η Ελένη είναι μαλακισμένη. (ee e-*le*-nee *ee*-ne ma-la-kee-*sme*-nee) (*Eleni is an asshole.*)

However, it doesn't always carry a negative tone. Among friends, it can be used as a *friendly* greeting:

Πού είσαι ρε μαλάκα; (poo *ee*-se re ma-*la*-ka) (*Where have you been, man?*)

Μαλάκα, τι κάνεις; (ma-*la*-ka tee *ka*-nees) (*Hey, man, how are you?*)

WARNING

Still, I would advise caution when using this word, especially if you're not a native Greek speaker. If used incorrectly, it could lead to misunderstandings or even heated exchanges.

Φιλοξενία

Φιλοξενία (fee-lo-kse-*nee*-a) is a word deeply intertwined with Greek culture. As mentioned earlier in this book, it derives from the words φίλος (*fee*-los) (*friend*) and ξένος (*kse*-nos) (*foreigner, stranger*). Essentially, φιλοξενία is the act of showing friendly behavior toward a guest or someone from another country.

CULTURAL WISDOM

In ancient Greece, hospitality was considered sacred. People honored Ξένιος Ζευς (*kse*-nee-os zefs), a protector of strangers, and Αθηνά Ξενία (a-the-*na* kse-*nee*-a), who also upheld this virtue. If a guest arrived at your home and wasn't treated with care, it was considered a sin and an insult to the gods.

This tradition has endured through the centuries. My grandmother, who lived in a village, would always set an extra plate on the table "for the stranger" — just in case someone arrived during the meal. This ensured that a guest would feel welcome and included.

REMEMBER

Because of this cultural mindset, Greeks take great pride in hospitality, whether in cafés, restaurants, or their homes. Visitors often receive exceptional treatment, making their experience warm and inviting.

Μεζές

The μεζές (me-*zes*) is a small appetizer dish, typically paired with drinks or served before the main meal. In plural form, it becomes μεζέδες (me-*ze*-des), as people rarely order just one. You can also use the diminutive form: μεζεδάκια (me-ze-*da*-kya) (*little meze dishes*).

Here are some examples of usage:

> **Φέρτε μας ένα μεζεδάκι, παρακαλώ.** (*fe*-rte mas *e*-na me-ze-*da*-kee pa-ra-ka-*lo*) (*Bring us a small appetizer, please.*)

> **Ορίστε οι μεζέδες σας.** (o-*ree*-ste ee me-ze-des sas) (*Here are your appetizers.*)

CULTURAL WISDOM

In Greece, drinking without something small to eat is uncommon. Even in bars, your drink is usually served with chips or nuts. While these aren't considered meze, they reflect a social drinking culture — one in which alcohol is enjoyed alongside food, making the experience more communal.

Etymologically, the word μεζές originates from Persian and Turkish, but it has been used in Greek for centuries.

Γλέντι

A γλέντι (*gle*-dee) is a celebration full of cheer, food, and dancing, in which people come together to have a great time. It's associated with traditional forms of entertainment rather than modern clubs or bars. Many times, there is live music with traditional instruments.

GRAMMATICALLY SPEAKING

The verb γλεντάω (gle-*da*-o) in the present tense means "to revel." In the past tense, γλέντησα (*gle*-dee-sa), and the future tense, θα γλεντήσω (tha gle-*dee*-so), it translates to "I celebrated" and "I will celebrate," respectively.

Examples of usage include the following:

Το γλέντι κράτησε μέχρι το πρωί. (to *gle*-dee *kra*-tee-se *me*-khree to pro-*ee*) (*The celebration lasted until morning.*)

Φάγαμε, ήπιαμε, και γλεντήσαμε . . . περάσαμε πάρα πολύ ωραία. (*fa*-ga-me *ee*-pya-me ke gle-*dee*-sa-me . . . pe-*ra*-sa-me *pa*-ra po-*lee* o-re-a) (*We ate, drank, and celebrated . . . we had an amazing time.*)

Εντάξει

The word εντάξει (e-da-ksee) essentially means OK or alright. You may hear:

Είσαι εντάξει; (*ee*-se e-*da*-ksee) (*Are you alright?*)

Όλα εντάξει. (*o*-la e-*da*-ksee) (*Everything is fine.*)

If someone tells you **Δεν είσαι εντάξει** (den *ee*-se e-*da*-ksee), it means you aren't acting properly or keeping your word.

TIP

In casual spoken language, Greeks also shorten it to *ντάξει* or *νταξ*, especially in informal conversation.

Γύρος

Gyros is food — a beloved food, which absolutely deserves a spot on any list of favorite Greek words!

The word γύρος (*yee*-ros), meaning something that turns, refers to the circular motion in which the meat is cooked. It's placed on a vertical rotisserie, slowly turning around a flame to ensure even cooking on all sides.

For many, just hearing the word γύρος is enough to make their mouth water — which is why it definitely belongs among Greece's most cherished culinary terms!

Ηλιοβασίλεμα

The word ηλιοβασίλεμα (ee-lyo-va-*see*-le-ma) translates to "sunset." Sunset, when the sky is clear, is a magical time. The sky bursts into vibrant colors, creating a stunning, almost dreamlike atmosphere.

Watching the sun set over the Aegean Sea is breathtaking — it looks as if the sun is sinking right into the water. This beauty has made Greek sunsets a tourist attraction on their own.

In Santorini island, you'll find one of the most spectacular sunsets in the world. Many visitors come to Greece — especially to the islands — to get married at sunset or organize photography sessions precisely at that moment.

Chapter **19**

Ten Greek Expressions About Love

D o you have a Greek partner? Then this chapter is especially for you. How many times has your partner tried to express their feelings with incomprehensible Greek words, only to attempt translating them afterward? Surely many! So now it's time to give them a little surprise. Choose one of the following words or phrases and say it to them the next time you see each other. You'll definitely see the surprise painted on their face.

Σε Αγαπώ

Here we are talking about deep emotions. **Σε αγαπώ** (se a-ga-*po*) means "I love you," but it's a profound expression. It describes the bond that develops between two people who have shared a lot and have worked on their relationship extensively. It's also a feeling you can have for friends, siblings, or even your pet.

If you want to find out if your partner loves you, you can ask:

Με αγαπάς; (me a-ga-*pas*) (*Do you love me?*)

And they may respond:

> **Σε αγαπώ.** (se a-ga-*po*) (*I love you.*)

More often you see this phrase with an apostrophe: **Σ'αγαπώ** (s'a-ga-*po*).

TIP

The verb **αγαπάω/αγαπώ** (a-ga-*pa*-o/a-ga-*po*) belongs to the B1 type, meaning it follows the pattern of verbs ending in **-αω/-ω**. For more details, look at Chapter 4.

REMEMBER

Here are some more examples:

> **Ο Νίκος αγαπάει την Ελένη.** (o *nee*-kos a-ga-*pa*-ee teen e-*le*-nee) (*Nikos loves Eleni.*)

> **Ο μπαμπάς αγαπάει τα παιδιά του.** (o ba-*bas* a-ga-*pa*-ee ta pe-*dya* too) (*The dad loves his children.*)

The noun form is **αγάπη** (a-*ga*-pee), meaning "love." You can refer to someone you love as **αγάπη μου** (a-*ga*-pee moo), which means "my love."

Αγάπη is also used as a female name.

CULTURAL WISDOM

Σε Σκέφτομαι

Σε σκέφτομαι (se *ske*-fto-me) means *I'm thinking of you.* The pronoun **σε** (se) indicates that the thought is directed toward the person you're speaking to. You can send or say this phrase to someone you care about, expressing affection or concern. It's not exclusively romantic — it can also express general human connection and care.

Additionally, the verb **σκέφτομαι** (*ske*-fto-me) refers to the broader process of thinking. Examples include the following:

> **Η Βασιλική σκέφτεται την Ειρήνη.** (ee va-see-lee-*kee ske*-fte-te teen ee-*ree*-nee) (*Vasiliki is thinking about Irini.*)

> **Αλέξανδρε, σε σκέφτομαι όλη μέρα.** (a-*le*-ksa-ndre, se *ske*-fto-me o-lee *me*-ra) (*Alexander, I think about you all day.*)

> **Ο μαθητής σκέφτεται πώς θα λύσει την άσκηση των μαθηματικών.** (o ma-thee-tees *ske*-fte-te pos tha *lee*-see teen *a*-skee-see ton ma-thee-ma-tee-*kon*) (*The student is thinking about how to solve the math problem.*)

From this verb comes the noun **σκέψη** (*ske*-psee), meaning "thought."

Μου Λείπεις

If you miss someone, you can say μου λείπεις (moo *lee*-pees) (*I miss you*) — this phrase expresses longing or the feeling of absence when someone isn't around. This phrase can be used in personal relationships — between friends, family members, or romantic partners.

You can also use μου λείπει (moo *lee*-pee) to say you miss a place or an experience. Examples include these:

> **Μου λείπει η Ελλάδα.** (moo *lee*-pee ee e-*la*-da) (*I miss Greece.*)
>
> **Μου λείπει το σχολείο.** (moo *lee*-pee to skho-*lee*-o) (*I miss school.*)

GRAMMATICALLY SPEAKING

The verb λείπω (*lee*-po) means to be absent, so if we were to be completely precise, μου λείπεις literally means "You are absent from me" or "You are missing from my life." Which, honestly, makes the expression even more romantic!

Σε Θέλω

This phrase often expresses strong romantic or passionate desire, as σε θέλω (se *the*-lo) directly translates to "I want you." It typically carries romantic or intimate connotations — it's not something you would say to friends or family.

WARNING

Be careful! If a colleague at work tells you σε θέλω λίγο (se *the*-lo *lee*-go), it simply means "I need you for a moment" or "I want to talk to you briefly." Don't misinterpret their words, or you may end up in an amusing or awkward situation!

Μου Αρέσεις

Μου αρέσεις (moo a-*re*-sees) means "I like you" and can be used during flirtation or to express admiration for your romantic partner. While it often refers to physical appearance, it can also express attraction to a person's overall character — both body and soul.

When used in the third person— **μου αρέσει** (moo a-*re*-see) — it means "I like" and can describe anything that brings you joy. Examples include these:

> **Μου αρέσει το παγωτό.** (moo a-*re*-see to pa-go-*to*) (*I like ice cream.*)

Μου αρέσει η θάλασσα. (moo a-*re*-see ee *tha*-la-sa) (*I like the sea.*)

Μου αρέσει το φαγητό της μαμάς. (moo a-*re*-see to fa-yee-*to* tees ma-*mas*) (*I like Mom's food.*)

Σε Γουστάρω

Σε γουστάρω (se goo-*sta*-ro) (*I'm really into you, I fancy you*) is more slang and conveys intense attraction or admiration. Γουστάρω (goo-*sta*-ro) implies strong enthusiasm for something or someone.

CULTURAL WISDOM

You need to have a certain level of familiarity with someone to use this phrase, as it can sound quite bold or unusual if used in the wrong context.

Είσαι Όμορφος, Είσαι Όμορφη

If you want to give a genuine compliment or express admiration toward your partner, commenting on their appearance is always a great choice.

>> Όμορφος (*o*-mo-rfos) is the masculine form, used when addressing a man.

>> Όμορφη (*o*-mo-rfee) is the feminine form, used when addressing a woman.

So the phrase είσαι όμορφος (*ee*-se o-mo-rfos) means "you are handsome" and the phrase είσαι όμορφη (*ee*-se o-mo-rfee) means "you are beautiful."

Ψυχή Μου

The word ψυχή (psee-*hee*) means "soul," and ψυχή μου (psee-*hee* moo) translates to "my soul." It's a sweet and affectionate term often used to address a loved one, though not necessarily a romantic partner. You can hear grandparents referring to their grandkids like this, mothers to their kids, and so on.

CULTURAL WISDOM

The concept of the soul holds deep significance in Greek culture, appearing in literature, philosophy, and theology since Homer's era (eighth century BCE). Given its rich heritage, ψυχή naturally found its way into romantic expressions.

Καρδιά Μου

A heartfelt expression of love! Καρδιά (ka-*rdya*) means "heart," and καρδιά μου (ka-*rdya* moo) translates to "my heart." Since the heart is a vital organ, calling someone your heart conveys immense emotional value.

Other affectionate terms include μάτια μου (*ma*-tya moo) (*my eyes*), reflecting how precious someone is — just like one's own eyes. These phrases are commonly found in romantic song lyrics.

A softer version of καρδιά μου is καρδούλα μου (ka-*rdoo*-la moo), meaning "my little heart."

Ζωή Μου

I'm closing the list of Greek romantic phrases with ζωή μου (zo-*ee* moo) meaning "my life." Calling someone your life expresses the idea that they are your everything. While it may seem intense, Greek romantic culture is known for its passion and deep emotions. People openly speak about their feelings with boldness and sincerity.

Chapter **20**

Ten Greek Words That Can't Be Translated

I can say that this is the most difficult chapter for me. The words in it don't translate directly into English, but their meaning is strongly connected to the way Greeks think and speak. For this reason, in this chapter I not only explain words to you but also entire concepts of Greek everyday life.

Ρε

Ρε (re) is a shortened version of the word μωρέ (mo–re), which originally meant "fool." Although few Greeks know this original meaning, ρε is a word that appears in most people's daily vocabulary. For example:

Πώς είσαι ρε φίλε; (pos ee-se re fee-le) (How are you, re, friend?)

Πού πας ρε; (poo pas re) (Where are you going, re?)

Depending on the tone of voice and context, it can express intensity or annoyance:

Τι κάνεις ρε; Γιατί πειράζεις τον σκύλο; (tee ka-nees re; ya-tee pee-ra-zees ton skee-lo) (What are you doing, re? Why are you bothering the dog?)

It can be added as an informal greeting:

Γεια ρε! (ya re) (*Hey, re!*)

Or it can express surprise:

Αχ ρε! Χάλασε το αυτοκίνητο. Τι θα κάνουμε; (ah re! *kha*-la-se to af-to-*kee*-nee-to. tee tha *ka*-noo-me) (*Oh, re! The car broke down. What will we do?*)

CULTURAL WISDOM

When you're in Greece, you'll hear ρε many times during the day. However, you must be careful in its usage. It's quite informal, and if used incorrectly, it may sound aggressive. Personally, I suggest avoiding it, but it's important to know its use because you'll hear it everywhere.

Άντε

A word whose meaning changes depending on tone and situation is άντε (*a*–de). It doesn't have a specific English translation, but it's used to add emotion or emphasis to phrases.

Its most common use is encouraging:

Άντε, πάμε να φύγουμε! (*a*-de, *pa*-me na *fee*-goo-me) (*Ante, let's go!*)

Άντε, ελάτε! Σας περιμένουμε! (*a*-de, e-*la*-te! sas pe-ree-*me*-noo-me) (*Ante, come on! We're waiting for you!*)

Secondly, it can express irony:

Η γιαγιά μου είναι η Μαντόνα. (ee ya-*ya* moo *ee*-ne ee ma-*do*-na) (*My grandma is Madonna.*)

Άντε, αλήθεια; (*a*-de, a-*lee*-thya) (*Ante, really?*)

In more colloquial language, άντε can be used instead of "go":

Νίκο, άντε να φέρεις ένα ποτήρι νερό στη γιαγιά σου. (*nee*-ko *a*-de na *fe*-rees *e*-na po-*tee*-ree ne-*ro* stee ya-*ya* soo) (*Nikos, ante, bring a glass of water to your grandma.*)

Μεράκι

Have you ever seen someone preparing a meal for their family with all the love and care they can muster? A musician singing while savoring each note? A carpenter carefully carving wood, pouring passion and dedication into their craft?

That feeling — the deep fulfillment and joy you experience when doing something with your heart and soul — is μεράκι (me-*ra*-kee). There is no direct translation into English. It's a general sense of enthusiasm, devotion, and wholehearted effort. One thing is certain: Anything done with μεράκι is done exceptionally well. Here are some examples:

> **Η Μάρθα** *έκανε πάντα τη δουλειά της με μεράκι.* (ee *ma*-rtha *e*-ka-ne *pa*-da tee doo-*lya* tees me me-*ra*-kee) (*Martha always did her work with meraki.*)
>
> **Το κορίτσι** *ζωγραφίζει πάνω σε ένα βότσαλο με πολύ μεράκι.* (to ko-*ree*-tsee zo-gra-*fee*-zee *pa*-no se *e*-na vo-tsa-lo me po-*lee* me-*ra*-kee) (*The girl is painting on a pebble with great meraki.*)

Έρωτας

It's time to get romantic. Have you ever felt those butterflies in your stomach whenever you see someone who excites you? The thrill of getting a reply to your message? The nervous anticipation before meeting them?

In Greek, this intense and passionate feeling is called έρωτας (*e*-ro-tas). It represents the first phase of attraction — different from love, which develops gradually, and more than simple interest.

CULTURAL WISDOM

In ancient Greece, Eros was the god of love, striking people with his arrows to make them fall in love. The Greek verb is ερωτεύομαι (e-ro-*tev*-o-me) (*to fall in love*), and you can say είμαι ερωτευμένος (*ee*-me e-ro-tev-*me*-nos) (for men) and είμαι ερωτευμένη (*ee*-me e-ro-tev-*me*-nee) (for women) (*I am in love*). While "I am in love" is the closest English phrase, it doesn't fully capture the essence of eros.

Φιλότιμο

Φιλότιμο (fee-*lo*-tee-mo) is a word with an extremely broad meaning, making it one of the hardest to translate. I'll describe it so you can grasp its essence.

A person with φιλότιμο acts with conscience, dignity, and honor. They go beyond what is required — not for personal gain but because it's the right thing to do.

A φιλότιμος (fee-*lo*-tee-mos) person — φιλότιμος for men, φιλότιμη (fee-*lo*-tee-mee) for women — will always do their best to help others, put in extra effort for the sake of morality, and never break their word. People around them respect and value them because they recognize their integrity and dedication. Here are some examples:

> Ο Κοσμάς είναι φιλότιμος άνθρωπος και δεν θα σε εξαπατήσει. (o ko-*smas ee*-ne fee-*lo*-tee-mos *an*-thro-pos ke den tha se e-ksa-pa-*tee*-see) (*Kosmas is a filotimos man, and he would never deceive you.*)

> Στις μέρες μας έχει χαθεί το φιλότιμο. (stees *me*-res mas *e*-hee kha-*thee* to fee-*lo*-tee-mo) (*Nowadays, filotimo is disappearing.*)

Κέφι

When you enjoy yourself with your whole body, mind, and heart — when nothing can hide your excitement — you can say that you are having fun with κέφι (*ke*-fee).

> Η χθεσινή βραδιά ήταν γεμάτη κέφι — χορέψαμε, τραγουδήσαμε, και περάσαμε πολύ καλά! (ee khthe-see-*nee* vra-*dya ee*-tan ye-*ma*-tee *ke*-fee — kho-*re*-psa-me, tra-goo-*dee*-sa-me, ke pe-*ra*-sa-me ka-*la*) (*Last night was full of kefi — we danced, sang, and had a great time!*)

If you say Είμαι κεφάτος (*ee*-me ke-*fa*-tos) (for men) or Είμαι κεφάτη (*ee*-me ke-*fa*-tee) (for women), it means you're in a good mood:

> Η Έλλη είναι κεφάτη. Από το πρωί κάνει τις δουλειές της και τραγουδάει. (ee *e*-lee *ee*-ne ke-*fa*-tee. a-*po* to pro-*ee ka*-nee tees doo-*lyes* tees ke tra-goo-*da*-ee) (*Elli is in a good mood. Since morning, she has been doing her chores and singing.*)

The opposite of this word is άκεφος (*a*-ke-fos) (for men) and άκεφη (*a*-ke-fee) (for women) — someone who has no κέφι at all:

> Σήμερα είμαι άκεφος και δεν θα πάω πουθενά. (*see*-me-ra *ee*-me *a*-ke-fos ke den tha *pa*-o poo-the-*na*) (*Today, I am in a bad mood and won't go anywhere.*)

Λεβέντης

This word is best described through a description rather than a sentence. Etymologically, it comes from Persian and Turkish but has been fully integrated into Greek.

Λεβέντης (le-*ve*-dees) describes a masculine, strong, and handsome man who possesses bravery, courage, and honesty — someone who doesn't fear hardships or dangers. This term is exclusively used for men; it's uncommon to hear it as a descriptor for a woman.

Παλικάρι

Παλικάρι (pa-lee-*ka*-ree) is very similar to λεβέντης (see the previous section) and comes from ancient Greek. It describes a young man who has a strong presence, power, sincerity, and courage.

GRAMMATICALLY SPEAKING

The word το παλικάρι is grammatically neutral even though it describes young men.

Often, older people use this word when addressing young men they don't know:

> Παλικάρι μου, μπορείς να με βοηθήσεις να περάσω τον δρόμο; (pa-lee-*ka*-ree moo bo-*rees* na me vo-ee-*thee*-sees na pe-*ra*-so ton *dro*-mo) (*Young man, can you help me cross the street?*)

An interesting variation is το γεροντοπαλίκαρο (to ye-ro-do-pa-*lee*-ka-ro), which describes an older man who has never married.

Θαλπωρή

Imagine being in an environment where you feel safe, warm, loved, and cared for. Your whole body and mind are at peace, and you're flooded with a sense of fulfillment and happiness. That is precisely what the word θαλπωρή (tha-lpo-*ree*) describes. Here are some examples:

> Η Ελένη έχει ανάγκη από θαλπωρή και πήγε στο σπίτι των γονιών της. (ee e-*le*-nee *e*-hee a-*na*-gee a-*po* tha-lpo-*ree* ke *pee*-ye sto *spee*-tee ton go-n*yon* tees) (*Eleni needed thalpori, so she went to her parents' house.*)

Ξάπλωσε στο ζεστό, μαλακό του κρεβάτι και ένιωσε τη θαλπωρή να τον τυλίγει.
(*ksa*-plo-se sto ze-*sto* ma-la-*ko* too kre-*va*-tee ke *e*-nyo-se tee tha-lpo-*ree* na ton
tee-*lee*-yee) (*He lay down on his warm, soft bed and felt thalpori envelop him.*)

Κελεπούρι

Το κελεπούρι (to ke-le-*poo*-ree) can be described as a great opportunity. It can be used to refer to both people and objects of exceptional value. Here are some examples:

Η γυναίκα του Πάνου είναι πραγματικό κελεπούρι. Είναι ευγενική, δυναμική, και όμορφη. (ee yee-*ne*-ka too *pa*-noo *ee*-ne pra-gma-tee-*ko* ke-le-*poo*-ree. *ee*-ne ev-ye-nee-*kee*, dee-na-mee-*kee*, ke o-mo-rfee) (*Panos' wife is truly a kelepouri. She is kind, strong, and beautiful.*)

Το σπίτι που αγόρασαν είναι κελεπούρι — μεγάλο, φωτεινό, και σε καλή τιμή.
(to *spee*-tee poo a-*go*-ra-san *ee*-ne pra-gma-tee-*ko* ke-le-*poo*-ree — me-*ga*-lo, fo-tee-*no*, ke se ka-*lee tee*-mee) (*The house they bought is a kelepouri — big, bright, and at a great price.*)

Chapter **21**

Ten Greek Phrases That Will Make You Sound More Fluent

n this chapter, I share ten expressions that are used daily by Greeks in colloquial speech and will make you sound like you know the tricks of the Greek
language.

Να'σαι Καλά

The phrase **Να'σαι καλά** (Na se ka–*la*) means "Be well." It's used as a general wish
or as a response to a compliment, like in the following examples where you wish
well to your interlocutors.

> **Έκανες πολύ καλή δουλειά.** (*e*-ka-nes po-*lee* ka-*lee* doo-*lya*) (*You did a great job.*)
>
> **Να'σαι καλά.**

> **Έχεις ωραία μαλλιά.** (*e*-hees o-*re*-a ma-*lya*) (*You have beautiful hair.*)
>
> **Να'σαι καλά.**

It can also mean "You're welcome" when someone thanks you for something:

> **Ευχαριστώ για τη βοήθεια.** (ef-kha-ree-*sto* ya tee vo-*ee*-thee-a) (*Thanks for the help.*)
>
> **Να'σαι καλά.**

GRAMMATICALLY
SPEAKING

The **'σαι** with the apostrophe is the verb **είσαι** (*ee*-se) (*you are*), which is the second person of the verb **είμαι** (*ee*-me) (*to be*). I explain more in Chapter 4.

Για Πες

The phrase **για πες** (ya pes) is used to start a conversation and show interest in what the other person is saying. It means "Tell me more" or "Go on, keep talking." It's informal and used as follows:

> **Δεν φαντάζεσαι τι έγινε σήμερα!** (den fa-*da*-ze-se tee *e*-yee-ne *see*-me-ra) (*You won't believe what happened today!*)
>
> **Για πες . . .**

Here's another example:

> **Για πες, θα έρθεις στην εκδρομή τη Δευτέρα;** (ya pes, tha *e*-rthees steen e-kdro-*mee* teen def-*te*-ra) (*Tell me, are you coming on the trip on Monday?*)

Κοίτα Να Δεις . . ./Άκου Να Δεις . . .

The phrase **κοίτα να δεις** (*kee*-ta na dees . . .) literally means "Look to see," while **άκου να δεις** (*a*-koo na dees . . .) literally means "Listen to see." Although the literal meaning doesn't make much sense, these expressions are used in different ways:

>> At the beginning of a sentence to explain something in a strong or strict manner:
>>
>> **Κοίτα/Άκου να δεις, αν το ξανακάνεις αυτό χωρίζουμε!** (*kee*-ta/*a*-koo na dees, an to ksa-na-*ka*-nees af-*to* kho-*ree*-zoo-me) (*Look/Listen, if you do this again, we're breaking up!*)

>> At the beginning of a sentence when introducing something very interesting:

Άκου να δεις τι έγινε προχθές! Μου έκλεψαν την τσάντα! (*a*-koo na dees tee e-yee-ne pro-*khthes*! moo e-kle-psan teen *tsa*-da) (*Listen to what happened the other day! My bag was stolen!*)

» As an exclamation when someone tells you a story and you want to show strong interest:

Πήγαμε εκδρομή και χάλασε το αυτοκίνητο. (*pee*-ga-me e-kdro-*mee* ke *kha*-la-se to af-to-*kee*-nee-to) (*We went on a trip, and the car broke down.*)

Κοίτα/Άκου να δεις!

Μια Χαρά

Μια χαρά (mya kha-*ra*) means "Just fine" or "Very well." The word χαρά (kha-*ra*) alone means "joy," so when you say Είμαι μια χαρά (*ee*-me mya kha-*ra*), you're essentially saying "I'm good." It's a nice alternative response to the question Τι κάνεις; (tee *ka*-nees) (*How are you?*) For example:

Τι κάνεις, Μαρία; (tee *ka*-nees ma-*ree*-a) (*How are you, Maria?*)

Μια χαρά.

Όπως Θέλεις

If someone asks for your permission or opinion on something and you don't want to take a stance, you can say όπως θέλεις (*o*-pos *the*-lees), meaning "As you wish." For example:

Θέλω να κάνω τατουάζ σε όλο το σώμα. (*the*-lo na *ka*-no ta-too-*az* se *o*-lo to *so*-ma) (*I want to get a full-body tattoo.*)

Όπως θέλεις.

However, depending on the tone, it can also be ironic, implying disagreement. In the preceding example, if you don't agree with your friend's choice, you might say Όπως θέλεις in a way that subtly expresses disapproval.

Να Σου Πω . . .

Another way Greeks start sentences is by saying Να σου πω (na soo po), which literally means "Let me tell you." It's an introductory phrase that prepares the listener for an important question.

Here are some examples:

Να σου πω, ξέρεις πού είναι ο μπλε φάκελος; (na soo po, *kse*-rees poo *ee*-ne o ble *fa*-ke-los) (*Let me ask you, do you know where the blue folder is?*)

Να σου πω, τηλεφώνησες στη Γιαγιά εχθές; (na soo po, tee-le-*fo*-nee-ses stee ya-*ya* e-khthes) (*Let me ask you, did you call Grandma yesterday?*)

Α Πα Πα!

The phrase Α πα πα! (a pa pa) doesn't have a direct translation — it's more of an exclamation used to express disapproval, rejection, or shock. Sometimes, it's also used as a reaction to gossip.

Here is one example:

Να βάψω τα μαλλιά μου ξανθά; (na *va*-pso ta ma-*lya* moo ksa-*ntha*) (*Should I dye my hair blonde?*)

Α πα πα! Δεν σου πηγαίνει. (a pa pa! den soo pee-*ye*-nee) (*A pa pa! It doesn't suit you.*)

And here's another:

Είδες το αγόρι της Κάτιας; (*ee*-des to a-*go*-ree tees *ka*-tyas) (*Did you see Katia's boyfriend?*)

Α πα πα! Δεν ταιριάζουν καθόλου. (a-pa-pa! den te-*rya*-zoon ka-*tho*-loo) (*A pa pa! They don't match at all.*)

Πω Πω!

This exclamation doesn't have a specific meaning on its own — it depends on tone and context. Greeks use it frequently to express different emotions:

>> Admiration: **Πω πω! Κοίτα ένα ωραίο σπίτι!** (po po! *kee*-ta *e*-na o-*re*-o *spee*-tee) (*Wow! Look at that beautiful house!*)

>> Disappointment or frustration: **Πω πω! Κάηκε το φαγητό!** (po po! *ka*-ee-ke to fa-yee-*to*) (*Oh no! The food is burned!*)

>> Surprise: **Πω πω! Δεν περίμενα να έρθεις τόσο γρήγορα!** (po po! den pe-*ree*-me-na na e-rthees *to*-so gree-go-ra) (*Wow! I didn't expect you to arrive so fast!*)

Και Μη Χειρότερα!

This phrase is used as a reaction to bad news, expressing hope that things won't get any worse. Here is one example of its usage:

> **Η κόρη μου δέχεται μπούλινγκ στο σχολείο.** (ee *ko*-ree moo *de*-he-te *boo*-ling sto skho-*lee*-o) (*My daughter is being bullied at school.*)

> **Και μη χειρότερα!** (ke mee hee-*ro*-te-ra) (*Let's hope it doesn't get any worse!*)

Here's another example:

> **Έπιασε φωτιά το δάσος!** (e-pya-se fo-*tya* to *da*-sos) (*The forest caught fire!*)

> **Και μη χειρότερα!** (ke mee hee-*ro*-te-ra) (*Hopefully, it won't get worse!*)

Αν Δεν Κάνω Λάθος . . .

This phrase means "If I'm not mistaken." It's used when expressing a fact or opinion while acknowledging the possibility of being incorrect. Here are two examples:

> **Αν δεν κάνω λάθος η Ειρήνη γεννήθηκε το 1992.** (an den *ka*-no *la*-thos ee ee-*ree*-nee ye-*nee*-thee-ke to *hee*-lya e-nya-*ko*-sya e-ne-*nee*-da *dee*-o) (*If I'm not mistaken, Irene was born in 1992.*)

> **Αν δεν κάνω λάθος η τσάντα είναι στο σαλόνι.** (an den *ka*-no *la*-thos ee *tsa*-da *ee*-ne sto sa-*lo*-nee) (*If I'm not mistaken, the bag is in the living room.*)

5

Appendixes

Appendix **A**
Mini-Dictionaries

Greek-English Mini-Dictionary

A

αγαπάω (a-ga-*pa*-o): to love

αγάπη (a-*ga*-pee) f: love

αγαπημένος/αγαπημένη/αγαπημένο (a-ga-pee-*me*-nos/a-ga-pee-*me*-nee/a-ga-pee-*me*-no) m/f/n: favorite

άγιος/αγία (*a*-yee-os/a-*yee*-a) m/f: saint

αγοράζω (a-go-*ra*-zo): to buy

αγόρι (a-*go*-ree) m: boy

αδελφή (a-de-*lfee*) f: sister

αδέλφια (a-*de*-lfya) n: siblings

αδελφός (a-de-*lfos*) m: brother

αεροδρόμιο (a-e-ro-*dro*-mee-o) n: airport

αεροπλάνο (a-e-ro-*pla*-no) n: airplane

αλήθεια (a-*lee*-thya) f: truth

αλλά (a-*la*): but

άνδρας (*a*-dras) m: man

άνοιξη (*a*-nee-ksee) f: spring

απλός/απλή/απλό (a-*plos*/a-*plee*/a-*plo*) m/f/n: simple

Από πού είσαι; (A-*po* poo *ee*-se): Where are you from?

αποθήκη (a-po-*thee*-kee) f: storage room

απορρυπαντικό (a-po-ree-pa-dee-*ko*) n: detergent

Απρίλιος (a-*pree*-lee-os) m: April

αριστερά (a-ree-ste-*ra*): left

αρνί (ar-*nee*) n: lamb

αρραβωνιάζομαι (a-ra-vo-*nya*-zo-me): to get engaged

αρχίζω (a-*rhee*-zo): to begin

αυγό (av-*go*) n: egg

Αύγουστος (*av*-goo-stos) m: August

αύριο (*av*-ree-o) n: tomorrow

Β

βάζω πλυντήριο (*va*-zo plee-*dee*-ree-o): to do the laundry

βιβλίο (vee-*vlee*-o) n: book

βλέπω (*vle*-po): to see

βλέπω τηλεόραση (*vle*-po tee-le-*o*-ra-see): to watch TV

βοηθάω (vo-ee-*tha*-o): to help

βοήθεια (vo-*ee*-thee-a) f: help

βράδυ (*vra*-dee) n: evening

βρίσκω (*vree*-sko): to find

βροχή (vro-*hee*) f: rain

βρύση (*vree*-see) f: faucet

Γ

γάλα (*ga*-la) n: milk

γάμος (*ga*-mos) m: wedding

γαμπρός (ga-*bros*) m: groom

γεια (ya): hello

γεια σας (ya sas): hello (formal)

γεια σου (ya soo): hello (informal)

γεια χαρά (ya kha-*ra*): bye

γελάω (ye-*la*-o): to laugh

γεμίζω (ye-*mee*-zo): to fill

γεύμα (*yev*-ma) n: meal

γιαγιά (ya-*ya*) f: grandmother

γιορτάζω (yo-*rta*-zo): to celebrate

γιορτή (yo-*rtee*) f: celebration

γιος (yos) m: son

γλώσσα (*glo*-ssa) f: language, tongue

γράμμα (*gra*-ma) n: letter

γραφείο (gra-*fee*-o) n: office

γράφω (*gra*-fo): to write

γρήγορα (*gree*-go-ra): quickly

γρήγορος/γρήγορη/γρήγορο (*gree*-go-ros/*gree*-go-ree/*gree*-go-ro) m/f/n: fast

γυαλί (ya-*lee*) n: glass

γυναίκα (yee-*ne*-ka) f: woman

γυρίζω (yee-*ree*-zo): to return

Δ

δάσκαλα (da-*ska*-la) f: teacher

δάσκαλος (*da*-ska-los) m: teacher

δέκα (*de*-ka): ten

Δεκέμβριος (de-*ke*-mvree-os) m: December

δέντρο (*de*-ndro) n: tree

δεξιά (de-ksee-*a*): right

Δευτέρα (def-*te*-ra) f: Monday

δημαρχείο (dee-ma-*rhee*-o) n: town hall

δημιουργώ (dee-mee-oo-*rgo*): to create

διαβάζω (dya-*va*-zo): to read

διάβαση πεζών (dee-*a*-va-see pe-*zon*) f: pedestrian crossing

διάλειμμα (*dee*-a-lee-ma) n: break

διάλογος (*dee*-a-lo-gos) m: dialogue

διαμέρισμα (dya-*me*-ree-sma) n: apartment

διασκέδαση (dya-*ske*-da-see) f: entertainment, fun

διασταύρωση (dee-a-*stav*-ro-see) f: intersection

διάφορος/διάφορη/διάφορο (*dya*-fo-ros/*dya*-fo-ree/*dya*-fo-ro) m/f/n: various, different

δίνω (*dee*-no): to give

δίπλα (*dee*-pla): next to

δουλεύω (doo-*lev*-o): to work

δρόμος (*dro*-mos) m: road

δύο (*dee*-o): two

δώρο (*do*-ro) n: gift

E

εβδομάδα (ev-do-*ma*-da) f: week

εγώ (e-*go*): I

εδώ (e-*do*): here

εικόνα (ee-*ko*-na) f: image, picture

είμαι (*ee*-me): to be

εισιτήριο (ee-see-*tee*-ree-o) n: ticket

εκατό (e-ka-*to*): one hundred

ελεύθερος/ελεύθερη/ελεύθερο (e-*lef*-the-ros/e-*lef*-the-ree/e-*lef*-the-ro) m/f/n: single, free

ελπίδα (e-*lpee*-da) f: hope

ελπίζω (e-*lpee*-zo): to hope

εμπρός (e-*mbros*): forward

ένα (*e*-na): one

εννιά (e-*nya*): nine

ενοικιάζω (e-nee-kee-*a*-zo): to rent

έξι (*e*-ksee): six

εορτάζω (e-o-*rta*-zo): to celebrate (religious)

εορτή (e-o-*rtee*) f: feast

επτά/εφτά (e-*pta*/e-*fta*): seven

εργάζομαι (e-*rga*-zo-me): to work

εργασία (e-rga-*see*-a) f: work

εργοστάσιο (e-rgo-*sta*-see-o) n: factory

ερωτεύομαι (e-ro-*tev*-o-me): to fall in love

εστιατόριο (e-stee-a-*to*-ree-o) n: restaurant

ετοιμάζω (e-tee-*ma*-zo): to prepare

έτοιμος/έτοιμη/έτοιμο (*e*-tee-mos/*e*-tee-mee/*e*-tee-mo) m/f/n: ready

ευθύς/ευθεία/ευθύ (ef-*thees*/ef-*thee*-a/ef-*thee*) m/f/n: straight ahead

ευτυχία (ef-tee-*hee*-a) f: happiness

ευτυχισμένος/ευτυχισμένη/ευτυχισμένο (ef-tee-hee-*sme*-nos/ef-tee-hee-*sme*-nee/ef-tee-hee-*sme*-no) m/f/n: happy

ευχαριστώ (ef-kha-ree-*sto*): thank you

Z

ζακέτα (za-*ke*-ta) f: jacket

ζάχαρη (*za*-kha-ree) f: sugar

ζεστός/ζεστή/ζεστό (ze-*stos*/ze-*stee*/ze-*sto*) m/f/n: hot, warm

ζεσταίνω (ze-*ste*-no): to warm up

ζευγάρι (zev-*ga*-ree) n: couple

ζητάω οδηγίες (zee-*ta*-o o-dee-*gee*-es): to ask for directions

ζωγραφίζω (zo-gra-*fee*-zo): to draw

ζωή (zo-*ee*) f: life

ζώνη (*zo*-nee) f: belt

ζωντανή μουσική (zo-da-*nee* moo-see-*kee*) f: live music

H

ή (ee): or

ημέρα (ee-*me*-ra): day

Θ

Θέλεις να με παντρευτείς; (*the*-lees na me pa-dref-*tees*): Will you marry me?

θέλω (*the*-lo): to want

θερμοκρασία (ther-mo-kra-*see*-a) f: temperature

θρησκευτικός γάμος (three-skef-tee-*kos* ga-mos) m: religious wedding

θυμάμαι (thee-*ma*-me): to remember

θυμός (thee-*mos*) m: anger

I

Ιανουάριος (ee-a-noo-*a*-ree-os) m: January

ιερός/ιερή/ιερό (ee-e-*ros*/ee-e-*ree*/ee-e-*ro*) m/f/n: holy

ιεροτελεστία (ee-e-ro-te-le-*stee*-a) f: ritual

ικανότητα (ee-ka-*no*-tee-ta) f: ability

ιστορία (ee-sto-*ree*-a) f: history, story

Ιούνιος (ee-*oo*-nee-os) m: June

Ιούλιος (ee-*oo*-lee-os) m: July

K

καθαρίζω (ka-tha-*ree*-zo): to clean

κάθε (*ka*-the): each

καθημερινά (ka-thee-me-ree-*na*): daily

κάθισμα (*ka*-thee-sma) n: seat

κάθομαι (*ka*-tho-me): to sit down

καθυστερώ (ka-thee-ste-*ro*): to be late, to delay

και (ke): and

καιρός (ke-*ros*) n: weather

καλοκαίρι (ka-lo-*ke*-ree) n: summer

καλός/καλή/καλό (ka-*los*/ka-*lee*/ka-*lo*) m/f/n: good, nice

καναπές (ka-na-*pes*) m: couch

κάνω (*ka*-no): to do

κάνω μπάνιο (*ka*-no *ba*-nyo): to take a bath

κάνω ποδήλατο (*ka*-no po-*dee*-la-to): to ride a bike

καπνίζω (ka-*pnee*-zo): to smoke

καρδιά (ka-rdya) f: heart

καρέκλα (ka-*re*-kla) f: chair

καρύδι (ka-*ree*-dee) n: walnut

καταλαβαίνω (ka-ta-la-*ve*-no): to understand

κατάστημα (ka-*ta*-stee-ma) n: store

κατεβαίνω (ka-te-*ve*-no): to go down, to descend

κατοικίδιο (ka-tee-*kee*-dee-o) n: pet

καφές (ka-*fes*) m: coffee

καφετέρια (ka-fe-*te*-ree-a) f: café

κείμενο (*kee*-me-no) n: text

κερνάω (ke-*rna*-o): to treat someone

κήπος (*kee*-pos) m: garden

κινητό (kee-nee-*to*) n: cell phone

κλαίω (*kle*-o): to cry

κλειδί (klee-*dee*) n: key

κλειστός/κλειστή/κλειστό (klee-*stos*/klee-*stee*/klee-*sto*) m/f/n: closed

κλιματιστικό (klee-ma-tee-stee-*ko*) n: air conditioner

κομμάτι (ko-*ma*-tee) n: piece

κόρη (*ko*-ree) f: daughter

κορίτσι (ko-*ree*-tsee) n: girl

κόσμος (*ko*-smos) m: people, world

κουβέρτα (koo-*ve*-rta) f: blanket

κουζίνα (koo-*zee*-na) f: kitchen

κούκλα (*koo*-kla) f: doll

κουμπάρος/κουμπάρα (koo-*ba*-ros/koo-*ba*-ra) m/f: best man/maid of honor

κουρασμένος/κουρασμένη/κουρασμένο (koo-ra-*sme*-nos/koo-ra-*sme*-nee/koo-ra-*sme*-no) m/f/n: tired

κουρέας (koo-*re*-as) m: barber

κούρεμα (*koo*-re-ma) n: haircut

κουτί (koo-*tee*) n: box

κωμωδία (ko-mo-*dee*-a) f: comedy

Λ

λαμπάδα (la-*ba*-da) f: decorated candle

λαχανικό (la-kha-nee-*ko*) n: vegetable

λέγομαι (*le*-go-me): to be called, to be named

λέω (le-o): to say, to tell
λεωφόρος (le-o-fo-ros) f: avenue
λίγο (lee-go): a little
λίστα (lee-sta) f: list
λουλούδι (loo-loo-dee) f: flower

M

μαγειρεύω (ma-yee-re-vo): to cook
μάγουλο (ma-goo-lo) n: cheek
μαζί (ma-zee): together
μαθαίνω (ma-the-no): to learn
μάθημα (ma-thee-ma) n: lesson, class
μαθητής/μαθήτρια (ma-thee-tees/ ma-thee-tree-a) m/f: student
Μάιος (ma-ee-os) m: May
μακαρόνια (ma-ka-ro-nya) n, plural: pasta
μακριά (ma-kree-a): far
μαμά (ma-ma) f: mom
μανάβικο (ma-na-vee-ko) n: greengrocer
μαρούλι (ma-roo-lee) n: lettuce
Μάρτιος (ma-rtee-os) m: March
Με λένε . . . (me le-ne): My name is . . .
μέλι (me-lee) n: honey
μένω (me-no): to live
μερικές φορές (me-ree-kes fo-res): sometimes
μέρος (me-ros) n: place, part
μεσημέρι (me-see-me-ree) n: noon, lunchtime
μηδέν (mee-den) n: zero
μήνας (mee-nas) m: month
μητέρα (mee-te-ra) f: mother
μουσική (moo-see-kee) f: music
μπαμπάς (ba-bas) m: dad

N

ναι (ne): yes
ναός (na-os) m: temple, church
νερό (ne-ro) n: water
νησί (nee-see) n: island
νιόπαντρος/νιόπαντρη (nyo-pa-dros/nyo-pa-dree) m/f: newlywed
νιπτήρας (nee-ptee-ras) m: sink
Νοέμβριος (no-e-mvree-os) m: November
νομίζω (no-mee-zo): to think, to believe
νύφη (nee-fee) f: bride
νύχτα (nee-khta) f: night

Ξ

ξανά (ksa-na): again
ξενοδοχείο (kse-no-do-hee-o) n: hotel
ξέρω (kse-ro): to know
ξύλο (ksee-lo) n: wood

O

οδός (o-dos) f: street
οκτώ (o-kto): eight
Οκτώβριος (o-kto-vree-os) m: October
όμορφος/όμορφη/όμορφο (o-mo-rfos/o-mo-rfee/o-mo-rfo) m/f/n: beautiful
όνομα (o-no-ma) n: name
ονομαστική γιορτή (o-no-ma-stee-kee yo-rtee) f: name day
όπως (o-pos): like, as
όρεξη (o-re-ksee) f: appetite
όταν (o-tan): when
ούζο (oo-zo) n: ouzo

ουρανός (oo-ra-*nos*) m: sky

ούτε (*oo*-te): neither, nor

Π

παιδί (pe-*dee*) n: child

παίζω (*pe*-zo): to play

παιχνίδι (pe-*khnee*-dee) n: toy, game

πάλι (*pa*-lee): again

πανεπιστήμιο (pa-ne-pee-*stee*-mee-o) n: university

παντρεύομαι (pa-*drev*-o-me): to get married

παπούτσι (pa-*poo*-tsee) n: shoe

πάππους (pa-*poos*) m: grandfather

παραδοσιακή μουσική (pa-ra-do-see-a-*kee* moo-see-*kee*) f: traditional music

παράθυρο (pa-*ra*-thee-ro) n: window

Παρασκευή (pa-ra-skev-*ee*) f: Friday

παράσταση (pa-*ra*-sta-see) f: performance

παρουσιάζω (pa-roo-see-*a*-zo): to present

Πάσχα (*pa*-skha) n: Easter

πατάτα (pa-*ta*-ta) f: potato

πατέρας (pa-*te*-ras) m: father

πατούσα (pa-*too*-sa) f: foot

πάω (*pa*-o): to go

Πέμπτη (*pe*-mbtee) f: Thursday

πέντε (*pe*-nde): five

περνάω (pe-*rna*-o): to pass time, to spend time

περπατάω (pe-rpa-*ta*-o): to walk

πέρυσι (*pe*-ree-see): last year

πιάτο (*pya*-to) n: plate

πίνω (*pee*-no): to drink

πιστεύω (pee-*stev*-o): to believe

πίτα (*pee*-ta) f: pie

πλατεία (pla-*tee*-a) f: square

πλένω (*ple*-no): to wash

πλούσιος/πλούσια/πλούσιο (*ploo*-see-os/*ploo*-see-a/*ploo*-see-o) m/f/n: rich

πλύσιμο (*plee*-see-mo) n: washing, laundry

ποδήλατο (po-*dee*-la-to) n: bicycle

πόδι (*po*-dee) n: leg

πόλη (*po*-lee) f: city

πόρτα (*po*-rta) f: door

πότε (*po*-te): when

πουκάμισο (poo-*ka*-mee-so) n: shirt

πρέπει (*pre*-pee): must, should

πριν (preen): before

πρόσκληση (*pro*-sklee-see) f: invitation

πρόσφατα (*pro*-sfa-ta): recently

πρόταση (*pro*-ta-see) f: proposal

πρόταση γάμου (*pro*-ta-see *ga*-moo) f: marriage proposal

πρωί (pro-*ee*) n: morning

πρώτος/πρώτη/πρώτο (*pro*-tos/*pro*-tee/*pro*-to) m/f/n: first

Ρ

ραντεβού (ra-de-*voo*) n: appointment, date

ρίχνω (*ree*-khno): to throw

ρούχο (*roo*-kho) n: clothes

ρωτάω (ro-*ta*-o): to ask

Σ

Σάββατο (*sa*-va-to) n: Saturday

Σεπτέμβριος (se-*pte*-mvree-os) m: September

σηκώνω (see-*ko*-no): to lift, to raise

σημείωση (see-*mee*-o-see) f: note

σήμερα (*see*-me-ra): today

σκάλα (*ska*-la) f: stairs

σκέφτομαι (*ske*-fto-me): to think

σκηνή (skee-*nee*) f: scene, stage

σκυλί (skee-*lee*) n: dog

σκύλος (*skee*-los) m: dog

σοκολάτα (so-ko-*la*-ta) f: chocolate

σπίτι (*spee*-tee) n: house, home

σπουδάζω (spoo-*da*-zo): to study (at university)

στάση (*sta*-see) f: stop

στέλνω (*ste*-lno): to send

στενοχωριέμαι (ste-no-kho-*rye*-me): to get upset

στρώμα (*stro*-ma) n: mattress

στρώσιμο (*stro*-see-mo) n: setting (table, bed)

σχολείο (skho-*lee*-o) n: school

σώμα (*so*-ma) n: body

T

ταβέρνα (ta-*ve*-rna) f: taverna

τάρτα (*ta*-rta) f: tart

τέσσερα (*te*-se-ra): four

Τετάρτη (te-*ta*-rtee) f: Wednesday

τηλεόραση (tee-le-*o*-ra-see) f: television

τι (tee): what

Τι κάνεις; (tee *ka*-nees): How are you?

τιμή (tee-*mee*) f: price, honor

τοίχος (*tee*-khos) m: wall

τουαλέτα (too-a-*le*-ta) f: toilet

τραγουδώ (tra-goo-*do*): to sing

τραπέζι (tra-*pe*-zee) n: table

τραυματίζομαι (trav-ma-*tee*-zo-me): to get injured

τρέχω (*tre*-kho): to run

τρία (*tree*-a): three

Τρίτη (*tree*-tee) f: Tuesday

τρόπος (*tro*-pos) m: way, manner

τσάντα (*tsa*-da) f: bag, purse

τσιγάρο (tsee-*ga*-ro) n: cigarette

τυρί (tee-*ree*) n: cheese

τώρα (*to*-ra): now

Y

υγεία (ee-*yee*-a) f: health

Φ

φαγητό (fa-yee-*to*) n: food

Φεβρουάριος (fe-vroo-*a*-ree-os) m: February

φθινόπωρο (fthee-*no*-po-ro) n: autumn

φίλος/φίλη (*fee*-los/*fee*-lee) m/f: friend

φοράω (fo-*ra*-o): to wear

φούρνος (*foo*-rnos) m: bakery, oven

φρέσκος/φρέσκια/φρέσκο (*fre*-skos/*fre*-skya/*fre*-sko) m/f/n: fresh

φτιάχνω (*ftya*-khno): to make

φυσικός/φυσική/φυσικό (fee-see-*kos*/fee-see-*kee*/fee-see-*ko*) m/f/n: natural

φωνή (fo-*nee*) f: voice

X

χαίρετε (*he*-re-te): hello (formal)

χαίρομαι (*he*-ro-me): to be glad, to enjoy

Χαίρω πολύ. (*he*-ro po-*lee*): Nice to meet you.

χαλάω (kha-*la*-o): to ruin, to spoil, to break

χαμογελάω (kha-mo-ye-*la*-o): to smile

χαρά (kha-*ra*) f: joy

χάρτης (*kha*-rtees) m: map

χειμώνας (hee-*mo*-nas) m: winter

χέρι (*he*-ree) n: hand

χορός (kho-*ros*) m: dance

χρώμα (*khro*-ma) n: color

χτες (khtes): yesterday

χτυπάω (khtee-*pa*-o): to hit, to knock

χώρα (*kho*-ra) f: country

χωριό (kho-*ryo*) n: village

χωρίς (kho-*rees*): without

Ψ

ψάρι (*psa*-ree) n: fish

ψέμα (*pse*-ma) n: lie (falsehood)

ψηλά (psee-*la*): high

ψηλός/ψηλή/ψηλό (psee-*los*/psee-*lee*/ psee-*lo*) m/f/n: tall

ψησταριά (psee-sta-*rya*) f: grill

ψυγείο (psee-*yee*-o) n: refrigerator

ψυχή (psee-*hee*) f: soul

ψώνια (*pso*-nya) n, plural: shopping

ψωνίζω (pso-*nee*-zo): to shop

Ω

ώρα (*o*-ra) f: time, hour

ωραίος/ωραία/ωραίο (o-*re*-os/o-*re*-a/ o-*re*-o) m/f/n: nice, beautiful

ωστόσο (o-*sto*-so): however, nevertheless

English-Greek Mini-Dictionary

A

a little: λίγο (*lee*-go)

ability: ικανότητα (ee-ka-*no*-tee-ta) f

again: πάλι (*pa*-lee)

air conditioner: κλιματιστικό (klee-ma-tee-stee-*ko*) n

airplane: αεροπλάνο (a-e-ro-*pla*-no) n

airport: αεροδρόμιο (a-e-ro-*dro*-mee-o) n

anger: θυμός (thee-*mos*) m

apartment: διαμέρισμα (dia-*me*-ree-sma) n

appetite: όρεξη (*o*-re-ksee) f

appointment, date: ραντεβού (ra-de-*voo*) n

April: Απρίλιος (a-*pree*-lee-os) m

(to) ask: ρωτάω (ro-*ta*-o)

(to) ask for directions: ζητάω οδηγίες (zee-*ta*-o o-dee-*yee*-es)

August: Αύγουστος (*av*-goo-stos) m

autumn: φθινόπωρο (fthee-*no*-po-ro) n

avenue: λεωφόρος (le-o-*fo*-ros) f

B

bag, purse: τσάντα (*tsa*-da) f

bakery, oven: φούρνος (*foo*-rnos) m

barber: κουρέας (koo-*re*-as) m

(to) be: είμαι (*ee*-me)

(to) be called, named: λέγομαι (*le*-go-me)

(to) be glad, enjoy: χαίρομαι (*he*-ro-me)

(to) be late, delay: καθυστερώ (ka-thee-ste-*ro*)

beautiful

beautiful: όμορφος/όμορφη/όμορφο (*o*-mo-rfos/*o*-mo-rfee/*o*-mo-rfo) m/f/n

before: πριν (preen)

(to) begin: αρχίζω (ar-*hee*-zo)

(to) believe: πιστεύω (pee-*stev*-o)

belt: ζώνη (zo-nee) f

best man/maid of honor: κουμπάρος/κουμπάρα (koo-*ba*-ros/koo-*ba*-ra) m/f

bicycle: ποδήλατο (po-*dee*-la-to) n

blanket: κουβέρτα (koo-*ve*-rta) f

body: σώμα (*so*-ma) n

book: βιβλίο (vee-*vlee*-o) n

box: κουτί (koo-*tee*) n

boy: αγόρι (a-*go*-ree) m

break: διάλειμμα (dee-*a*-lee-ma) n

bride: νύφη (*nee*-fee) f

brother: αδελφός (a-de-*lfos*) m

but: αλλά (a-*la*)

(to) buy: αγοράζω (a-go-ra-zo)

bye: γεια χαρά (ya kha-*ra*)

C

café: καφετέρια (ka-fe-*te*-ree-a) f

(to) celebrate: γιορτάζω (yo-*rta*-zo)

(to) celebrate (religious): εορτάζω (e-o-*rta*-zo)

celebration: γιορτή (yo-*rtee*) f

cell phone: κινητό (kee-nee-*to*) n

chair: καρέκλα (ka-*re*-kla) f

cheek: μάγουλο (*ma*-goo-lo) n

cheese: τυρί (tee-*ree*) n

child: παιδί (pe-*dee*) n

chocolate: σοκολάτα (so-ko-*la*-ta) f

cigarette: τσιγάρο (tsee-*ga*-ro) n

city: πόλη (*po*-lee) f

(to) clean: καθαρίζω (ka-tha-*ree*-zo)

closed: κλειστός/κλειστή/κλειστό (klee-*stos*/klee-*stee*/klee-*sto*) m/f/n

clothes: ρούχο (*roo*-kho) n

coffee: καφές (ka-*fes*) m

color: χρώμα (*khro*-ma) n

comedy: κωμωδία (ko-mo-*dee*-a) f

(to) cook: μαγειρεύω (ma-yee-*rev*-o)

couch: καναπές (ka-na-*pes*) m

country: χώρα (*kho*-ra) f

couple: ζευγάρι (zev-*ga*-ree) n

(to) create: δημιουργώ (dee-mee-oo-*rgo*)

(to) cry: κλαίω (*kle*-o)

D

dad: μπαμπάς (ba-*bas*) m

daily: καθημερινά (ka-thee-me-ree-*na*)

dance: χορός (kho-*ros*) m

daughter: κόρη (*ko*-ree) f

day: ημέρα (ee-*me*-ra) f

December: Δεκέμβριος (de-*ke*-mvree-os) m

decorated candle: λαμπάδα (la-*ba*-da) f

detergent: απορρυπαντικό (a-po-ree-pa-dee-*ko*) n

dialogue: διάλογος (dee-*a*-lo-gos) m

(to) do: κάνω (*ka*-no)

(to) do the laundry: βάζω πλυντήριο (*va*-zo plee-*dee*-ree-o)

dog: σκύλος (*skee*-los) m

dog: σκυλί (skee-*lee*) n

doll: κούκλα (*koo*-kla) f

door: πόρτα (*po*-rta) f

(to) draw: ζωγραφίζω (zo-gra-*fee*-zo)

(to) drink: πίνω (*pee*-no)

E

each: κάθε (*ka*-the)

Easter: Πάσχα (*pa*-skha) n

egg: αυγό (av-*go*) n

eight: οκτώ (o-*kto*)

entertainment, fun: διασκέδαση (dya-*ske*-da-see) f

evening: βράδυ (*vra*-dee) n

F

factory: εργοστάσιο (e-rgo-*sta*-see-o) n

(to) fall in love: ερωτεύομαι (e-ro-*tev*-o-me)

far: μακριά (ma-kree-*a*)

fast: γρήγορος/γρήγορη/γρήγορο (*gree*-go-ros/*gree*-go-ree/*gree*-go-ro) m/f/n

father: πατέρας (pa-*te*-ras) m

faucet: βρύση (*vree*-see) f

favorite: αγαπημένος/αγαπημένη/αγαπημένο (a-ga-pee-*me*-nos/a-ga-pee-*me*-nee/a-ga-pee-*me*-no) m/f/n

feast: εορτή (e-o-*rtee*) f

February: Φεβρουάριος (fe-vroo-*a*-ree-os) m

(to) fill: γεμίζω (ye-*mee*-zo)

(to) find: βρίσκω (*vree*-sko)

first: πρώτος/πρώτη/πρώτο (*pro*-tos/*pro*-tee/*pro*-to) m/f/n

fish: ψάρι (*psa*-ree) n

five: πέντε (*pe*-nde)

flower: λουλούδι (loo-*loo*-dee) n

food: φαγητό (fa-yee-*to*) n

foot: πατούσα (pa-*too*-sa) f

forward: εμπρός (e-*bros*)

four: τέσσερα (*te*-se-ra)

fresh: φρέσκος/φρέσκια/φρέσκο (*fre*-skos/*fre*-skya/*fre*-sko) m/f/n

Friday: Παρασκευή (pa-ra-skev-*ee*) f

friend: φίλος/φίλη (*fee*-los/*fee*-lee) m/f

G

garden: κήπος (*kee*-pos) m

(to) get engaged: αρραβωνιάζομαι (a-ra-vo-*nya*-zo-me)

(to) get injured: τραυματίζομαι (trav-ma-*tee*-zo-me)

(to) get married: παντρεύομαι (pa-*drev*-o-me)

(to) get upset: στενοχωριέμαι (ste-no-kho-*rye*-me)

gift: δώρο (*do*-ro) n

girl: κορίτσι (ko-*ree*-tsee) n

(to) give: δίνω (*dee*-no)

glass: γυαλί (ya-*lee*) n

(to) go: πάω (*pa*-o)

(to) go down, descend: κατεβαίνω (ka-te-*ve*-no)

good, nice: καλός/καλή/καλό (ka-*los*/ka-*lee*/ka-*lo*) m/f/n

grandfather: πάππους (pa-*poos*) m

grandmother: γιαγιά (ya-*ya*) f

greengrocer: μανάβικο (ma-*na*-vee-ko) n

grill: ψησταριά (psee-sta-*rya*) f

groom: γαμπρός (ga-*bros*) m

H

haircut: κούρεμα (*koo*-re-ma) n

hand: χέρι (*he*-ree) n

happiness: ευτυχία (ef-tee-*hee*-a) f

happy: ευτυχισμένος/ευτυχισμένη/ευτυχισμένο (ef-tee-hee-*sme*-nos/ef-tee-hee-*sme*-nee/ef-tee-hee-*sme*-no) m/f/n

heart: καρδιά (ka-*rdya*) f

hello: γεια (ya)

hello (formal): γεια σας (ya sas)

hello (formal): χαίρετε (*he*-re-te)

hello (informal): γεια σου (ya soo)

(to) help: βοηθάω (vo-ee-*tha*-o)

help: βοήθεια (vo-*ee*-thee-a) f

here: εδώ (e-*do*)

high: ψηλά (psee-*la*)

history, story: ιστορία (ee-sto-*ree*-a) f

(to) hit, knock: χτυπάω (khtee-*pa*-o)

holy: ιερός/ιερή/ιερό (ee-e-*ros*/ee-e-*ree*/ee-e-*ro*) m/f/n

honey: μέλι (*me*-lee) n

hope: ελπίδα (e-*lpee*-da) f

(to) hope: ελπίζω (e-*lpee*-zo)

hot, warm: ζεστός/ζεστή/ζεστό (ze-*stos*/ze-*stee*/ze-*sto*) m/f/n

hotel: ξενοδοχείο (kse-no-do-*hee*-o) n

house, home: σπίτι (*spee*-tee) n

How are you?: Τι κάνεις; (tee *ka*-nees)

however, nevertheless: ωστόσο (o-*sto*-so)

I

I: εγώ (e-*go*)

image, picture: εικόνα (ee-*ko*-na) f

intersection: διασταύρωση (dee-a-*stav*-ro-see) f

invitation: πρόσκληση (*pro*-sklee-see) f

island: νησί (nee-*see*) n

J

jacket: ζακέτα (za-*ke*-ta) f
January: Ιανουάριος (ee-a-noo-*a*-ree-os) m
joy: χαρά (kha-*ra*) f
June: Ιούνιος (ee-*oo*-nee-os) m
July: Ιούλιος (ee-*oo*-lee-os) m

K

key: κλειδί (klee-*dee*) n
kitchen: κουζίνα (koo-*zee*-na) f
(to) know: ξέρω (*kse*-ro)

L

lamb: αρνί (a-r*nee*) n
language, tongue: γλώσσα (*glo*-ssa) f
last year: πέρυσι (*pe*-ree-see)
(to) laugh: γελάω (ye-*la*-o)
(to) learn: μαθαίνω (ma-*the*-no)
left: αριστερά (a-ree-ste-*ra*)
leg: πόδι (*po*-dee) n
lesson, class: μάθημα (*ma*-thee-ma) n
letter: γράμμα (*gra*-ma) n
lettuce: μαρούλι (ma-*roo*-lee) n
lie, falsehood: ψέμα (*pse*-ma) n
life: ζωή (zo-*ee*) f
(to) lift, raise: σηκώνω (see-*ko*-no)
like, as: όπως (*o*-pos)
list: λίστα (*lee*-sta) f
(to) live: μένω (*me*-no)
live music: ζωντανή μουσική (zo-da-*nee* moo-see-*kee*) f
(to) love: αγαπάω (a-ga-*pa*-o)
love: αγάπη (a-*ga*-pee) f

M

(to) make: φτιάχνω (*ftya*-khno)
man: άνδρας (*a*-dras) m
map: χάρτης (*kha*-rtees) m
March: Μάρτιος (*Ma*-rtee-os) m
marriage proposal: πρόταση γάμου (*pro*-ta-see *ga*-moo) f
mattress: στρώμα (*stro*-ma) n
May: Μάιος (*ma*-ee-os) m
meal: γεύμα (*yev*-ma) n
milk: γάλα (*ga*-la) n
mom: μαμά (ma-*ma*) f
Monday: Δευτέρα (def-*te*-ra) f
month: μήνας (*mee*-nas) m
morning: πρωί (pro-*ee*) n
mother: μητέρα (mee-*te*-ra) f
music: μουσική (moo-see-*kee*) f
must, should: πρέπει (*pre*-pee)
My name is . . . : Με λένε . . . (me *le*-ne)

N

name: όνομα (*o*-no-ma) n
natural: φυσικός/φυσική/φυσικό (fee-see-*kos*/fee-see-*kee*/fee-see-*ko*) m/f/n
neither, nor: ούτε (*oo*-te)
never: ποτέ (po-*te*)
newlywed: νιόπαντρος/νιόπαντρη (*nyo*-pa-dros/*nyo*-pa-dree) m/f
next to: δίπλα (*dee*-pla)
nice, beautiful: ωραίος/ωραία/ωραίο (*o*-re-os/*o*-re-a/*o*-re-o) m/f/n
Nice to meet you: Χαίρω πολύ. (*he*-ro po-*lee*)
night: νύχτα (*nee*-khta) f

nine: εννιά (e-*nya*)

noon, lunchtime: μεσημέρι (me-see-*me*-ree) n

note: σημείωση (see-*mee*-o-see) f

November: Νοέμβριος (no-*e*-mvree-os) m

now: τώρα (*to*-ra)

O

October: Οκτώβριος (o-*kto*-vree-os) m

office: γραφείο (gra-*fee*-o) n

one: ένα (*e*-na)

one hundred: εκατό (e-ka-*to*)

or: ή (ee)

ouzo: ούζο (*oo*-zo) n

P

(to) pass time, spend time: περνάω (pe-*rna*-o)

pasta: μακαρόνια (ma-ka-*ro*-nya) n, plural

pedestrian crossing: διάβαση πεζών (dee-*a*-va-see pe-*zon*) f

people, world: κόσμος (*ko*-smos) m

performance: παράσταση (pa-*ra*-sta-see) f

pet: κατοικίδιο (ka-tee-*kee*-dee-o) n

pie: πίτα (*pee*-ta) f

piece: κομμάτι (ko-*ma*-tee) n

place, part: μέρος (*me*-ros) n

plate: πιάτο (*pya*-to) n

(to) play: παίζω (*pe*-zo)

potato: πατάτα (pa-*ta*-ta) f

(to) prepare: ετοιμάζω (e-tee-*ma*-zo)

(to) present: παρουσιάζω (pa-roo-see-*a*-zo)

price, honor: τιμή (tee-*mee*) f

proposal: πρόταση (*pro*-ta-see) f

Q

quickly: γρήγορα (*gree*-go-ra)

R

rain: βροχή (vro-*hee*) f

(to) read: διαβάζω (dya-*va*-zo)

ready: έτοιμος/έτοιμη/έτοιμο (*e*-tee-mos/*e*-tee-mee/*e*-tee-mo) m/f/n

recently: πρόσφατα (*pro*-sfa-ta)

refrigerator: ψυγείο (psee-*yee*-o) n

religious wedding: θρησκευτικός γάμος (three-skef-tee-*kos* ga-mos) m

(to) remember: θυμάμαι (thee-*ma*-me)

(to) rent: ενοικιάζω (e-nee-kee-*a*-zo)

restaurant: εστιατόριο (e-stee-a-*to*-ree-o) n

(to) return: γυρίζω (yee-*ree*-zo)

rich: πλούσιος/πλούσια/πλούσιο (*ploo*-see-os/*ploo*-see-a/*ploo*-see-o) m/f/n

(to) ride a bike: κάνω ποδήλατο (*ka*-no po-*dee*-la-to)

right: δεξιά (de-ksee-*a*)

ritual: ιεροτελεστία (ee-e-ro-te-le-*stee*-a) f

road: δρόμος (*dro*-mos) m

(to) ruin, spoil, break: χαλάω (cha-*la*-o)

(to) run: τρέχω (*tre*-kho)

S

saint: άγιος/αγία (*a*-yee-os/a-*yee*-a) m/f

Saturday: Σάββατο (*sa*-va-to) n

(to) say, tell: λέω (*le*-o)

scene, stage: σκηνή (skee-*nee*) f

school: σχολείο (skho-*lee*-o) n

seat: κάθισμα (*ka*-thee-sma) n

(to) see: βλέπω (*vle*-po)

(to) send: στέλνω (*ste*-lno)

September: Σεπτέμβριος (se-*pte*-mvree-os) m

setting (table, bed): στρώσιμο (*stro*-see-mo) n

seven: επτά/εφτά (e-*pta*/e-*fta*)

shirt: πουκάμισο (poo-*ka*-mee-so) n

shoe: παπούτσι (pa-*poo*-tsee) n

(to) shop: ψωνίζω (pso-*nee*-zo)

shopping: ψώνια (*pso*-nya) n, plural

siblings: αδέλφια (a-*de*-lfya) n, plural

simple: απλός/απλή/απλό (a-*plos*/a-*plee*/a-*plo*) m/f/n

(to) sing: τραγουδώ (tra-goo-*do*)

single, free: ελεύθερος/ελεύθερη/ελεύθερο (e-*lef*-the-ros/e-*lef*-the-ree/e-*lef*-the-ro) m/f/n

sister: αδελφή (a-de-*lfee*) f

(to) sit down: κάθομαι (*ka*-tho-me)

six: έξι (*e*-ksee)

sky: ουρανός (oo-ra-*nos*) m

(to) smile: χαμογελάω (kha-mo-ye-*la*-o)

(to) smoke: καπνίζω (ka-*pnee*-zo)

solution: λύση (*lee*-see) f

sometimes: μερικές φορές (me-ree-*kes* fo-*res*)

son: γιος (yos) m

soul: ψυχή (psee-*hee*) f

spring: άνοιξη (*a*-nee-ksee) f

square: πλατεία (pla-*tee*-a) f

stairs: σκάλα (*ska*-la) f

stop: στάση (*sta*-see) f

storage room: αποθήκη (a-po-*thee*-kee) f

store: κατάστημα (ka-*ta*-stee-ma) n

straight ahead: ευθύς/ευθεία/ευθύ (ef-*thees*/ef-*thee*-a/ef-*thee*) m/f/n

street: οδός (o-*dos*) f

student: μαθητής/μαθήτρια (ma-thee-*tees*/ma-*thee*-tree-a) m/f

(to) study at university: σπουδάζω (spoo-*da*-zo)

sugar: ζάχαρη (*za*-kha-ree) f

summer: καλοκαίρι (ka-lo-*ke*-ree) n

T

table: τραπέζι (tra-*pe*-zee) n

(to) take a bath: κάνω μπάνιο (*ka*-no *ba*-nyo)

tall: ψηλός/ψηλή/ψηλό (psee-*los*/psee-*lee*/psee-*lo*) m/f/n

tart: τάρτα (*ta*-rta) f

taverna: ταβέρνα (ta-*ve*-rna) f

teacher: δάσκαλος/δάσκαλα (*da*-ska-los/da-*ska*-la) m/f

television: τηλεόραση (tee-le-*o*-ra-see) f

temperature: θερμοκρασία (the-rmo-kra-*see*-a) f

temple, church: ναός (na-*os*) m

ten: δέκα (*de*-ka)

text: κείμενο (*kee*-me-no) n

thank you: ευχαριστώ (ef-kha-ree-*sto*)

(to) think: σκέφτομαι (*ske*-fto-me)

(to) think, believe: νομίζω (no-*mee*-zo)

three: τρία (*tree*-a)

(to) throw: ρίχνω (*ree*-khno)

Thursday: πέμπτη (*pe*-mbtee) f

ticket: εισιτήριο (ee-see-*tee*-ree-o) n

time, hour: ώρα (*o*-ra) f

tired: κουρασμένος/κουρασμένη/κουρασμ ένο (koo-ra-*sme*-nos/koo-ra-*sme*-nee/koo-ra-*sme*-no) m/f/n

today: σήμερα (*see*-me-ra)

together: μαζί (ma-*zee*)

toilet: τουαλέτα (too-a-*le*-ta) f

tomorrow: αύριο (*av*-ree-o, to)

town hall: δημαρχείο (dee-ma-rhee-o) n

toy, fame: παιχνίδι (pe-khnee-dee) n

traditional music: παραδοσιακή μουσική (pa-ra-do-see-a-kee moo-see-kee) f

(to) treat (someone): κερνάω (ke-rna-o)

tree: δέντρο (de-dro) n

truth: αλήθεια (a-lee-thya) f

Tuesday: Τρίτη (tree-tee) f

two: δύο (dee-o)

U

(to) understand: καταλαβαίνω (ka-ta-la-ve-no)

university: πανεπιστήμιο (pa-ne-pee-stee-mee-o) n

V

various, different: διάφορο/διάφορη/διάφορο (dya-fo-ros/dya-fo-ree/dya-fo-ro) m/f/m

vegetable: λαχανικό (la-kha-nee-ko) n

village: χωριό (kho-ryo) n

voice: φωνή (fo-nee) f

W

(to) walk: περπατάω (pe-rpa-ta-o)

wall: τοίχος (tee-khos) m

walnut: καρύδι (ka-ree-dee) n

(to) want: θέλω (the-lo)

(to) warm up: ζεσταίνω (ze-ste-no)

(to) wash: πλένω (ple-no)

washing: πλύσιμο (plee-see-mo) n

(to) watch TV: βλέπω τηλεόραση (vle-po tee-le-o-ra-see)

water: νερό (ne-ro) n

way, manner: τρόπος (tro-pos) m

(to) wear: φοράω (fo-ra-o)

weather: καιρός (ke-ros) m

wedding: γάμος (ga-mos) m

Wednesday: Τετάρτη (te-ta-rtee) f

week: εβδομάδα (ev-do-ma-da) f

what: τι (tee)

when: όταν (o-tan)

when: πότε (po-te)

Where are you from?: Από πού είσαι; (a-po poo ee-se)

Will you marry me?: Θέλεις να με παντρευτείς; (the-lees na me pa-dre-ftees)

window: παράθυρο (pa-ra-thee-ro) n

winter: χειμώνας (hee-mo-nas) m

without: χωρίς (kho-rees)

woman: γυναίκα (yee-ne-ka) f

wood: ξύλο (ksee-lo) n

work: εργασία (e-rga-see-a) f

(to) work: δουλεύω (doo-lev-o)

(to) work: εργάζομαι (e-rga-zo-me)

(to) write: γράφω (gra-fo)

Y

yes: ναι (ne)

yesterday: χτες (khtes)

Z

zero: μηδέν (mee-den)

Appendix B
Verb Tables

This appendix shows the conjugation of the present tense (enestotas), past simple tense (aoristos), and future simple tense (stigmieos melodas) as well as the subjunctive mood. It also includes a list of basic irregular verbs. For more details about Greek verbs, see Chapter 4.

Regular Greek Verbs

Type A Verbs
For example: αγοράζω (to buy)

	Present	Past Simple	Future Simple
εγώ (I)	αγοράζω	αγόρασα	θα αγοράσω
εσύ (you, singular/informal)	αγοράζεις	αγόρασες	θα αγοράσεις
αυτός, αυτή, αυτό (he, she, it)	αγοράζει	αγόρασε	θα αγοράσει
εμείς (we)	αγοράζουμε	αγοράσαμε	θα αγοράσουμε
εσείς (you, plural/formal singular)	αγοράζετε	αγοράσατε	θα αγοράσετε
αυτοί, αυτές, αυτά (they — masculine, feminine, neuter)	αγοράζουν(ε)	αγόρασαν/αγοράσανε	θα αγοράσουν(ε)

Type B1 Verbs
For example: μιλάω (to speak)

	Present	Past Simple	Future Simple
εγώ (I)	μιλάω	μίλησα	θα μιλήσω
εσύ (you, singular/informal)	μιλάς	μίλησες	θα μιλήσεις
αυτός, αυτή, αυτό (he, she, it)	μιλά/μιλάει	μίλησε	θα μιλήσει
εμείς (we)	μιλάμε	μιλήσαμε	θα μιλήσουμε
εσείς (you, plural/formal singular)	μιλάτε	μιλήσατε	θα μιλήσετε
αυτοί, αυτές, αυτά (they — masculine, feminine, neuter)	μιλάνε/μιλούν(ε)	μίλησαν/μιλήσανε	θα μιλήσουν(ε)

Type B2 Verbs
For example: προσπαθώ (to try)

	Present	Past Simple	Future Simple
εγώ (I)	προσπαθώ	προσπάθησα	θα προσπαθήσω
εσύ (you, singular/informal)	προσπαθείς	προσπάθησες	θα προσπαθήσεις
αυτός, αυτή, αυτό (he, she, it)	προσπαθεί	προσπάθησε	θα προσπαθήσει
εμείς (we)	προσπαθούμε	προσπαθήσαμε	θα προσπαθήσουμε
εσείς (you, plural/formal singular)	προσπαθείτε	προσπαθήσατε	θα προσπαθήσετε
αυτοί, αυτές, αυτά (they — masculine, feminine, neuter)	προσπαθούν(ε)	προσπάθησαν/προσπαθήσανε	θα προσπαθήσουν(ε)

Type AB Verbs
For example: ακούω (to hear)

	Present	Past Simple	Future Simple
εγώ (I)	ακούω	άκουσα	θα ακούσω
εσύ (you, singular/informal)	ακούς	άκουσες	θα ακούσεις
αυτός, αυτή, αυτό (he, she, it)	ακούει	άκουσε	θα ακούσει
εμείς (we)	ακούμε	ακούσαμε	θα ακούσουμε
εσείς (you, plural/formal singular)	ακούτε	ακούσατε	θα ακούσετε
αυτοί, αυτές, αυτά (they — masculine, feminine, neuter)	ακούν(ε)	άκουσαν/ακούσανε	θα ακούσουν(ε)

Type Γ1 Verbs
For example: έρχομαι (to come)

	Present
εγώ (I)	έρχομαι
εσύ (you, singular/informal)	έρχεσαι
αυτός, αυτή, αυτό (he, she, it)	έρχεται
εμείς (we)	ερχόμαστε
εσείς (you, plural/formal singular)	έρχεστε/ερχόσαστε
αυτοί, αυτές, αυτά (they — masculine, feminine, neuter)	έρχονται

Type Γ2 Verbs
For example: κοιμάμαι (to sleep)

	Present
εγώ (I)	κοιμάμαι
εσύ (you, singular/informal)	κοιμάσαι
αυτός, αυτή, αυτό (he, she, it)	κοιμάται
εμείς (we)	κοιμόμαστε
εσείς (you, plural/formal singular)	κοιμάστε/κοιμόσαστε
αυτοί, αυτές, αυτά (they — masculine, feminine, neuter)	κοιμούνται

The Subjunctive Mood

For Verb Types A, B1, B2, AB

	A	B1	B2	AB
εγώ (I)	να αγοράσω	να μιλήσω	να προσπαθήσω	να ακούσω
εσύ (you, singular/informal)	να αγοράσεις	να μιλήσεις	να προσπαθήσεις	να ακούσεις
αυτός, αυτή, αυτό (he, she, it)	να αγοράσει	να μιλήσει	να προσπαθήσει	να ακούσει
εμείς (we)	να αγοράσουμε	να μιλήσουμε	να προσπαθήσουμε	να ακούσουμε
εσείς (you, plural/formal singular)	να αγοράσετε	να μιλήσετε	να προσπαθήσετε	να ακούσετε
αυτοί, αυτές, αυτά (they — masculine, feminine, neuter)	να αγοράσουν(ε)	να μιλήσουν(ε)	να προσπαθήσουν(ε)	να ακούσουν(ε)

Irregular Greek Verbs

Some Greek verbs don't follow the rules to form the simple past and simple future tenses. These verbs are called irregular verbs. Unfortunately, the only thing you can do to learn them is to memorize. The following table shows you a few irregular Greek verbs in the present, past simple, and future simple tenses.

Present Tense	Past Simple	Future Simple
λέω (to say)	είπα	θα πω
τρώω (to eat)	έφαγα	θα φάω
βλέπω (to see)	είδα	θα δω
πηγαίνω (to go)	πήγα	θα πάω
φέρνω (to bring)	έφερα	θα φέρω
δίνω (to give)	έδωσα	θα δώσω
παίρνω (to take)	πήρα	θα πάρω
μένω (to stay)	έμεινα	θα μείνω
έρχομαι (to come)	ήρθα	θα έρθω
γράφω (to write)	έγραψα	θα γράψω
τρέχω (to run)	έτρεξα	θα τρέξω
πίνω (to drink)	ήπια	θα πιω
μαθαίνω (to learn)	έμαθα	θα μάθω
ανεβαίνω (to climb/go up)	ανέβηκα	θα ανέβω

Appendix C
Answer Key

The following pages provide you with the answer keys to the Fun & Games activities at the end of the chapters.

Chapter 3: Tackling Basic Grammar

Masculine: Λίβανος, Καναδάς, Μαυρίκιος, Παναμάς

Feminine: Αγγλία, Αμερική, Γερμανία, Ταϊλάνδη

Neutral: Μεξικό, Βέλγιο, Ιράκ, Περού, Πουέρτο Ρίκο

Chapter 4: Grammar Beyond the Basics

Present (Enestotas)	Past Simple (Aoristos)	Future Simple (Steegmieos Melodas)
αγοράζω	αγόρασα	θα αγοράσω
δουλεύω	δούλεψα	θα δουλέψω
μιλάω	μίλησα	θα μιλήσω
μπορώ	μπόρεσα	θα μπορέσω
τρώω	έφαγα	θα φάω
ακούω	άκουσα	θα ακούσω
προσπαθώ	προσπάθησα	θα προσπαθήσω
αγαπάω	αγάπησα	θα αγαπήσω

Chapter 5: Getting Started with Basic Expressions

Πώς σε λένε; — Με λένε Ελένη.

Τι δουλειά κάνεις; — Είμαι δικηγόρος.

Είσαι παντρεμένη; — Όχι, είμαι ελεύθερη.

Πώς είστε κύριε Γιώργο; — Είμαι καλά.

Έχεις αδέλφια; — Ναι, έχω δύο αδέλφια.

Τι γλώσσες μιλάς; — Μιλάω ελληνικά και αγγλικά.

Από πού είσαι; — Είμαι από την Ελλάδα.

Chapter 6: Figuring Out Numbers, Dates, and Times

6:10 Η ώρα είναι έξι και δέκα.

6:45 Η ώρα είναι επτά παρά τέταρτο.

6:00 Η ώρα είναι έξι ακριβώς.

6:15 Η ώρα είναι έξι και τέταρτο.

6:35 Η ώρα είναι επτά παρά είκοσι πέντε.

6:30 Η ώρα είναι έξι και μισή.

Chapter 7: Speaking Greek at Home

1. Table: τραπέζι
2. Sofa: καναπές
3. Bed: κρεβάτι
4. Chair: καρέκλα
5. Bookshelf: βιβλιοθήκη
6. TV: τηλεόραση
7. Closet: ντουλάπα

Chapter 8: Moving Around

1. Από το σπίτι προχώρα ευθεία
2. Στρίψε δεξιά
3. Στρίψε αριστερά

4. Στρίψε αριστερά

5. Στρίψε δεξιά

6. Το σούπερ μάρκετ είναι στο αριστερό σου χέρι

Chapter 9: Shopping Made Easy

Clothing: παλτό, φόρεμα, μπλούζα, καπέλο

Groceries: ντομάτα, μαρούλι, αχλάδι, πορτοκάλι, καρότο

Supermarket: κρασί, απορρυπαντικό, χαρτί υγείας, καφές, γιαούρτι

Chapter 10: Days and Nights Out

κυρίως πιάτο

ελληνικός καφές

ταινία τρόμου

κέντρο διασκέδασης

λαϊκή μουσική

παραδοσιακοί χοροί

Chapter 11: Your Body and Your Health

1. **κεφάλι:** head

2. **στήθος:** chest

3. **παλάμη:** palm

4. **γόνατο:** knee

5. **κοιλιά:** stomach

6. **μπούτι:** thigh

7. **πατούσα:** foot

Chapter 12: Let's Talk about Business

1. Desk: **γραφείο**

2. Documents: **αρχεία**

3. Phone: **τηλέφωνο**

4. Computer: **υπολογιστής**

5. Desk chair: καρέκλα γραφείου

6. Printer: εκτυπωτής

Chapter 13: Planning a Trip

διακοπές

κράτηση

χωριό

διαμονή

ευρώ

βουνό

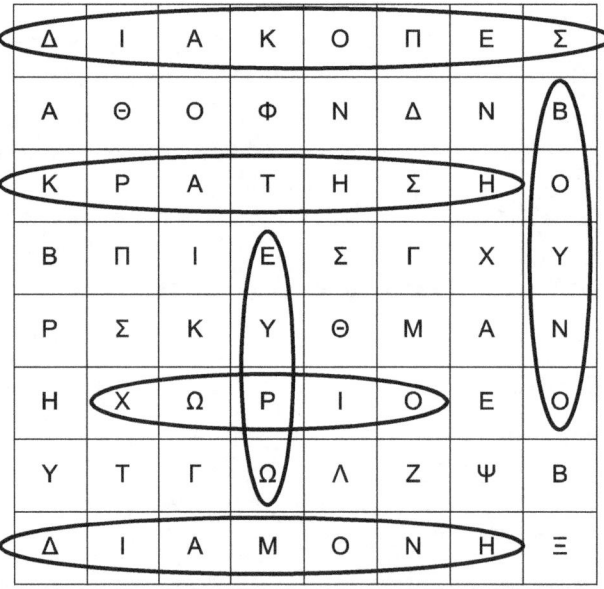

© John Wiley & Sons, Inc.

Chapter 14: Getting Around: Planes, Trains, Taxis, and More

Taxi: ταρίφα, ταξιτζής, ταξίμετρο

Ferry: λιμάνι, κατάστρωμα, καμπίνα

Airplane: αεροδρόμιο, απογείωση, αφίξεις, πτήση

Train: πλατφόρμα, σταθμός, βαγόνι

Chapter 16: Understanding Greek Traditions

σουβλίζω το αρνί

κερνάω τους φίλους μου

λίστα καλεσμένων

Μεγάλη Εβδομάδα

πάντα άξιοι

πρόταση γάμου

Index

αυτή τη στιγμή (at this moment), 101
αυτή την ώρα (at this time), 101
αυτί (ear), 164
αυτό (it), 48
αυτοί (they, masculine), 48
αυτοκίνητο (car), 28, 124
αυτός (he), 48
αφίξεις (arrivals), 206
Αφροδίτη (Aphrodite), 216
αχλάδι (pear), 139

B

βαγόνι (wagon, carriage), 208
Βάζω πλυντήριο (I do the laundry), 113
βαλίτσα (suitcase), 197
βαμβακερό (cotton), 133
Βελγίδα (Belgian; female), 81
Βέλγιο (Belgium), 81
Βέλγος (Belgian; male), 81
βελούδινο (velvet), 133
βέρες (wedding rings), 227
βιβλίο (book), 28
βιβλιοθήκη (bookshelf), 111
βίζα (visa), 196
βιογραφικό σημείωμα (resume, CV), 188
Βίον ανθόσπαρτον! (Wishing a life full of flowers), 227
βλέπω (to see), 46
βόλεϊ (volleyball), 178
βουνό (mountain), 196
βούρτσα τουαλέτας (toilet brush), 112
βούτυρο (butter), 140
βράδυ (evening), 107
βρύση (faucet/tap), 112
τα βυζαντινά προσκυνήματα της Θεσσαλονίκης (Byzantine pilgrimage sites of Thessaloniki, The), 218

Γ

γάλα (milk), 140, 154
γάλα σε σκόνη (baby formula), 141
γαλακτοκομικά (dairy products), 138, 140
Γαλλία (France), 80
Γαλλίδα (French; female), 80
γαλλικά (French language), 80, 81
Γάλλος (French; male), 80
γαλοπούλα (turkey), 139
γάμος (wedding), 225–229
γάμπα (calf), 165
γαμπρός (groom), 226
γάντια (gloves), 134
γαρίδα (shrimp), 140
γάτα (cat), 28
γεια (hello), 75–76
Γεια μας! (Cheers!), 244
γεια σας (hello), 76
γεια σου (hello to you), 76
γεια χαρά (bye), 89
Γείτσες! (Bless you!), 244
γεμιστά, 148
γενικός ιατρός (general practitioner), 171
γεννητικά όργανα (genitals), 165
Γερμανία (Germany), 80
Γερμανίδα (German; female), 80
γερμανικά (German language), 80, 81
Γερμανός (German; male), 80
γεροντοπαλίκαρο, 259
για μωρά (for babies), 141
Για πες (Tell me more/Go on, keep talking), 262
γιαγιά (grandmother), 86
γιαούρτι (yogurt), 140
γιατρός (doctor), 85, 170–174
γιορτή (celebration), 230
γιός (son), 87
γκαράζ (garage), 30

γλάστρες (flowerpots), 108
γλέντι, 158, 246–247
γλουτοί (glutes), 164
γλυκό κρασί (sweet wine), 220
γλυπτική (sculpture), 218
γλώσσα (language), 80
γλώσσα (tongue), 164
γόνατο (knee), 165
γραβάτα (tie), 134
γραμμάριο (gram), 142
γραμματέας (secretary), 85, 185
γραμμή (track, line), 208
γραφείο (office), 183
γράφω (to write), 46
γυμναστήριο (gym), 178
γυμναστική (workout), 178
γυναικολόγος (gynecologist), 171
γύρος, 247

Δ

Δανή/Δανέζα (Danish; female), 81
Δανία (Denmark), 81
δανικά/δανέζικα (Danish language), 81
Δανός (Danish; male), 81
δάπεδο (floor), 108
δάσκαλος/δασκάλα (male/female teacher), 84
δάχτυλα (fingers), 164
δε(ν), 61
δέκα (ten), 92
δεκαεννιά/δεκαεννέα (nineteen), 93
δεκαέξι (sixteen), 93
δεκαεπτά/δεκαεφτά (seventeen), 93
δεκαοκτώ/δεκαοχτώ (eighteen), 93
δεκαπέντε (fifteen), 92
δεκατέσσερα (fourteen), 92
δεκατρία (thirteen), 92
Δεκέμβριος (December), 97

μαθαίνω (to learn), 46

Μάιος (May), 97

μακριά (far), 121

μαλάκας/μαλακισμένη, 245

μαλλιά (hair), 163

μάλλινο (wool), 133

μάνατζερ (manager), 184

Μαντείο των Δελφών (Oracle of Delphi), 217

μαξιλάρι (pillow), 109

μαρούλι (lettuce), 139

Μάρτιος (March), 97

μας (our), 42

μάτι (eye), 163

μάτια μου (my eyes), 253

μαύρο (black), 133

Με λένε . . . (My name is . . .), 77

Μεγάλη Εβδομάδα (Holy Week), 230

μέγεθος (size), 132

μεζεδάκια, 246

μεζεδοπωλείο, 149

μεζές, 246

μενού (menu), 150, 226

μένω (to live, to stay), 46

μεράκι, 257

μεσημέρι (midday), 106

μέσο μεταφοράς (means of transportation), 123–127

μετά (after), 102

μετρητά (cash), 201

μετρό (subway), 124

μέτωπο (forehead), 163

μηδέν (zero), 92

μήλο (apple), 138

μήνας (month), 97

μητέρα/μαμά (mother, mom/ mum), 86

μηχανάκι (motobike), 124

μηχανικός (engineer), 85

Μια χαρά (Just fine), 263

μιλάω (to speak), 46

Μιλάω . . . (I speak . . .), 82

μίτινγκ (meeting), 184

μόλις (just now), 101

μονάδα εντατικής θεραπείας (ΜΕΘ) (intensive care unit [ICU]), 175

Μονή Αγίου Νεκταρίου (Saint Nektarios Monastery), 218

μονόκλινο (single room, with one bed), 197

μοσχάρι (beef), 139

μοτοσικλέτα (motorcycle), 124

μου (my), 41

Μου αρέσεις (I like you), 251–252

Μου είναι μεγάλο (It's too big for me), 132

Μου είναι μικρό (It's too small for me), 132

Μου κάνει (It fits me), 133

Μου λείπεις (I miss you), 251

μουσακάς, 148

μουσείο (museum), 219–220

μουσική (music), 157, 226

μπαγκέτες (baguettes), 140

μπακαλιάρος (cod), 140

μπαλκόνι (balcony), 108

μπαμπάς (father), 29

μπανάνα (banana), 138

μπανιέρα (bathtub), 112

μπάνιο (bathroom), 108, 112–113

μπαρ (bar), 157

μπάσκετ (basketball), 178

μπισκότα (cookies), 141

μπλε (blue), 133

μπλούζα (blouse), 134

Μπορείτε να με βοηθήσετε; (Can you help me?), 119

Μπορείτε να μου προτείνετε κάτι; (Can you recommend something?), 150

μπορώ (to be able), 47

μπότες (boots), 134

μπουκάλι (bottle), 142

μπούτι (thigh), 165

μπουφάν (jacket), 134

μπουφές (buffet), 30

μπράτσο (arm), 164

μπρίκι (briki), 154

μπρόκολο (broccoli), 139

μπύρα (beer), 141

Μυκήνες (Mycenae), 217

μύτη (nose), 163

μωρομάντηλα (baby wipes), 141

N

Να ευτυχίσετε! (May you be happy!), 227

Να ζήσετε! (May you live long and happily!), 227

Να σου πω (Let me tell you), 264

Να χαίρεσαι το όνομά σου (Enjoy your name!), 230

Να'σαι καλά (Be well/You're welcome), 261–262

Ναι, παρακαλώ (yes, please), 134

ναύλο (fare), 212

νερό (water), 28, 141

νεροχύτης (sink), 112

νησί (island), 196

νηστεία (fasting), 231

νιόπαντροι (newlyweds), 227

νιπτήρας (sink), 112

Νοέμβριος (November), 97

νομικός σύμβουλος (legal advisor), 185

νόμισμα (currency, coin), 201

νοσηλευτής/νοσηλεύτρια/ νοσοκόμος/νοσοκόμα (male/ female nurse), 84, 174

νοσοκομείο (hospital), 174–175

νούμερο (number), 91, 132

ντεντλάιν (deadline), 184

ντολμαδάκια, 148

ντομάτα (tomato), 139

ντόπιος (local), 196

ντουζιέρα (showerhead), 112

ντουλάπα (wardrobe/closet), 110

About the Author

Eirini Argyrouli was born in Athens in 1992. She studied the Greek language at the University of Athens and the University of Amsterdam, specializing in Ancient Greek and Greek language teaching.

She worked as a project manager at the academic publishing house De Gruyter Brill in the Netherlands. She later continued her studies in management at Lund University in Sweden.

In 2022, she founded Greek Learning Hub, an online school dedicated to teaching the Greek language to people worldwide. After conducting research, she developed her own teaching methodology, which she successfully applies at her school.

Eirini continues to be inspired by her students' needs and interests, creating and working toward the promotion of the Greek language. To learn more about Eirini and the Greek Learning Hub, visit Greeklearninghub.com.

Dedication

To my spiritual father, Konstantinos Stratigopoulos, whose deep love for the Greek language has been a guiding light in my journey.

Author's Acknowledgments

I am deeply grateful to my teachers who nurtured my love for the Greek language and its teaching. My heartfelt thanks go to Professor Sophia Papaiôannou from the University of Athens, Professor Irene de Jong from the University of Amsterdam, and Professor Hans Knutsson from Lund University. Their wisdom and guidance have been invaluable, and I will always cherish the knowledge they have imparted to me.

I would like to express my deepest gratitude to Jennifer Yee at Wiley for granting me the opportunity to write this book and to Georgette Beatty for her exceptional collaboration and mentorship. These two remarkable women made my writing journey both smooth and rewarding. I am also sincerely thankful to Kristie Pyles and Kelly Henthorne from the Wiley family for their unwavering support and to Georgia Mouzakiti for her meticulous attention to the final touches.

A portion of this book was written in the cozy living room of my dear childhood friend, Paris Dapolas, whose hospitality and support I greatly appreciate. I am equally thankful to Georgios Konstantinou, who shared my enthusiasm for this project and provided invaluable encouragement.

Above all, I wish to express my profound gratitude to my beloved parents, my siblings, and Nikoletta Tsiarta. Their unwavering support and faith in me mean more than words can convey.

Publisher's Acknowledgments

Senior Acquisitions Editor: Jennifer Yee
Senior Managing Editor: Kristie Pyles
Development Editor: Georgette Beatty
Copy Editor: Kelly D. Henthorne
Technical Editor: Georgia Mouzakiti

Production Editor: Bharaneedharan Murthy
Cover Image: © travnikovstudio/Getty Images